The Widow

The Widow

NOLA DUNCAN & LIBBY HARKNESS

EBURY
PRESS

An Ebury Press book
Published by Random House Australia Pty Ltd
Level 3, 100 Pacific Highway, North Sydney NSW 2060
www.randomhouse.com.au

First published by Ebury Press in 2013

Addresses for companies within the Random House Group can be found at
www.randomhouse.com.au/offices

National Library of Australia
Cataloguing-in-Publication Entry

Duncan, Nola
The widow/Nola Duncan and Libby Harkness

ISBN 978 1 74275 864 0 (pbk)

Duncan, Nola
Man–woman relationships
Spouses – Australia – Biography

Other Authors/Contributors:
Harkness, Libby

306.872

Cover design by Christa Moffitt, Christabella Designs
Cover image courtesy Trevillion Images
Internal design by Midland Typesetters
Typeset in Sabon 12/15pt by Midland Typesetters, Australia
Printed in Australia by Griffin Press, an accredited ISO AS/NZS 14001:2004
Environmental Management System printer

Random House Australia uses papers that are natural, renewable and
recyclable products and made from wood grown in sustainable forests.
The logging and manufacturing processes are expected to conform to the
environmental regulations of the country of origin.

Contents

Authors' Note

Michael and Linda's letters, and Michael's poems and sonnets, have been transcribed with their original punctuation and grammar.

Some names and places have been changed. For legal reasons it has not been possible to reproduce Linda's letters in full.

Clouds

They are stippled today, tentative and feather light
Not a bold statement, more a nudge, a gentle reminder,
Saying all is not settled, all is not obvious.
The heavens could still darken to overcast grey,
Or the cloud-dust could just huff away, vanish,
Leaving clear sky and raw, revealing sunlight.

They are streaky today, testament to recent motion.
A still tableau, belying the high winds of origin.
A static, vectorial spread, quietly awaiting dispersal.
They will not change, till the forces that formed them
    change
When they slowly deform, then reform, then transform
To a totally new conformation.

They are woolly today, billowing and fluffy.
Proud clouds. Clouds that love being clouds.
Playful, prominent, full of cloudy enjoyment,
They writhe, they twist, they swirl and squirm,
Daring the wind to blow them away, and
Flaunting their constantly changing forms.

They are stormy today, densely menacing,
But curiously thrilling and exciting.
They hide in their folds a cosmic energy
Which trembles and teeters on the edge of eruption,
Which in time, unchallenged, must finally release
To thrash and flash to eventual satiety.

MIW 6.xi.96

Prologue

The talk turned to Michael's life support. Switching it off no longer appeared to be a matter of if, but when. It was our second family conference with the doctors since Michael's heart had failed him the previous night, and the morning had not brought any better news.

The family had arrived at the hospital in anxious dribs and drabs; two children who lived interstate were still on their way. The rest of us – three of Michael's four children, two of my three, the Intensive Care Unit doctor and another resident, a nurse and our local rector – gathered in a special room the hospital reserved for such difficult conferences. Until the doctor in Canberra Hospital's ICU had contacted Michael's cardiologist and been given the full picture of the parlous state of Michael's heart, she had been rather careful to be noncommittal about exactly how bad things might be. However, having consulted the cardiologist that morning, she was clear about the prognosis: there was very little hope.

The brain damage question loomed large. They didn't use the word 'vegetable' but they said that the tests they had done indicated there was no brain activity. This was of course a real concern to us all; Michael was an intellectual man and very proud. We had to try to come to terms with the fact that his brilliant mind was gone. The ventilator was the only thing keeping his body breathing. We talked about withdrawing ventilation and what would happen if he survived and recovered but had no functioning brain. 'Well, if Dad can't do two cryptic crosswords a day, then he's certainly not going to want to live,' Michael's daughter Catherine said firmly.

'Your father will not be doing any more crosswords.' The doctor's tone was kind but her message was clear.

How did I not know how bad his heart was? This question hung in the air, but was not uppermost in my mind right then; consumed as I was by shock, I was still operating on the fuzzy edge of reality.

The decision was made to turn off his life support. That's when something rather unexpected, and in truth rather disconcerting, happened. The rector, who up to this point had not participated in the conversation, interjected earnestly. 'I wonder if I could just say something here . . .' We all went quiet and turned to look at him expectantly. 'Perhaps we should wait and give some more thought to the possibility of a miracle happening.'

There was a collective uncomfortable shifting in our seats. We had just been through a tortuous discussion about turning off Michael's life support and the decision had been made. Now we were being asked to think about miracles!

At that point, my daughter, Marlana, intervened, bless her. Marlana, a trained nurse, had been acting as a bit of a mediator between the doctors and the rest of us. She turned to the doctors: 'Let me be clear about this; there's not going to be any miracle, is there.'

It was more of a statement than a question. She then listed all the things that were wrong with Michael. He had suffered multiple organ failure; he was having seizures; his heart was not responding to any of the drugs; he was brain dead.

The doctors confirmed that the only miracle would be the survival of his body's shell. The Michael we knew was gone.

So he was moved to an isolation room where we could say goodbye to him before the life support was removed. Most of the family were gathered in that room. Unfortunately, Marlana's husband was on a flight back from the United States and was not going to make it in time; nor was my daughter Claudine, flying in from Darwin, or Michael's daughter Christine, coming from Cairns.

The medical staff kept Michael going until we were ready. I sat very still beside the bed, thinking about the moment I might be ready. I wasn't sure I'd ever be ready. I didn't want to let go because I knew it was the end. I would never see him again.

I have no sense of how long we were there. We talked to him, held his hand and stroked his forehead. He was seventy-six but still a good-looking man. My good-looking man. I wasn't crying at that point. Adam, Michael's younger son, was so distressed he decided he could not stay; Marlana had an infected eye and a nurse had been applying ointment to it for most of the day, but she was crying so much her tears kept washing out each new application. The other children were quietly stoic.

They'd taken out all but one IV line, the one delivering morphine, when we'd decided to withdraw treatment. Heavy sedation had stopped the seizures; his colour was good and he looked peaceful. Finally, they switched off the ventilator.

Dr Michael Westfield, my lovely man, was gone from my life. He died at 9 pm on 6 August 2010.

The
Widow

The Last Day

When I look back, I can see the signs that Michael's health was a lot worse than he ever mentioned to me. He had recovered extremely well from the massive heart failure that had nearly taken his life in 1994. However, when he was diagnosed with endocarditis, an inflammation of the inner lining of the heart, in 2008, his recovery was long and slow. The endocarditis had damaged his mitral valve and it was necessary to have surgery to replace yet another valve.

After this illness he tired easily and avoided walking any distance. He had taken to parking the car as close as he could to wherever we were going so that not too much walking was involved. I should have been more alert to these changes. Obviously I knew he had a heart condition, I just didn't know how bad it really was. And he chose not to tell me.

My first real warning that all was not well came shortly before he suffered the cardiac arrest that took his life. Marlana, who now ran her own chocolate-making business, had booked a trip to the Hunter Valley Chocolate Festival in New South Wales. I was going along to help her and had spent the day at her home packing chocolates and loading them into the car. Her husband was in the United States on business and the children were staying with grandparents while she was away. We decided it would be a good idea for her to have dinner with us and to sleep over that night, and then we could make an early start in the morning.

I rang Michael to let him know that Marlana would be staying over and he said he would make extra for dinner. It had been a long day and after dinner Marlana went off to have a shower. Michael and I relaxed and discussed our upcoming trip to Broome in Western Australia at the end of the month, a holiday that included attending 'Opera Under the Stars', an annual event, and one we always enjoyed. We had previously stayed at a fairly pricey resort, but this year we decided to stay somewhere a little less expensive and Michael had just that day paid for our accommodation.

'Well, if it doesn't work out, we can always go back to the other resort next year,' I said.

'I think if you go next year, you'll be going on your own,' he replied quietly. A bit startled, I looked over at him, frowning with concern. He looked relaxed in his favourite chair in the corner of our family room.

'Why do you say that? It's not like you to talk like that.'

'Well, I don't think I'm going to make it.'

'Are you not as well as I think you are?'

'Perhaps not . . .'

I was quietly pondering this conversation when suddenly the force of the cardiac arrest threw Michael's head back. Startled, I jumped up and unsuccessfully tried to rouse him. I raced to get Marlana out of the shower.

'Come, quickly – something's happened to Michael!'

Marlana wrapped a towel around herself and we rushed back to him. He was unconscious and Marlana said we had to get him onto the floor so we wrested him, none too gently, out of the chair – he was a big man and, with him being a dead weight, it wasn't easy. Marlana took over and, although distressed, immediately ripped open his shirt and started cardiopulmonary resuscitation (CPR) while I called the ambulance. I gave the details to the operator, who said the ambulance would be on its way and to turn on the outside light; he also explained that as the local fire brigade was closer it was standard procedure to call them and they would probably arrive before the ambulance.

Poor Marlana was finding it heavy-going. Michael was a large man with a barrel chest, which made it difficult to get effective strength into the chest compressions. The difficulty was compounded because Marlana had a carpel tunnel injury and her wrists were weak. Michael's colour was getting worse and Marlana was upset and crying, but still working away. The operator at the ambulance centre told me to stay on the line and I was able to pass messages between him and Marlana, who was by now almost at the point of exhaustion.

It seemed like an eternity, but in reality it must have been a matter of minutes, before I heard the siren. 'The firies are coming,' Marlana yelled. 'Get something for me to put on.' By this time her towel had fallen off and she was naked; I put a dressing gown around her heaving shoulders.

Three large firemen came in; one immediately took over CPR from Marlana while the other two pushed back the furniture. They rotated CPR between them, each pumping really hard for a couple of minutes until the Intensive Care Unit's paramedic team arrived and started shocking Michael with the defibrillator. They worked on him for about twenty minutes and the longer it went on the worse it looked.

By then the room was quite crowded and Marlana went out to make some phone calls to family members and I watched distractedly, as everyone focused on getting Michael breathing.

I was grateful that at least he was still alive when they finally put him into the ambulance. There wasn't enough room for me to accompany him, so Marlana and I drove to the hospital in her car. Catherine, Michael's daughter, who had arrived moments before, also drove to the hospital. Once there, we were told that although they had resuscitated him in Emergency, he had not regained consciousness and he was to be transferred to the ICU.

The doctor from Emergency asked what had happened and I did my best to recall the order of events. He asked me about Michael's health. Had he been unwell? I said 'no' because as far as I was concerned his cardiologist had told him he was doing fine. Well, that's what Michael had told me. They must have known there was more going on but could not be sure until they had spoken to his specialist.

We were eventually taken up to the ICU and were allowed to see him, two at a time. By then he was sedated with morphine and the ventilator was quietly pumping his chest in and out. He looked like he was sleeping; the intravenous lines injecting him with multiple medications snaked from his body. He was also covered with a cooling blanket, which Marlana told me was helpful in decreasing brain damage.

The children – Catherine, and Michael's sons Anthony and Adam, and my Matthew and Marlana – were there with me waiting for the first family conference with the doctors. In shock, we talked quietly among ourselves, trying to have a calm, general conversation. When the ICU doctor arrived she talked about how they might proceed. She wanted to be sure about the level of brain damage and needed to wait for Michael's medical history before making any decisions. She suggested we go home for a few hours while they carried out some more tests.

At about 6 am, Marlana and I drove home, her car still stuffed with chocolates. You could smell their sweetness, a reminder of normality lost. At home the house felt cold and empty. Marlana mopped the floor in the family room and then we moved the furniture back. I made a cup of tea but I don't remember drinking it.

I thought I might try for a couple of hours' sleep, although I was wide awake and knew it was unlikely to come, even if I did close my eyes. It was almost dawn by the time I entered the bedroom. I could see the bed with the covers neatly turned down. Michael was a creature of habit and early every evening he would turn them down in preparation for us going to bed later. And there it was – a reminder of him: the covers he had turned sometime before dinner the night before.

But tonight only one of us slipped between the sheets.

Bereavement

My darling Michael
How blessed I was to have the privilege
To love you and to spend 29 years of my life with you;
Your love in return was a precious gift.
It was an honour to love and care for you
till the end of your life.
Wait for me.

Funeral notice, *Canberra Times*, 11 August 2010

Michael and I had talked a lot about funerals and read books on the subject, but while we had talked about what each of us might want, the one important thing we had never actually made a decision about was cremation or burial. Whatever it was, we wanted to be together. I was now faced with the decision of what he had really wanted. The one thing we had agreed on was a cardboard coffin. That meant finding a funeral director who would accommodate this wish, because not all will.

I dressed Michael in a short-sleeved shirt, trousers and shoes and socks. I put a pen in his pocket; he always had a pen in his pocket. It was nothing fancy, just as he would have been dressed for any ordinary day. But it wasn't an ordinary day and he didn't look the same; I was anxious that none of the children saw him like that. I wanted them to remember him as he was after the life support had been removed; his colour was good at that time and he looked very peaceful.

Marlana heeded my advice and didn't go to view him. Claudine went because she hadn't managed to see him in the hospital. Catherine wanted to see him too and so I called her. 'Catherine, if you want to go, go, but my advice is to remember your father as he was when we last saw him in hospital.'

In the end I decided to have a private cremation followed by a memorial service. I had requested no flowers but wanted them for the coffin. I didn't like the tone of the floral arrangements available through the funeral home, so Catherine offered to collect some native flowers from a friend's farm and she made posies for each of the grandchildren to put on the coffin at the crematorium. I knew Michael would have liked the natives and it was a way of involving the grandchildren, who all drew pictures to put on the coffin as well.

Surprisingly, I hadn't cried the night Michael had died. Maybe it was the shock or disbelief. I did cry a lot during the week of planning for the memorial service, but it was often due more to frustration than grief: my computer had chosen this time to fail. I was not receiving emails, nor could I send them. We were preparing eulogies, the funeral director was sending through funeral notices for proofing and the company undertaking the printing of the service booklet was trying to send proofs for editing, and I was getting very anxious as time was short.

Claudine did her best to work her way through many different providers of internet 'expertise', none of whom were at all helpful in resolving the problem; and playing the sympathy card about the funeral for my husband did not work either. I finally called a computer troubleshooter who had previously done some work for us. It seems he either had more clout with my internet provider or knew the right questions to ask, or both. With my email working, my stress levels lowered.

The actual planning for the funeral itself went remarkably well considering there was such a blended family involved. For the most part everyone seemed either to agree, or be prepared to acquiesce, to whatever my wishes were.

I chose the people I wanted to give eulogies: Anthony on behalf of Michael's children; Matthew on behalf of my children; Bruce Graham, a former colleague of Michael's from the university; and another family friend.

I thought it appropriate to have the memorial service at the church where we had worshipped together for nearly thirty years; the rector of that church and a retired clergy friend of Michael's conducted the service.

One of our shared passions was poetry and I selected a special poem called 'Clouds', which Michael had written for me in 1996. It was too long to be read out during the service so I included it in the Order of Service booklet. Reading this poem again, I recalled how we would lie on a picnic rug somewhere, often by our favourite place, Lake Burley Griffin, and gaze up at the scudding clouds. At the bottom were Michael's neat initials – MIW. It was the way he signed all the beautiful poems and sonnets he had written to me during our long and happy marriage.

The day of the funeral dawned cold and bleak, which was rather how I felt as I stepped out in widow's black to go to the church packed to overflowing with our families, friends, former colleagues and old students. My good friend Pru, whom I had met at the university in 1976, but who had since moved to my home town of Perth, flew over for the funeral. My brother's wife and my niece also came over from Perth.

There were tears and smiles as Matthew read his eulogy.

Mum and Michael were married in 1981 and thus we – Marlana, Claudine and I – became stepchildren with no clear idea of what that would entail. Of the homes we lived in, my favourite was the smallest. It had a fireplace and a good kitchen and Michael cooked; we'd have dinner together after Michael said grace. I was not especially religious but you make allowances.

Three decades later, Ulrika, Susan [his wife and daughter] and I live in a small house with a fireplace and a good kitchen and we have dinners together after saying grace. I'm not especially religious but you make allowances.

On the right day, when it's cold outside and warm inside and pots are simmering and I have a tea towel draped over my shoulder, as Michael used to while he cooked, I think of that house and I like to think this is Michael's influence, because that is what I want it to be.

Marlana, Claudine and I had different experiences with Michael. Marlana was the youngest and formed the closest bond with him. She was young enough to have had bedtime stories read to her by Michael. Michael guided Marlana through school and two university degrees, correcting every essay she wrote, never complaining about correcting the same spelling mistakes over and over. She is astonished by this generosity, the rest of us more so. Michael and Marlana remained close, sharing recipes and their garden vegetables and conversation and, most importantly, time. Michael told me how much he enjoyed seeing Marlana develop from child to adult to mother.

Each of us remembers the winter days and the smell of soup or stew through the house. Just as often something more exotic was on offer. We watched Michael make bread. We are all good cooks and all of us put that down to Michael.

We loved Michael's humour: gentle, elegant and witty. Most of all I loved his facial expressions – the twitch of the mouth, the sideways look, the adoption of doleful mien and low, serious tone or both eyebrows raised in mock surprise. Whatever it was, I would find myself smiling before he uttered a word as much out of anticipation as anything. And I would look at my mum and see her laughing, helplessly. At those times I'd think, how wonderful.

Coupled with that was Michael's formidable intellect. What a mind. Great insight, great range and depth over any subject. One could be intimidated by such a person, but such was Michael's lightness of touch with language that no one was ever made to feel inferior.

While our experiences as stepchildren may have been different, we share a common understanding of what made Michael important to us.

Foremost was his love and respect for our mum. He brought her joy. Together Mum and Michael gave us a loving and secure home base. Next was Michael's patience and generosity. Michael was forgiving of faults of people no matter how they behaved.

Claudine I know felt keenly the time and expense associated with Mum's annual visits to Queensland or Darwin, but Michael always encouraged their time together.

For all the things we loved about Michael, and there were many, it was as much what he didn't do that was important. He never raised his voice to any of us. He was not judgmental. He gave us space. He never preached. And by virtue of this restraint, he affected our lives profoundly, because he became an example of the power that patience and understanding could have on others.

Consequently he was respected and admired by every person in our heavily blended and somewhat complex family. For there was nothing not to like.

Most of all he made our mum happy. For three decades, they walked on the bright side of the road, supporting each other and supporting us and their church and community. For that we are grateful.

Michael was a beautiful person.

Such a wonderful eulogy moved me to later write a note to Matthew in which I recalled a story I had heard about the late Australian poet Philip Hodgins. Philip knew he was dying of leukaemia and asked the author, poet and play-wright Peter Goldsworthy if he would write his eulogy. Just before he died he asked Peter if he had, by any chance, written the eulogy and if so would he mind sending him a copy so he could read it, which Peter did. A week later Peter received a very nice bottle of wine with a card attached that read, 'That is a eulogy to die for.'

I told Matthew that had Michael read his eulogy, he too would have said it was a 'eulogy to die for', and it was.

At the service a friend handed out memory cards for anyone who wanted to record something special about Michael. The dozens of cards that came back showed the depth of people's love and respect for my Michael. It was quite overwhelming and very comforting.

What a special person has departed your life! These are the traits that spring to mind when I turn my thoughts to dear Michael: gentleman; cheeky and funny; devoted husband; family man; humility; earthy; honest; fair; engaged; present; measured; mature. What a package!

There was nothing superficial about Michael. He was a man who had 'depth', and his personable nature fostered the impression that no matter what you were talking about, Michael was totally enthralled with the conversation. I always felt uplifted after a loud, robust conversation with him.

I remember Michael for his thoughtfulness and his tremen-dous support in a time of need. His wit and marvellous use of language. His friendship and wonderful sociability.

My dearest memory of Michael is of both of you, Nola, and your deep love and respect for each other. I remember all the times you drove me home from church, our discussions and the one that stands out above all was when I was saying I didn't know what to do with some pain and heartache and Michael said very simply 'Let go and let God.'

My memories of Michael are many and various: Mozart, Sibelius, Joan Baez, anti-authoritarian, talk-fests, hours of Dylan Thomas and the residents of *Under Milk Wood* and a host of other poets, mutual recitations of Goonery nonsense with sound effects. But most of all a marvellous, modest, witty and entertaining, outstanding intellect and a remarkable, compassionate nature.

I truly believed I had been married to the most wonderful man in the world. How was I going to live the rest of my days without him?

Friends and family gradually departed over the next few days and suddenly I was alone. I felt strange and flat; I sort of went on autopilot for a while. For the most part, people left me to grieve. I did not change anything in the bedroom; it stayed exactly the way it had been when Michael died – only his medications were removed from the bedside table because of the grandchildren. Other than that, his clothes stayed untouched, his shorts and tops – all washed and pressed ready to go to Broome – remained where they were.

The ashes were ready to collect a week after the funeral but I couldn't get up the energy to go and get them; I finally did so about a month later and put them on the bedside table until I decided what I was going to do with them.

In spite of a strange kind of listlessness, I made myself do the things that had to be done, and initially there was quite a lot to do. I sent out two hundred thank-you letters and set about putting Michael's pressing financial affairs in order. I'd had my first instance of dealing with bureaucracy and its indifference to death with the computer problem before the funeral; now I was to deal with it on a much wider scale.

My first encounter with the 'death problem' was with American Express. Michael had a number of credit cards – I never worked out why he had so many and he never told me – and I sent three cards to Amex with a copy of the death certificate, as they requested, and asked them to cancel them.

After a month or so I hadn't heard from them, so I phoned to ask if the cards had been cancelled. I was passed from one person to another and finally I was told that two of them had been cancelled, but the third would have to be dealt with by his bank. The person I spoke to also mentioned that one of the cards had a credit of eighty dollars.

I was then passed to the legal department, who told me I had to send another copy of Michael's death certificate, and a copy of his will, in order to retrieve the eighty dollars. They wanted me to fax the documents, but as I didn't have a fax machine, I sent both by certified mail. Weeks went by and I still had not heard back. I made another call – a very unpleasant one, as it turned out – to another unhelpful person in the legal department, who told me they had not received the documents.

As I had sent them by certified mail, I told her they must have received them. At this point we were almost having a screaming match. She asked me the address to which I had sent the documents and I told her I'd sent them to the Amex post office box number. She then replied triumphantly that certified mail could not be sent to a post office box and she told me she was going to hang up, which she did.

I phoned the post office and quoted the number of my certified mail and was given both the time and the name of the person who had signed for them. I then wrote a letter to Amex informing them that I had been advised this was a matter that I could take to the Small Claims Court and this I would do if I did not, at the very least, and as a courtesy, receive some response from them within a reasonable time.

They responded with an unsigned (but initialled) letter informing me 'without prejudice' that they were unable to locate the copy of the will and would I kindly re-forward it, and other supporting documents, via fax. My son-in-law helpfully faxed the documents.

I also sent a copy of the Renunciation of Probate by the Public Trustee, to 'avoid any further obfuscation on your part'. I thanked them for apologising for any inconvenience they'd caused me and suggested that perhaps they could also apologise for the distress.

Time passed and again I did not hear anything; another letter was sent advising them that if they did not respond to my correspondence within two weeks from the date on the letter, I would take the matter to the Small Claims Court.

This letter elicited a telephone call from Amex telling me that they had sent the cheque, but had sent it to the Public Trustee Office, even though I had advised them that the public trustee had provided a Renunciation of Probate.

I then rang the Public Trustee Office, and spoke with a very helpful person who said he was so glad I had called – yes, they had received the cheque, it had been sent to the wrong address. They had therefore had to retrieve Michael's documents from the archives to determine to whom the cheque should be sent.

I know it was only eighty dollars, but it was the principle.

Then there was the matter of the third credit card that had to be cancelled at the bank. On my first visit I took a copy of the death certificate. Unfortunately, it was not certified by a Justice of the Peace. Once I'd had this done I returned to the bank and was told that the card would be cancelled.

Then I received a statement from the bank and not only had the card not been cancelled, the bank had accepted a direct debit. I went back to the bank. While I waited, the teller phoned someone in 'cards' and 'cards' said they had not received a copy of the death certificate. I told him I had provided the certified certificate some weeks previously. He was very sorry but they did not seem to have it. We had a very heated conversation – at this point I was past worrying about being overheard.

'Is this bank usually so cavalier with important documents? A death certificate is an important document, you know.'

'Mrs Westfield, the quickest and easiest way to sort this out is for you to provide us with another copy of the death certificate.'

'Well, that may be the quickest and easiest way for you but it is certainly not the quickest and easiest way for me, so I suggest that you start looking for that document,' I said and marched out, aware that the eyes of everyone in the bank were looking my way. Because I am small of stature some people may think I look a bit meek, but I can stand on my dig with the best of them when pushed – and I was severely pushed!

I then wrote a very nasty letter to the bank's head office in Melbourne. I said that I did not know if they actually had a customer service department, but if they did not, they should consider opening one, as from my experience they certainly needed it. I didn't have a name to whom I could address the letter, so it probably found its way into a rubbish bin.

Trawling through the bank's website I found an email address to which one could write a brief complaint (or a compliment!) and there was a promise of a response within three days. Surprisingly, a woman from the bank did respond and after I gave her my tale of woe she said she would look into the matter. And she did. Funnily enough, the death certificate was miraculously found.

By the time I came round to dealing with Medibank, I was feeling quite frazzled. Medibank was irritating but not obstructive. I told the woman behind the counter that I wanted to cancel my *late* husband's membership and gave her his card. She tapped away on her computer and then, looking up at me expectantly, asked, 'Why do you want to cancel his membership?'

I visited both Michael's GP and cardiologist. I wanted to try to understand what had happened. Michael had visited his GP quite recently to get the all-clear for the Broome trip and he was told there was no reason not to go. He had not been to see his cardiologist for a year although he kept saying he must make an appointment to do so.

I was aware that his health was not great – and hadn't been since the endocarditis – but I was not aware of just how bad it was. Until his heart failure in 1994, Michael had enjoyed quite robust health and he wasn't a complainer when he had a cold or a bout of flu, which he rarely did.

The lead-up to the life-threatening endocarditis had actually begun in November 2007. Michael had contracted a nasty virus that had made him quite ill and he had very bad headaches. He had also injured his back while lifting something heavy doing voluntary work at the church. His back pain was accompanied by a lot of other unexplained symptoms but our doctor was away for Christmas and the locums did not appear to be well-informed and did not come up with any believable diagnosis.

By the end of January I was seriously worried about him as he could hardly walk, had come out in a rash and was feverish. I finally managed to get him a cancellation appointment at the Chronic Pain Clinic, where the doctor pronounced Michael very ill.

'I know!' I replied sharply.

He went by ambulance straight to hospital, where they dosed him for three days with strong antibiotics for an infection. Once the causal organism was identified, they switched to a more targeted intravenous antibiotic and after four weeks he was considered well enough to go home and be treated there for another four weeks.

His cardiologist then discovered that the blood infection had affected the mitral valve between the atrium and ventricle on the left side. In May he had successful cardio-thoracic surgery to replace the valve and came home with many restrictions and a rehabilitation program. It was quite a stressful time but he survived. He also lost 18 kilos. Michael liked good food and loved cooking and he had gradually put on a bit of weight over the years, but being a tall man he carried it well and I never said anything about it. Everyone told him he looked much better without the weight, which I think Michael found a bit embarrassing.

'No one told me I was fat before,' he said, rather bemused.

During my visit to the cardiologist, he looked at me directly and said, 'The last time I saw Michael, I was very disappointed that the valve was not working as well as I would have liked. I changed his medication as I thought that might improve things.'

It must have improved things somewhat because Michael didn't go back. Surely he would have done so otherwise? I asked him if Michael was aware that things were not going too well.

'Yes,' he said, 'Michael was well aware of the state of his heart.'

This was information Michael had chosen not to share with me, for whatever reason. I thought about that conversation we had never finished on the night he died, when he hinted that I might have to go to the opera in Broome on my own the following year. Was he about to tell me the real state of his health? Knowing Michael, probably not, but this out-of-character comment had startled me and I certainly would have pressed the issue if I'd had the chance.

One thing the cardiologist did tell me was that anyone with Michael's heart condition could go suddenly, as Michael had, or they could linger and have a slow, uncomfortable death. I think he made his point; Michael was fortunate in death.

Reflections

Time passed. I wasn't sleeping very well, although I'd never been a good sleeper. But I'd always looked forward to waking up to Michael bringing me my morning coffee in bed. He'd even brought me coffee the day he died. Sometimes a poem, a card, a piece of prose or a sonnet accompanied the coffee. He wrote of life and love so beautifully. He was an early riser and I could picture him sitting in his study in the breaking dawn composing something meaningful for me with which to start my day.

Morning sonnet

Forbid that I should treat you as a slave
And love you as a sundry form of leisure.
An equal, open sharing, this I crave;
That each bring to the other living pleasure.
I long that you may find the liberty
To liberate all treasures of your heart
Without some awful fear of injury
That might confine expression on your part.
O Nola love, though longing beats so strong.
We have each other such a little time.
And yet I see that living we belong,
Contributors to life and not to crime.
In all-devouring joy I cannot say

That love for you condemns in any way.
MIW 3.i.92

Or he could make me smile with some silly ditty:

Stretch forth your hand and take the cup
Preparatory to getting up
For your kind senior lecturer, he,
Has brought you some fresh made cof-fee

Sometimes when Michael went away to conferences or on university business, he would leave propped up on the bedside table an envelope containing a love note or poem for each day he was away.

But that lovely life – life as I knew it – was gone. Also gone was my appetite and I lost a lot of weight. A friend invited me to dinner – it was the most beautiful dinner and I just couldn't eat it. I sat there feeling awful because I almost always eat what is put in front of me.

When another friend invited me to afternoon tea, I was pleased to go as her husband had been seriously ill in hospital when Michael died. He was making a good recovery and I wanted to see him to say how pleased I was that he was getting better. But when I arrived on the doorstep and he opened the door, I looked at him, up and about again while Michael was dead, and the words wouldn't come, only racking sobs. I stood there, a weeping mess, and could not go in.

Nor could I watch television in the evenings as I found this a very lonely experience. That's a funny thing for someone who is a bit of a loner to say, but it is different when you're watching TV with someone who is interested in the same things, particularly the news or some political item. Michael and I were political junkies so we would always make comments to each other about what was happening with whatever government was in power. Once I even made a comment to his empty chair. So I read, worked on my craft interests, did some housework and listened to the radio instead.

It was quite some time before I could go back to my voluntary job at the op shop. I did take up bridge lessons, which I enjoyed. I had stopped going to lawn bowls, even though I had been a very enthusiastic bowler. I found people were discomfited dealing with someone grieving after a death. My daughter Claudine, a sweet, emotionally attuned woman and a very good lawn bowler herself, came down from Newcastle in New South Wales, where she had moved to be closer to me after Michael died. She spent some time with me; I think she saw it as her role to get me back on the bowling green and that by coming with me I would not be on my own and I might get back some confidence. So I did start to play again, but not as often or with as much enjoyment as before.

In no time it was Christmas and I went with Marlana and her husband, David, and their children to Merimbula on the New South Wales south coast, which was lovely. They felt it would be best if my first Christmas on my own was somewhere away from Canberra. Michael had for years cooked a huge Christmas dinner for as many of the family who wished to come and I did not particularly want to take up where he left off. Leaving town was a less painful option.

But at home, alone, it was the memories that sustained me during my first year of widowhood. Michael had never given me an engagement ring – we had no money in those early years and while he had given me a ring with gemstones, it was more of a dress ring. But six months before he died, he gave me a diamond and sapphire ring. He said he realised he had never bought me a proper engagement ring. I looked at that ring a lot.

I brought out all the beautiful cards, letters, poems and messages he'd written to me over the years and sorted them into categories: birthday, Valentine's Day and anniversary messages (Michael rarely bought commercial cards and when he did he would add his own prose); general love messages and notes; poems and sonnets.

I pored over photographs; I listened over and over to the tape of him playing the classical guitar piece 'Spanish Romance', and any tape with him talking so I could hear his voice. Michael had a beautifully modulated voice – cultured, but not plummy.

I listened to the tape of our wedding many times; it was one of the happiest days of my life. A very cold day, 6 June 1981. We were unable to marry in the Anglican Church because we were both divorced, so we were married in the Uniting Church; Michael's brother Bill and my friend Pru were our witnesses, and Pru also sang at the service. There was no best man and Marlana, aged nine, was my little bridesmaid. Matthew gave me away.

Michael was forty-six and I was thirty-nine.

The Early Years

I grew up in Perth in a loving home environment with my two older brothers. My parents were very kind and gentle people. My mother was a violinist and my father was a flautist, and although my father had a public service position, he'd also played in the West Australian Symphony Orchestra in its formative years.

Sport was something I enjoyed, but my mother tried to make sure I had a breadth of other interests. I had elocution lessons, music lessons and I learnt all types of dance. But in spite of being given every opportunity to do anything I wanted, my main interest at that time was to leave school. It was only later in life that I regretted not going further with my education and would have dearly loved to have gone to university.

My first job after leaving school was as a receptionist/typist. It was very mundane and although I wanted to spread my wings, I didn't have enough money to go anywhere. My solution was to join the Australian Air Force and I was sent to Melbourne. It was 1959 and I was eighteen. It was probably the worst decision of my life. I quickly discovered that I did not fit into military life; I was not comfortable with the culture or the behaviour. I had, up to that point, led a rather sheltered life and the experience was certainly a major culture shock. I was also very homesick.

I met my first husband, Des, in Melbourne. He was also in the Air Force, and was studying for a degree in electrical engineering as part of his officer training – I think his officer status may have been part of the attraction. I was twenty and he was twenty-two when we married. He had joined the Air Force when he was quite young and was well inculcated into military culture by the time I met him. He was already used to bossing people around, and the trouble is that when you boss people around at work, for some it's hard to break the habit when you get home.

After we married we were posted to Amberley in Queensland, and soon after arriving I found I was pregnant with Matthew. Shortly afterwards, Des was posted to France. Prior to taking up this posting he had been required to learn French at a language school in Melbourne for six months. The France posting was 'unaccompanied' – in other words, I was not invited. Newly married, newly pregnant and with my husband about to leave me for the next seventeen months, I was naturally very unhappy.

It was also quite clear that Des found me a bit of a nuisance, and I was sent back to my parents in Perth to await the baby's arrival. I stayed with them until Matthew was fourteen months old. Looking back, it cannot have been easy for my parents, but they never complained. I did feel that I had been abandoned, and I think perhaps that even way back then, it was the beginning of the end of our marriage.

After France, Des was posted to Williamtown in New South Wales, where Claudine was born, then to Melbourne, followed by a posting to Washington DC, again unaccompanied. I found myself without my husband again and this time it was to be for eleven months and with two small children. After Des left for Washington I felt quite resentful, and, in a rare display of assertiveness, I decided that if I sold the car and rented the house, the children and I could join him. With the assistance both practically and financially, of my parents, that's what I did – a decision, I might add, that Des did not view enthusiastically.

On our return to Australia we were posted to Edinburgh in South Australia, which I found miserable, followed by Melbourne, where Marlana was born. It is difficult for military wives to put down serious roots with the constant moving, but in Melbourne I made some good friends. I joined an amateur musical theatre group, which I loved; it was an outlet from my domestic life of days filled with housework and looking after young children.

One evening while Des was eating his dinner *and* reading a magazine, I was regaling him with my day with the kids and it was obvious I was boring him. 'You're not listening to a word I'm saying,' I said crossly.

He looked up at me, as if surprised at the remark. 'Nola, I'm not interested in ninety per cent of what you do or say.' A mean remark, reminding me just how much I was struggling in this marriage. I never found out the ten per cent he *was* interested in.

When Matthew was due to go to high school I wanted to send him to private school. Des did not have a problem with this as long as I paid for it. To do this I had to get a job and I found one quite quickly in an insurance company, and loved it. It gave me a great sense of independence and new people to talk to.

Des's next posting was to Dayton, Ohio, in the US, for twelve months. The children and I went with him on this occasion and it was a happy time. The change was good for our marriage, and I met some wonderful women who became my friends. All too soon we were returning home – but where was home? Des had been posted to Canberra. I wanted to go back to Melbourne; I thought Des might be able to commute for a time. But he would not have a bar of that idea and so my lovely home in Melbourne was sold and we moved to Canberra.

I was offered an administrative job at the university; however, what I really wanted was to be at the university as a student, not an employee. I decided I would go to night school and obtain university entrance. I wanted to study for an Arts degree; Political Science, English Literature, Australian Literature, or anything, really – it all sounded exciting to me. I thought it was my turn to undertake some studies, but unfortunately what I wanted did not fit in with Des's plans for himself that year. So, once again, my plans went on hold and I knew that nothing was ever going to change. When Des's next posting – to Richmond in New South Wales – came round, I refused to go. By this time I knew that while I was married to Des, I was never going to have the opportunity to do any of the things I wanted to do. I told him I wanted his move to Richmond to be the beginning of a formal separation. The word 'divorce' was not mentioned. I know he was surprised by my emphatic resolve; I had for so many years been the obedient wife, allowing myself to be dictated to. But Des had underestimated the level of my simmering discontent over the years and he certainly underestimated my preparedness to do something about it. I thought it was *my* time and I was ready to fly.

In the early years there were access issues with the children, and the two girls lived with Des for a time in Richmond, but eventually they all came back to Canberra. Des later happily remarried.

I have a tendency to keep correspondence and when I was going through all the letters, notes and poems Michael had written to me over the years, I came across a letter Des had written to me many years later. In it he said that he did not blame me for the break-up of our marriage and by the 'standards in which he would conduct a marriage now' he did not know how it had lasted as long as it had. He wanted me to understand that whatever he might feel about Michael personally, he thought he was a good man and he believed we had a happy marriage. He added that he was satisfied the children would have a good future and was pleased with the way Michael and I had guided Marlana into adulthood.

***

It was at the university that I first met Pru, who was to become a lasting friend. This was also where I met Michael. He was away on sabbatical at Cambridge University in the UK with his wife and family when I joined the Science Department in late 1976. I first saw him in January 1977; I thought he was a nice-looking man – he used to describe his looks as 'craggy'.

Michael was a biologist and we worked in the same department. He was a very popular member of staff and was also popular with the undergraduate students because he made himself available to them, which a lot of lecturers didn't do.

To me he was just one of the staff and we would talk at morning tea like everyone else. He was charming and seemed interested in talking to me. Of course, he was interested in talking to a lot of people. But I found it a welcome change to speak to a man who was interested in conversing with me on a range of subjects. The stimulus was rather intoxicating after all my years with Des, who didn't find me at all interesting to talk to.

Over time our conversations evolved to the more personal. I told him I was separated and he told me about his own marriage breakdown, although at the time he was still living with his wife. From his point of view, his marriage had become rocky after about seven years.

We became friends. We would share books, as we liked the same writers. We shared a love of poetry and classical music – Chopin, Tchaikovsky, Elgar. We were also of one mind politically – left-leaning. He was witty and made me laugh; he made everyone else laugh too, although some of his humour was darkly subtle and if you didn't get it immediately, you missed it altogether.

Eventually we started having the occasional lunch together down by Lake Burley Griffin. The lake was to feature in our relationship. It was a nice spot and only five minutes from the university; not being an academic like Michael, I only had an hour for lunch.

It was during those peaceful lunches by the lake that Michael started to tell me a bit about his background. He was the youngest of four boys and had grown up on a dairy farm in Queensland. His mother, Mary, was Scottish; she had a master's degree in linguistics and during the First World War was on the faculty at Glasgow University. After the war she knew she would be required to relinquish her position in favour of any returning soldier who might qualify for the job.

Michael's father, Jack, was Mary's second cousin and he'd been a stretcher-bearer in France. After he was demobbed he paid a visit to his Scottish relatives in Glasgow, where he met Mary. They corresponded when he returned to Australia and she eventually came out to Australia to marry him. Mary went from being an academic in Scotland to a dairy farmer's wife in country Australia. Michael said that she never complained about this massive change; she apparently had the capacity never to look back and regret – perhaps it was her hardy Scottish mettle.

Jack signed up for the Second World War and came back a broken man, dying relatively young, when Michael was only twelve; he and his mother ran the dairy farm themselves for several years.

None of his brothers had been to university, so Mary, being academically minded, wanted university for her youngest son. She could obviously tell he was wasted on a dairy farm so she sold the farm and they moved to Brisbane, where Legacy took him under its wing. Legacy, a charity established by a group of ex-servicemen after the First World War to help war widows, or their children, suffering financial hardship, put Michael through his final year of high school at Brisbane Boys' College. His academic prowess was immediately evident and he was there only a year before becoming dux of the school.

Apart from having brains, Michael was a talented sports-man. He played rugby and cricket. He was also a junior tennis champion – he'd represented Queensland in an inter-state competition called the Linton Cup for junior males. The team consisted of Roy Emerson at No. 1, Michael at No. 2, Rod Laver at No. 3 and Malcolm Anderson at No. 4. He could have continued with a tennis career but his mother had her heart set on an academic life for him. I think Michael, with his love of literature and romantic, poetic mind, would have been more suited to the arts, but he chose science, as there were no scholarships available in Arts.

After graduating from the University of Queensland, Michael went to work at the Department of Agriculture Research Station in Warwick in Queensland, as he had to repay the university scholarship he had received. He met his first wife, Margaret, a teacher, in Warwick. He then received a scholarship to do his PhD at Sydney University, after which he was offered an academic appointment in Canberra and the family moved to the ACT.

Our relationship changed from friendship to something more meaningful very gradually. We saw each other at work, we talked a lot, sometimes we had lunch together in the lunch room or at the lake; sometimes we went to lunch-time concerts at the School of Music, either the two of us, or with others. It was a very slow process of getting to know each other. The romance crept in with the poems he started to write to me.

Your Hand

Craft perfection, Nature's
moulded glove
Stretched towards, but never
touching; reaching

Yet the very living core, and
breaching

Inner reservoirs of whelming love
That such a hand so giving
and discreet
Might sometime take, accept
this hand of mine
Would be a gesture whole
and fully fine
Rendering generosity complete.

MIW 1978

Looking back, it seems a rather old-world courtship, and it took a long time to graduate to more than hand-holding. When, quite some time later, talk turned to marriage, we both decided to start the painful process of divorce. Because I thought it inappropriate to be working in the same department as someone I was seeing romantically, I transferred from my administrative position in the Science Department into another area of the university, but was still in administration.

We were slowly working our way towards marriage – well, we were certainly not going anywhere else as far as I was concerned – and Michael formally proposed on 7 December 1980, by the lake. Naturally I said yes. This time I was really in love; my feelings were so different from those I'd had with Des. Michael was a soulmate – we connected on so many levels. The day he proposed became a very special date in our anniversary calendar. We always celebrated it by going out to dinner or with a romantic picnic by the lake. The kids would ask where we were going – we usually had a bottle of wine with us – and we'd say we were celebrating. What were we celebrating? 'Pearl Harbor Day,' we'd tell them. Not necessarily a day to be celebrated, but it *was* Pearl Harbor Day and it was *our* day to celebrate.

Until Michael and I decided to get married, I had been living in the house I owned with Des and he was still based in New South Wales. Michael had moved into a little house we had bought together and was living quite spartanly; all he had was a bed, a table and a chair. We'd been very lucky to get that house; the real estate agent told us it was going to be repossessed by the bank. It needed a bit of work but it was in our price range.

I received some money from the sale of my home, and even though the federal government had brought in the new Family Law Act in 1975, which decreed assets were to be divided fifty–fifty, I still had to fight for my fifty per cent of our marital home. Michael wasn't prepared to fight for a share of anything he had with Margaret, which annoyed me a little at the time because I didn't think it was fair. He took the view that the line of least resistance was the best way to go and in the end I accepted that decision. We did, after all, have each other.

Publicly, things were still very 'proper' sexually in 1981 and it's hard to believe it was only three decades ago and that we'd both been married before. When I moved into our little house two weeks before we married, Michael moved out until our wedding day, staying with his brother Bill, who was living in Canberra at the time.

And so we settled into married life. Marlana was still at primary school, and both she and Matthew, who was at university, lived with us. Claudine went flatting. Over the next five years we did a lot of work on that little house – painting, and landscaping the garden and adding a small extension.

Michael was head of his department by the time we moved to a larger home one suburb away. But we were never happy there – even though it ticked all the boxes of what we wanted in a house, it wasn't right for us, possibly because we had such special memories of our first house on which we had lovingly worked together and where we'd had our early married days.

One day when I was out walking I came across a nice flat vacant block of land around the corner from where we were living. It had a 'House and Land Package' sign on it. The builder was a bit desperate and was prepared to build a home to our design without progress payments, which was good for us because we wouldn't have any money until we sold the house we were living in, which we did surprisingly quickly.

Building the house had its own stresses but we got what we wanted, including a lovely fireplace where we could light roaring fires to keep us cosy in the freezing Canberra winters. We eventually moved in on Christmas Eve 1991. It was an exciting time. When we were not busy working in the garden we enjoyed sharing our new home with family and friends. I have wonderful memories of that time.

Michael retired in 1997, although he stayed on as a Visiting Fellow so he could look after his graduate students who were yet to complete. This enabled him to keep his office and use the library, but the work was unpaid, of course. I retired in 2000.

In 2006 we decided to sell our home and downsize to something more manageable. Although we had intended to see out our days in the lovely home we had built together, it was mostly the garden that made up our minds – we didn't want to be slaves to it. So we bought a very nice two-bedroom townhouse with a small courtyard garden in a new complex a twenty-minute drive from the city. It was here I thought we could live out our days in happy retirement. We were older, a bit slower, but we still shared a love of many things. And I never stopped loving Michael.

In Memory

Michael Westfield
10.6.1934–6.8.2010

It has been a lonely painful
year down here without
you my darling and I am so
grateful for the precious
memories I have of our life
together. I miss you so much.
Nola

Canberra Times, 6 August 2011

The Box

As the first anniversary of Michael's death approached, his ashes were still sitting on the bedside dresser. I had a conversation with Marlana about what I wanted to do with them. When Michael and I had talked about cremation, we had thought it might be nice to have our ashes scattered over the lake because it was a place of such significance to us. Marlana was horrified. 'We can't feed Michael to the carp!'

Over the months since Michael's death, I had talked with his children about the ashes; mostly they were not concerned about what I did with them, but the general consensus was that a plaque somewhere would be nice, so the grandchildren could visit with flowers. I decided to inter the ashes in the Memorial Gardens at the Woden Cemetery. It was not what I wanted, but as this would please the family, I decided it was probably the right thing to do. I wandered around the cemetery with the caretaker until I found a suitable garden area where I could place a rock, large enough for two plaques – one for now, one for later when I joined him. I also chose a memorial seat to go nearby with a little plaque that read:

This seat is a gift in memory of Michael Westfield;
please enjoy the memories and the silence of eternity.

I took the ashes to the funeral director and chose a small urn for some of them to go in and asked him to transfer the rest into the box the cemetery had given me. I had decided I wanted Father Pat, a priest from the Catholic church next door, to give the blessing at the interment of the ashes as he had been very good to us during Michael's protracted illness.

Pru flew over from Perth and she, Marlana and one of her little boys and I went down in our good clothes and smart shoes with some fresh plants, a spade and a garden fork. Father Pat gave the blessing and afterwards, our gardening done, we sat on the memorial seat for a while, contemplating life and death and friends and family.

Later, at home, Pru and I thought it was definitely time for some champagne, but try as we might, we could not get the cork out. Our efforts only succeeded in breaking it. Then we had to work on the broken cork with a corkscrew. We were laughing and getting hot and bothered, but we were determined; by the time we finally opened it we were already high without having touched a drop. I seemed to have crossed a threshold. Time to stop grieving and move forward.

Up to that point I hadn't changed anything at home, but now I decided it was time to knuckle down and do something about Michael's things. I started with his papers because I thought they would be the least painful.

We had brought many boxes from our previous home and they were stored in the garage. Michael had never discussed these boxes. I knew many of them contained research papers, but he never talked about what I should do with them after he died – assuming he died before me. I began to sort through them and send some papers off to people whom I thought would be interested in them; the rest I put aside for shredding.

Then I lifted down a large sealed box and found the name 'Linda' handwritten on it. I knew this girl Linda – she had been one of Michael's students from the 1990s, although she could hardly be called a girl. She was in her early thirties with a husband and three children. We often invited Michael's students to share a meal with us and Linda had been to our home several times.

I was momentarily confused. Would these be her research papers? But Michael hadn't kept the research papers of his other doctoral students. As I looked for something with which to open the box, I was trying to recall more about her. She had been doing a PhD. I didn't remember her as especially pretty. I knew she had a nickname and that it appeared to bear no relation to her real name, but I was uninterested in her and it had never occurred to me to ask her much about herself.

Using a pair of scissors like a knife, I scored the tape across the top of the box and opened it. On top of a pile of sealed manila envelopes was an over-full manila folder marked '1997', the contents of which spilt onto the garage floor. Looking down and without touching them I could see they were letters, and in Michael's very distinctive handwriting.

I picked one up and read the endearment: 'Dearest, darlingest, most wonderful Linda'. And another: 'Most precious Linda'. They all started this way. I knew what I was looking at; I just did not want to believe what I was reading, because to do so was to acknowledge a dreadful truth – the worst of truths – Michael had had an affair. It was a moment both surreal and confronting. This could not be happening.

I felt sick and dizzy; my vision momentarily blurred. I caught my breath, leant against the wall for support and slowly slid to the floor. I sat there stunned for a time, unable to read any further the letters I was holding. Then I reached into the box and started pulling out the dated, sealed envelopes – 1992, 1993, 1994, 1995 and 1996.

The heart failure year, 1994. I ripped open the envelope. Yes, the affair had been in full flight before his heart failed in September. Then I ripped open 1995 and could barely contain my grief when I read his January letters; as soon as I had nursed him back to health and he was able to return to work, he had gone straight back to the affair with her.

I started reading the letters that had fallen onto the floor. When I saw the dates I realised these were copies of letters Michael had written to Linda after she had left the university in the middle of 1997, having finished her PhD, and to my profound shock and disgust they were very sexually explicit. He was writing about his memories of their sexual experiences – apparently reliving them, trying to keep them alive.

I feel sure you recall sitting on my face sucking me while I licked you to orgasm . . .

My lips remember the unbelievably beautiful sensation of brushing and sucking your lower lips – the swollen outer ones and the soft slippery delicate inner ones, all enriched with your sensual, stimulating, extra special Linda odour – quite unique and unforgettable . . .

I sat in the stillness of the garage surrounded by envelopes containing their love letters; her letters in her untidy handwriting were there too. I then stood up and packed everything back in the box and took it inside. I was beside myself. I didn't know what to do; who could I tell? At that precise minute, no one, so mute was I with anguish and grief.

Then I went into the office and wrote an email to Pru.

19 August 2011

Subject: Grief or rage or both

Dear Pru,

Are you sitting down? If not I suggest you do.

What I'm about to tell you is something that, at the moment, I'm telling ONLY you. I will have to ponder my future actions and reactions.

As you know I have been going through Michael's papers. I opened a box today, which I thought were research papers, but not so, they were love letters between Michael and one of his PhD students. He had been having a raging affair for at least six years from 1992. I cannot find if, or indeed when, it ended.

Can you have pornographic letters or only pictures? Yes, you can: the dictionary says 'obscene literature' and that describes many of these letters very nicely. I have not read them all, as there are far too many; this was not just a shoebox, you understand, and anyway I got the drift pretty quickly.

The thing that makes me really angry is that after Michael's collapse in 1994, I sat by his hospital bed for six weeks and then nursed him once home for a couple of months, and after all that, it seems the affair resumed almost immediately.

So, where to from here?

Love, Nola

The same night I received a reply written very late after Pru had arrived home from an evening out with a friend. Naturally she was shocked at Michael's betrayal, and could not reconcile this behaviour with his outward persona. She could not believe he had not destroyed the letters. More importantly, she was worried about me.

'I wish I could be with you for I feel it is not good for you to be alone with a million thoughts swirling around in your mind and feeling impotent against the anger which you must surely feel. Try not to fall apart. I know you won't want to do anything drastic. If my arms were long enough they would extend down the fibre cables and hold you to reassure you of your worth, and that I would want to do anything I could to help you through the initial stages of this shock.' She promised to visit as soon as she could.

I too could not understand why Michael hadn't destroyed these letters: had he wanted me to find them? Given the intensity of the affair, I couldn't believe he'd forgotten they were there (and must have been for years).

Interestingly, around 1997–98, I had been aware of the possibility of a special friendship of Michael's. But it turns out I had the wrong woman. Around that time he seemed to be developing a close relationship with a woman called Annette, who was Linda's friend and flatmate. After Linda had left the university, Michael had spent a lot of time with Annette, supporting her through various work and health dramas, and driving her to appointments. Annette was first mentioned in the letters between Linda and Michael in 1993 and increasingly more so as the years went on. She, Linda and another friend of theirs, Kaye, had some sort of club that had met regularly at Annette's address. It was referred to in their correspondence as '41 Nicols', or just 'No. 41'. These meetings had been talk-fests on politics, literature, gay rights, music and any other issues of the day. Indeed, I had been invited a couple of times, but the invitations had then stopped – and now I knew why.

On my first, more cursory read of the letters I noted that he'd mentioned me quite a bit. Nothing really nasty, just rather unkind. But of course leaving those letters for me to find was the most unforgiveable thing of all.

In my response to Pru I said, 'You are right; the behaviour does not fit the persona. Anyway, I cannot murder him, as he's already dead. I think I can cope with the affair itself; what I cannot cope with is why he left me the letters, they are so terribly intimate, as I said, almost pornographic.'

During the tumult of the days that followed, my mood swung from anger to despair. I remembered that Michael had invited Linda to have dinner with us on her last night in Canberra. She had not been to our home for some years (or so I thought – I was to discover otherwise later, through the letters). I looked back on that invitation with outrage. Outrage at Michael's audacity in inviting her; similarly, her audacity in accepting. That he could invite her to our table knowing the depth of his dreadful secret beggared belief.

The betrayal, the lies, the hypocrisy ate me up. The hypocrisy took my breath away, and anger joined the pain in my heart. All those years he had lied to me and deceived me. Not my perfect man; not the perfect husband. I had idolised him and how the idol had fallen. I am by nature a reasonably calm person, rarely given to outward displays of anger, but I cast about for some way to vent this overwhelming feeling of darkness; I looked at the small urn on the dresser with his remaining ashes and was momentarily tempted to fling it in the rubbish. Instead I put it where I couldn't see it and vowed I would never have my ashes buried in the vacant spot next to his. And I tossed four copies of Linda's thesis in the bin (why on earth did we have four copies? No other student rated this level of thesis retention by Michael).

I abandoned reading the letters and turned my immediate attention to finding contact details for Linda. I wanted her to know that I had found the correspondence and knew about the affair. And I wanted her to know there and then. I searched through Michael's old emails and found an address for Annette. I emailed her asking for Linda's contact details. Nothing was forthcoming immediately so I eventually obtained the information from one of Linda's former colleagues, and wrote her a curt email saying I'd found the letters and asking her what she wanted me to do with them. I added that she had ruined my life.

A couple of days later, I received an email from Annette saying she'd had a 'cryptic text message' from Linda asking

Annette to ask me to send the 'papers' to her. She gave me her address. I had not heard from Annette for years. She apologised for not contacting me after Michael's death but blamed it on her aversion to telephones.

I decided it was time to write and tell her of my discovery. I wrote what I thought was a dignified letter, pointing out that while Michael had told Linda that I knew and accepted his deep love for her, nothing could be further from the truth; I'd had no idea about the affair, none whatsoever, for the whole six years. I told her of the very explicit sexual nature of many of the letters. I said I felt I had been betrayed by them all.

I did apologise for actually thinking she might have been 'the other woman' during the months after Linda had left, when he had spent such a lot of time with her – having coffee, driving her to work and so on. Not, I explained, that I'd said anything to Michael about my resentment, as my rational side knew they were simply friends, and that's what friends did for each other.

There was a lot more I could have written in my letter but it was all too painful. I ended up saying I was sorry that Linda did not have the courage to write to me, but had chosen to use her as intermediary, 'once again'. If Linda wanted the letters she was going to have to contact me herself.

I received a brief email from Annette in response, saying she was sorry about the pain I must be in but that I mattered more to Michael than anyone else and that he loved and respected me immensely. She promised to email again when she had more time.

I needed to talk to someone. I wanted to talk to my local minister, the Reverend Sally Parsons, whom I had always found approachable, but she was away for a week. So I looked at the list of counsellors in the phone book, randomly picked someone local and went to see her. As I had never been to a counsellor before, I had no idea what to expect and I was very disappointed. I only saw her once; she was not at all helpful and I considered it a waste of money.

I waited until Sally returned, and rang and asked if I could talk to her.

'Are you going to cry?' she asked.

'Probably.'

She had seen a lot of my grieving in the past year and no doubt thought I was going to talk about Michael. I was, but not in the way she expected.

Sally came to the house (no use crying in a café) – a small woman with a lovely smile. She was a good listener. 'What is it that they don't understand about the Commandments?'

It was, of course, a rhetorical question and one neither of us had an answer to.

One of the last things she said to me that day was that I was going to have to learn to forgive Michael; that I would never get over this if I didn't. In another email, Pru had also talked about forgiving him. She had written that it would take time for me to be able to do so, but she hoped that I might at least be able to relegate him to the edges of my consciousness. 'You do not want to be anchored to the knowledge of a part of Michael's past that is currently ruining your present and the prospect of a calm future.'

This I knew would be very hard; forgiving him even harder. Leaving those letters for me to find was such a cowardly act – he was dead so he couldn't see my unhappiness. Anyway, I didn't know what forgiving a dead person would achieve, and did not really want to think about it then.

What was I going to do about telling the family? How could I possibly tell them? I decided to talk to Michael's niece, Jane, in Melbourne. Jane was a general practitioner and I knew she had Mondays off so I rang and asked whether if I flew down to Melbourne, she could possibly meet me at the airport for lunch. She agreed, probably thinking I had some sort of urgent health problem I needed to discuss.

Jane was disturbed when I told her about her uncle's exploits, and her thoughts were immediately for me. Her advice was to get rid of all his things – anything that reminded me of him, including photos. We decided the children should be told and she offered to come up to Canberra to help me do this, if I felt I needed help. It was also decided not to tell Michael's older brothers, one of whom was her father and in his nineties, and the other of whom was over eighty. She rang me the next morning and said she had spoken to a medical colleague who had confirmed what we had discussed – the children definitely had to be told. It was too much of a burden for me to carry on my own.

But at the end of the day, I couldn't do it. I simply couldn't summon up the courage to tell them. How could I destroy their image of Michael when I hadn't come to terms with the revelations myself? I knew then that it would be some time before I could face breaking this news to them.

Shortly after this, Pru arrived. I had missed her when she moved to Perth to take up a position at a university, and I had never been more acutely aware of just how important her friendship and support were.

By the time she arrived I'd finally read all the letters, and had completely revised my original comment to her that I had been given a few mentions, nothing really nasty – just rather unkind. Unhappily, this turned out to be totally wrong.

There were so many shocks. Michael had confessed to Linda that he'd had affairs during his first marriage. This was news to me. He had even had an affair while he was on sabbatical with his wife and family in the UK, shortly before I met him.

He'd shared with Linda the love of the same things he had shared with me, such as the lake, which had also become *their* special place. And clouds. Imagine how devastated I was to find the poem 'Clouds', which I thought he'd written for me in 1996, had actually been written for her. It was the poem I had chosen for the Order of Service booklet at his funeral. I burnt with embarrassment and humiliation. His betrayal and lies cut very deep.

It was breathtaking how quickly the opening of a box had changed a perfect man into a serial adulterer and heartbreaker. It was as if I had been living with two totally different people for all those years. I'd never been much interested in astrology, but it occurred to me that as he was a Gemini – the sign of the twins – maybe there was something in it after all.

Pru and I went through some of the letters together and actually managed to have a laugh at a few of them – especially Linda's jealous hissy fits over Michael's friendships with other women, particularly Annette. We even laughingly pondered what I might do with the correspondence. Pru asked if I knew anyone at Mills & Boon. But of course we knew it wasn't Mills & Boon material: while there was no doubt that some of Michael's letters were beautifully written, their subject matter was often unbearably lewd and broke my heart.

Pru encouraged me to make changes around the house. I bought a new bed and redecorated my bedroom. I removed a large chair that Michael liked (and I didn't) from the living room, swapping it with my piano, which had been languishing unloved and untouched in the spare room. Pictures were removed, and books and other personal items were given away. But the pain could not be removed or given away.

Then, early in September, I received a long letter from Annette. She went on about my pain (how would she know?) and how much Michael had loved me – how after his heart failure he was even more appreciative of my love and care and would cry 'unashamedly' when he related how I had cared for him through the ups and downs of his surgery and recovery. *Really?* She talked about how much Michael and Linda valued their marriages and refused to admit that it was an affair they were having.

She said the Linda and Michael thing was some romantic 'notion' they had and as far as she knew there was only one sexual encounter and that was 'very late'. When Kaye had found out about this it had severely interrupted her friendship with them, but she herself was in an 'invidious position', being their 'dear friend', and she couldn't bring herself to ditch them.

To say I boiled with rage over this email would be an understatement. I spat chips and I couldn't wait to respond.

9 September 2011

Dear Annette,

Thank you for your email. I'm sure it was sent with the best of intentions. Unfortunately, it's just not possible to explain away a six-year love affair in a few lines.

I have now completed the painful task of reading all 741 letters between Michael and Linda and about half of the 161 emails between them and you. You suggested that the affair was not sexual until the end. I assume you believe this to be so because it is what you were told by Michael and Linda. Let me assure you, nothing was further from the truth, which means you too were lied to and deceived. The affair was sexual from at least 1993. Michael and Linda did not just engage in sex, they WROTE about it graphic detail. There are hundreds of letters and they are lewd and sordid and I attach some examples, for which I apologise because they are truly disgusting, but I'm sure you would not believe me otherwise.

None of the people who were my confidants, and who knew Michael well, would believe what had occurred had it not been for the letters. No doubt I was naive, certainly I was too trusting and I never thought Michael would be stupid enough to have an affair with a student; it could have ended badly for both of them but it did not, it only ended badly for me and his family.

Linda started to express her concern that Michael kept their affair 'secret' from me while she was being open with her husband. Michael, with his usual mastery with words, was able to convince Linda that the differences were much less than she thought. It was all lies. In short, he told Linda what she wanted to hear in those letters regarding my knowledge and understanding of the affair.

Had I known it would have been the end of our marriage and Michael would have been in no doubt about that. His solution was to lie, and on this occasion to Linda. And this, it seems, he did with consummate ease . . .

And now I come to you, Annette. I never read your emails to Michael. I considered them to be between the two of you and I deleted all of them after his death. However, I did come across a few emails in his sent box that he had failed to delete and it was disappointing to discover that you had filled the void when Linda had finished with him. In them he expressed his love for you. I none-the-less smile when in a particular letter of Linda's, (and heaven knows I've had little to smile about in the last fifteen months) Linda had a fit of jealousy about you.

And so, what of Linda, the living guilty party, getting on with life, enjoying her family, no pain, no regrets, no guilt, no shame and no morals.

And so, what of Michael, the dead guilty party, an older man falling for a younger woman to boost his ego and revive his flagging virility. What is the adage – there is no fool like an old fool.

Michael wrote many unkind things about me in his letters. But the most unkind, even cruel thing he did was to leave those letters for me to find. Why could he not let me die in blissful ignorance?

Kind regards,
Nola Westfield

*Attachments: Michael's letters of 6 September '93', 24 September '93, 7 October '93 and Linda's of 22 September '93.

Fire of Passion

Your love which sparked an
unquenched fire
In the forest of my life,
A searing, clearing, cleansing
flare
Since you became my wife.
Has given me a new spring
growth,
Green tips from black, burnt
bark.
A surge of rising, healing
Life
A light to banish dark.
O Nola, darling Nola, hear
The cry of joy I shout.
Passion's flame is spreading
still
And never will burn out.

MIW 6.vi.81

The Book

In classical Greek mythology, Pandora was the first woman on Earth. Zeus gave her a beautiful container, which she was ordered never to open. But, driven by the curiosity bestowed on her by the gods who had made her, she did open the box, and found that it contained all manner of evil. She tried to close the container, but it was too late – its contents had escaped and spread over the Earth. Today, the phrase 'to open a Pandora's box' means to perform an action that may seem small or innocuous, but that turns out to have severe and far-reaching consequences.

It was indeed a dark day for me, the day I opened that box. Initially I was pulling the letters out at random, reading some until, in despair and shock, I would say to myself, 'I'm not going to read anymore.' I would then wander around the house in a daze. But the box mocked me, drawing me back to its wretched contents again and again. The memories of our life together became more sullied with every letter I read.

After a few days, and still a bit dazed, I knew I wasn't going about the task in a methodical fashion. I decided to put the letters in date order and read through them all from the beginning. Then I added up the number of letters in each year – 741 in total, all handwritten – and dozens of emails written after Linda had left the university, with longer and longer gaps in between until the final one, just a few months before Michael died.

I went back and reread everything he had written for me since he'd met her – all the poems and love notes – but now I could no longer be sure what he was saying to me. The depth of the pain I felt is probably indescribable.

Then I bought a large notebook and went through the letters and poems again, carefully copying out pertinent extracts – sometimes quite lengthy ones – matching dates and making comments (often just one or two acid words) that expressed how I felt at the time. As I simmered away, I would often return to the notebook to make further comments as they occurred to me. I called it the Purple Book, due to the colour of its cover, not the colour of the content.

When I decided to write about this I knew I couldn't include all their correspondence. All 741 letters (or 'notes', as they called them), plus the dozens of emails and many poems Michael and Linda had written to each other, amounted to millions of words. The letters, all handwritten on foolscap paper, were often updated several times in a day and were usually many pages long. During university semesters, they hand-delivered their letters into their individual communication letterboxes at the university, or pushed them under the door of each other's room; dates often overlapped.

Their affair must have been very time-consuming – not just the assignations, but also their need to write in such detail about it. In 1993 alone they wrote 206 letters to each other. I suppose, being lovers, they wanted and needed this additional communication, but how had they got anything else done?

Michael was an early riser and would go from our bed to his home office, where I assumed he was attending to his university work. In fact, I now discovered, he must have been writing his passionate thoughts to Linda while I was still asleep or sipping the coffee he always brought me before I got up. He also wrote to her at other times during the day, and often last thing at night as well. It seems that Linda sometimes struggled under the weight of her other responsibilities, but Michael never mentioned any such struggle. This affair certainly involved an element of narcissism – perhaps all adulterous love affairs do.

It was six months before I felt emotionally strong enough to reveal Michael's secret to the children. By then I was thinking about writing a book about it, so I had to explain this to them as well. Their reactions were all different. I lacked the courage to tell each one personally. I had a discussion with Michael's eldest son, Anthony, and asked him if he would speak with his siblings and assure them that if they wanted to talk to me about what I was planning, I was certainly willing to be there for them. Only one took up that offer. Another expressed concern for his mother (Michael's first wife) and what effect putting all this in a book might have on her.

This was not an unreasonable concern, as Michael's letters revealed details about the several extra-marital affairs he had had during their marriage. Because I'd known nothing of these affairs, I assumed that his first wife would not have known either. However, I subsequently learnt that this was not the case, so some of the burden of guilt about revealing these earlier indiscretions was removed.

I spoke to my own children individually. Apart from their initial disbelief, one really did not want to know about it – she loved Michael and she wanted her memories of him kept intact. My son wanted to know why I would want to put it all in a book. I told him I hoped it would be a cathartic experience. He responded, 'Well, it might be a cathartic experience for you, but it is not going to be a cathartic experience for the rest of the family.'

I thought this response was a little harsh and, in fairness, he later softened that response, explaining that he was only anxious that I might be undertaking something that would cause me even greater distress. My other daughter, who also loved Michael very much, fortunately loved me more; Michael was swiftly off the pedestal she had him on and her concerns were solely for me.

Nearly all the letters I have selected to tell what Michael and Linda called 'The Chronicle of the Great Love' have been edited to some degree, some heavily as they were often repetitive. Those reproduced have been chosen to reflect the changing nature of their relationship over eighteen years, along with Michael's thoughts about me and the role I played in his life over this time.

The
Letters

1992

Purple Book: '97 letters in four months!'

How could this possibly be? Where on earth had he found the time? We had moved into our new home, the one we had designed to be exactly as we wanted, only nine months earlier, and were looking forward to our second Christmas there. It had been a very busy and exciting time in our lives; I had great memories of those months. We often had family and friends around to the house at weekends. Spring hadn't quite taken the chill off Canberra Sundays in September, so Michael would light a big fire in our wonderful open fireplace and we'd all gather around. He loved to cook, so he relished the new modern kitchen in which he could display his culinary skills to our guests. Summer was coming and we were planning and planting in the garden, and laying the lawn. It beggars belief that this is when he started his love affair.

The affair, or the beginning of what he and Linda later referred to as the Great Love or GL (*ad nauseam*), appears to date from early September 1992, though they started writing in earnest about it after a conference in Melbourne later in the month. Indeed, it may have begun earlier, but there are no letters before the beginning of September.

4 September

Michael: I have been very naughty. I knocked on your window; I saw the light on and wondered if you were present or just left the light on. No luck!

I am going a little bit crazy not seeing you, but it's good for my self-control isn't it. Being strong is my future and you must help me with that. I promise to make your responsibility easy to bear.

Hang in there Linda and keep those thoughts coming my way.

Love you, Michael

Linda's first letter to Michael, written on 8 September, was mostly about the bad relationship (though a professional one, this time, it appears) she'd had with her former doctoral supervisor. She'd been rereading a letter from him and said she felt down 'in the pool of misery/tragedies of my life'. Although he'd made things hard for her, she said, 'I remained a "good girl" to him – some of my friends and even my hubby told me I was crazy just letting him step on me.'

She went on to speculate that perhaps her supervisor had been insecure because of her 'accomplishments/awards'. She was confused about her personality: 'I'm not happy being boastful,' she said, claiming it was against the spirit in her. She bemoaned the fact she hadn't asserted herself against him, but added she didn't keep hurt feelings inside her. 'They just pop away – vanish in the air so easily. Maybe this is the reason I bubble with joy and enthusiasm every day.' She couldn't understand why anyone would see her as a threat because she loved people – 'I love to see the goodness in them. Do you think there is something wrong with me?'

Linda went on to ask Michael to spend a little time reading her letter, replying and checking her English, suggesting anything she should do differently. Already there appeared to be strong feelings between the two of them – not only did Michael have the temerity to sign off his first letter with 'Love you', but she ended hers with, 'I've never felt this wonderful feeling before that transcend into the care of the heart, mind, body and spirit. You have touched my heart and I have grown. May the light always shine in you.'

I had no idea how long they'd known each other when this was written, but surely it must have been some time, if Michael was already able to utter these two words to his student. It seemed that my apparently decent husband was embarking on a journey during which his outward respectability was to become a sham.

Linda wrote in her next note that she had much, much more on her mind that she wanted to share with Michael. She felt she talked to him 'like a friend, a sister, a father, a mother, a girlfriend, a guardian, an old person'. She asked herself why she could bestow such a range of characters on him and decided it was because he had such a strong aura, 'so powerful, so enduring and magical'.

That's a very flattering image of my husband; I'm sure it appealed to his ego. And no doubt the way she finished the letter also pleased him: 'Thank you for giving part of me in you and you will always be a part of me as long as I live.'

Having read Michael's response, in which he alluded to affairs he'd had during his first marriage, I wrote, quite aghast, in the Purple Book: 'Two extra-marital affairs!' I knew Michael had liked the company of women and was capable of forming deep friendships with them, but I was happy to accept that this was just part of the way he was. I certainly had no idea he'd had affairs when he was married to Margaret. In this letter he mentioned a girl called Edith. I was also aware of his friendship with someone called Edith, who, I think, had still been in the department when I'd started there – a rather quiet young thing. Sometime later she had moved to Melbourne, and Pru has since told me that there was talk she'd left because Michael had broken her heart. Knowing what I now know about Michael all these years later, I felt sad for Edith – she too had been betrayed.

22 September

Michael: Recalling my extramarital involvements threw up some interesting contrasts which I didn't speak about, but which I will now share with you. With Marie, the girl in NZ, it was an emotional storm which engulfed me after an innocent start. A big bursting passionate thing which could have become fully sexual. It was very nearly beyond my control and would certainly have led to separation and divorce had Marie herself not called it off. As you suggested, she probably couldn't face being responsible for the marriage break-up. But I emphasise again – it was a big and all consuming passion which could have increased if it had not been stifled by one of us.

My other affair with Edith was different. I deliberately set out to enjoy her company and to share insights, emotions and experiences with her, in a way I had never been able to do with Margaret, my wife. Perhaps I was seeking a dimension in the relationship which was lacking in my marriage, but it wasn't sexual.

I felt more of a betrayer, more unfaithful over my involvement with Edith than with the passionate time with Marie. With Edith I was sharing something that my wife might have enjoyed but I was denying her access to my thoughts. With one girl I looked for a superficial relationship and it rapidly became deeper. With the other, I really wanted a deep relationship but Eros got in the way for her. Freud had struck one but not the other.

Sharing is risky, deliciously risky, but only by letting out our thoughts can we be satisfied. 'The wine in the bottle does not quench thirst.' For now I am not thirsty but I will thirst again.

Poster Night

The magnolia blooms, untouched,
shows its perfection to the world
But try to hold it, experience
its tangible beauty, and it
bruises, spoils and tarnishes.

The butterfly flaunts its freedom
and embraces every flower, pond
and perch. But grasp it,
capture it, enfold it in your
covetous net, as it struggles,
sheds its gold-dust and becomes
a sad wounded, defeated thing.

And you Linda, so beautiful, so
generous and free, radiate your
sense of wonder and your zest
for living. But you must never
be caged, not for a moment,
lest you become sorrowful,
confused or compromised.
Live Linda. Live free

MIW 28.9.92

Although they appeared to have been declaring their love for
each other before the conference in Melbourne, it seemed
from Michael's letter of 30 September that this was where
the silly giddiness had started.

An affair within a university environment is not unusual
– they happen all the time, and universities are often
considered to be cesspools of sex and learning. In her book

The First Stone, Helen Garner wrote, 'The erotic will always dance between people who teach and learn.'

But a teacher's affair with a student is never considered appropriate. Michael was supposed to be a responsible person, and he comprehensively abrogated that responsibility when he embarked on this affair. He was old enough to be this girl's father, and maturity should have taught him the value of discretion and good judgment. In this affair he did not show either.

In one of Pru's emails to me after I found the letters she said, 'We both know these things happen in university situations – especially between students who become entranced by their clever, all-caring etc supervisor but the circumstances of yours and Michael's relationship and all you had been through I would have thought would have precluded such behaviour on Michael's part – and you both were devoted to one another.' Ah, but it seems one of us was less devoted than the other. While I was working hard so we had the money to help pay for our lovely new house, Michael was working hard wooing one of his students.

30 September

Michael: 'What a day this has been! What a rare mood I'm in. Why, it's almost like being in love . . .'

So goes the old song, and I understand those words well. I am so thankful that we were somehow thrown together. You have said some lovely things to me and I have opened my heart to you in a very self-revealing way. You have broadened my perspective on life in so many ways and I love you for it. I hesitate to use the word 'love' for fear of frightening you, but how can I describe it otherwise. Love expands one's life; it doesn't have to displace others that I love and my special feeling for you is a wonderful bonus for me. Oh, Linda, please understand what I say.

From the early damp morning and the flowers, the buses, the rosellas and the geese, to the shops and the trams and the snapshots and the art gallery – to the University, to dinner and all . . . it's been a nice day. One to store in the pleasant memory bank. I get a lump in my throat thinking about it, and the beginning of tears.

I knocked quietly on your door a few moments before writing this. I wanted to see you once more before going to bed to end the day. There was no light I could see, and my heart was thumping so hard it was almost a relief when you didn't answer. I hope tomorrow night you and I can talk a little; that your door, or mine, will open and we can discuss the millions of things on my mind.

I have many questions to ask before flying out on Tuesday. [Michael was going to the Philippines for an academic conference.]

May I say 'Goodnight and pleasant dreams Linda!' I am projecting loving thoughts in your direction now – catch them. How lovely you are!

On 3 October Linda replied, 'This should suggest a significant event in our lives . . . It has touched a part of my heart, a part of my spirit and added a different flavour in my mind.'

She went on to write that her experience with Michael should strengthen her bond with Roy, her academic husband, who had remained at their home, overseas, with their young children. I was bemused about this waffle. What she seemed to be saying was that her life with Roy was steeped in the routine practicalities of life and had become a bit boring, and Michael had 'awakened' something in her: 'I thought Roy would be my best friend forever. I should now prepare to be with him in a very wonderful way.' I wondered what kind of a person felt it was acceptable to use their lover to improve their relationship with their marriage partner. To me, these were morals and beliefs that were not normal.

However, Linda was a Catholic and had a lot of questions revolving around her feelings for Michael and the kisses they'd shared at the conference. Many of her questions were for God and why he had made things so complicated for her. 'I want peace but you gave me trouble,' she wrote, apparently admonishing God!

4 October

Michael: Now for the longest PS in the history of letter-writing.

PS I love you with my whole being. I have a rich mixture of passion, tenderness, fatherly love, but above all, a wonderful, spiritual sharing of minds which I hope can go on forever. Thursday night was a powerful energy sharing experience. Your love is thrilling, exciting and beautiful. We could have shared our bodies, but I was glad we did not. Mind you, it took hours for the pain to leave my loins. That part of me ached for you. I got a thrill every time you touched me in the car – that wasn't just accidental or incidental was it? Saying goodbye at your door was a wrench and I longed to kiss you.

Naturally I want to see you before I go, but if that is not to be, we will survive on notes.

I can't thank you enough for your advice about how we should behave towards one another in public. That will be just about all the time won't it – there will be precious few private moments, but I shall play it cool.

Linda, don't go to Yanco with just Lin – please. I want you to be safe. He is a fast driver and he must want you but he won't try anything if I am present.

Purple Book: 'Yanco. Lin.'

Yanco is a small town in southern New South Wales, about a four-hour drive from Canberra, where Michael had experimental plots. Lin was a Chinese doctoral student also under Michael's supervision. Michael went to Yanco regularly. He was often accompanied by his doctoral students, and I never considered the possibility of any impropriety if the student was female – but I now saw what a great opportunity these trips must have provided for him and Linda to go away together on scientific work. However, on this occasion, because Michael was off to the Philippines, despite his offer, he obviously wouldn't be able to go with Linda and Lin.

Two days later Linda woke feeling liberated from 'the pang of fear and guilt'. 'I read your letter and I'm thrilled that you're so far yet so near . . . I feel so secure and safe, protected and guarded, defended and loved, but most of all I felt the pureness of my body, heart, mind and spirit.'

Michael wrote notes for Linda while he was away. He quoted lines by the great romantic poets George Herbert, Tennyson, Wordsworth, Byron and Shakespeare, adding his own lines after each quote. But how distasteful to find that after these lines by Herbert –

Love bade me welcome, yet my soul drew back,
Guilty of dust and sin.
'You must sit down' says Love, 'and taste my meat'
So I did sit and eat

– Michael had written: 'Love's beckoning is so strong. I for one could not resist it. But I was strong too, my love. I could have taken us so much further, but you were not really ready, and I respect that. I think you will probably respect me more as well – I hope so. But, my darling, I am hot, hot, hot inside for you.'

Linda responded that she was happy to hear from Michael: 'Such a wonderful voice – you are reaching me through your voice and I'm quite relief from bursting.' But she was upset she wouldn't see him for the next few days – 'my heart just sink'.

I always looked forward to Michael returning from one of his trips. We would often go out to dinner and he would regale me with funny stories about the places he'd been and the people he'd met. And he talked a bit about his work. I would fill him in on news from the home front and give him any interesting magazine or newspaper articles I'd saved for him to read.

13 October

Michael: Being back from the Philippines has been a time of mixed feelings. I have had the utter thrill and delight of being back and seeing you. You looked so lovely, so warm and loving. But there was a tentativeness I couldn't understand. Could you not put your feelings down for me? Can't you trust me with those thoughts?

. . . I read your notes and was thrilled. But I couldn't understand the latter part of notes for 3 Oct – the day we got back from Melbourne. They were so disturbed and at the same time struggling to come to terms with an experience (our experience?) and trying to make future resolutions. My declared tangible love for you seemed to be accepted and rejected at the same time. Welcomed and abhorred. If only I had kept my love to myself, but I can't feel anything so strongly and not tell you about it. I am more honest with you than with any other person on earth.

Reading between the lines, you have become very protective of your marriage because you see dangers. I feel the same threats as you do but I feel my marriage is solidly built. But Linda, my love is not an invitation to abandon your marriage, or even to act treacherously . . . But we can and do share something special in each other. Why deny it? I can imagine sharing with you forever in a way that is no threat to the marriage of either of us.

15 October

Michael: What do I think love is?
I'm afraid of falling into the same trap
That has ensnared so many before me, but . . .
I think love is: the will to expend one's self for the purpose
    of nurturing one's own or another's spiritual growth.
In the light of our 'experience' (i.e. yours and mine) you
    have wondered and worried and expressed confusion.
    'Why did this happen?'
'How can this happen when I/you love my/your husband/
    wife?'
'Can you really love more than one person?'
'What's happening to me/us?'

I believe my definition shakes off our
self-limiting bonds. We can, *if*
it is our purpose, desire spiritual
growth for ourselves and for the
other person, in a close relationship with that person.
We can call it love without endangering ourselves
or the other person.

Purple Book: '"Self-limiting bonds!" So they're not endangering themselves or others. What a lot of self-serving nonsense.'

On 16 October Linda wrote about a TV program she'd seen on Abelard, the eleventh-century philosopher, and his young student, Heloise, and commented on their 'great love story'. This is where she began to see herself as Heloise to Michael's Abelard because of the way they too had expressed their feelings in letters and poems. 'How mighty were the words. What a nice history of love and passion, pain and suffering.' Lofty sentiments indeed.

By now Linda was declaring that she had never loved a man the way she loved Michael, deeply and unconditionally.

She was feeling 'fulfilment and true happiness . . . As I write this note, my body shivers and my face blushes; I feel like you're at my side, connected to me'.

This sounded like a clear invitation to me.

Sometimes, and I'm not sure why, Michael and Linda wrote parts of their notes to each other in the third person. The following day Michael wrote:

> I am concerned that I have demanded too much of Linda and she does so much for me inside. But thoughts that she might wish me to leave her alone to give her more space, when I desire to be so close, fills me with misgiving. She is strong, I know. She can look after herself I know. But I can't be seen to use my position to compel a loving response from her that she doesn't feel. I believe she does love me in a way far beyond/supervisor student closeness, bigger and of great substance. I am not able to forget that.
>
> I guess the thing I find the hardest to dismiss from my thoughts is that she is a beautiful young woman, full of energy, full of passion, full of life itself. I cannot say for certain that I am loving only the person Linda is; I also love the woman Linda is. Freud! Eros! Carnality? Sex! So in my completely honest moments I have to acknowledge that I am stirred and thrilled by this wonderful young woman. How easily this could be construed as *all* it is. An older man falling for a younger woman to revive his flagging virility. Please, please Linda, don't ever see me like that!

Then he reverted to the first person:

> I'll be honest with you. I won't deny the stirring in my body, but that's not all there is. I do want to share with you my spiritual thoughts, my insights and my vulnerability. I want to share with you because you understand, receive and appreciate those thoughts, and you give me so much in

return – wisdom, instinctive understanding and insights beyond your years.

Purple Book: 'Sex!'

I saw this letter as the first overt grooming for the next step – sex.

The letters over the next few days revolved around Linda and Lin's trip to Yanco. After the trip, Linda had revealed to Michael that her relationship with Lin was troubling her. She said her love for Michael made it necessary to confess to a bit of a flirtation she'd had with Lin. Because she couldn't be with Michael at Yanco, she'd diverted her attention to Lin, letting him hold her hand and even embracing him. She felt it was unfair because it was Michael she loved but Lin she shared time with. She observed, 'He doesn't know how we stand, but he . . . said to me "I think Michael likes you very much." . . . I want to help him so I give him encouragement.'

Linda commented on Lin's loneliness – his wife was in China – but said she didn't want to take advantage of his feelings towards her. I was becoming more and more amazed: was anyone here thinking of their marriage partner? This girl had a husband and children and she was coming on to a fellow student *and* embarking on an affair with their supervisor.

Linda was nervous about seeing Michael after her revelations about Lin. On 21 October she wrote a very long letter in which she asked why he loved her and why she loved him: 'It has never occurred in my mind that you are already old. Maybe that's the wonder of our love – a love that knows no bounds – no space, no time, no age, no place – nothing.'

She went on to say that she loved him more than a student–supervisor relationship would allow (which seemed clear, unless she was used to a very different kind of student–supervisor relationship to most students); they had a special cohesive closeness, 'because no matter how we try, we can't be physically together – it will only bring sadness and noise'. However, it was clear they *were* already physically together because she continued that she found it 'fulfilling' to kiss and embrace him, even if that was all they could do. She said that when she was close to him he made her shiver, and pleaded, 'Keep me away from danger. I need you to protect me. Michael, oh Michael please help me. Help me. HELP!'

Purple Book: 'Michael as the guardian protector!' This was to become a recurring theme in Linda's letters.

> Michael: The interesting, thought-provoking thing about the Abelard and Heloise story is that the real romance of the love story is the meeting of the minds in the letters and poems, not in the affair when they were younger and produced a baby. I'm sure you appreciate that, trying to balance the twin experiences of the recorded thoughts and the physical presence of a loving supervisor. A very nice PS to the Abelard and Heloise story is that 700 years later, about 150 years ago, both bodies were removed and buried in a single tomb in a cemetery in Paris.

Purple Book: 'Pure manipulation.' By constantly referring to Heloise and Abelard, Michael appeared to be trying to elevate the affair beyond its clandestine tawdriness.

After Linda had finished reading a book about Heloise and Abelard, which Michael had given her, she wrote, 'As you've said, it was the meeting of the minds that kept them going. But what of their spirits? They satisfied their physical desires but their love continued until they were older.' She then asked Michael if he would like to make their love the 'love story of the century'. But at the same time she questioned the love that they had for each other. What about the love she had for her husband? 'Can we really love two human beings at the same time?'

Purple Book: 'No!' Loving two people, in a romantic sense, at the same time is not a concept I have ever believed in.

On 23 October he took time out from his 'pressing duties' to read Linda's 'notes'. I wondered now exactly what those pressing duties had been. Me? His other students?

> I couldn't wait another minute to respond to the few (very few) uncertain notes in the beautiful story of a love observed. You can be *absolutely certain* that I love you, in a unique and powerful way. I am as positive and sure as I am of life itself. I will *never, ever* stop loving you. If it is to be a sacrificial love, then so be it . . . My mind is full of you and I feel ten feet tall just being aware of you . . . I adore you. Be beautiful for me.
>
> Don't torture yourself about being affectionate with Lin; in a very real way he is part of our circle, part of us . . . Come to think of it, if we want to conceal just how deep our love is for one another (you and me) it would be easiest in a close-knit threesome of people who spend a lot of time in each other's company.
>
> In relationships, people remain forever separate, no matter if they share houses, family, kitchens or beds. But this new creation which is not the sum of two personalities, but the capturing of essences, spirits in a new whole, stands apart from the everyday, tangible separateness of people. When we are separate – it is still there.
>
> Awesome isn't it!

Purple Book: 'Awesome!' This was such uncharacteristic language from a man of Michael's literacy. I found the last paragraph of this letter extraordinarily bleak. He had well and truly proved the truth of his comment that people 'remain forever separate' in relationships.

25 October

Michael: It would be sacrilege to try to capture in notes the events and responses of this evening, but I should write something. It is so beautiful and too brilliantly consuming to be adequately described. I will write of our love at great length one day. A lifetime has been compressed into two and a half hours.

A life's journey into a short walk by the lake. For a few short moments we were the only two people in the world. We were the original Adam and Eve. No other man but me, no other woman but you. The world's first embrace. Fresh, new, unique. Nothing else like it. Nothing to compare with it. Love's essences, the mingled distillate of our two souls.

I will write you a poem once I have internalised the experience. Poetry is the spontaneous overflow of powerful feelings: it takes its origin from the emotion recollected in tranquillity.

At the moment I am too full of emotional drugs, too high to be tranquil. Meanwhile, be my love's essence.

Dusk by the Lake
25.x.92

Reed stalks thrust at the evening sky,
Confident, proud, assured of their destiny.
Silhouettes, parallel, stiffened and upright
Directing our eyes to gaze towards heaven.

Heaven is here, here by the water.
Shimmering lights and cruising ducks.
All creation rests at that moment,
clasps us in its contented embrace.

Small flowers quietly show their display;

Unfold their petals, offer their scent.
Tiny creatures creep in the lush grass;
A solitary lark alone breaks the silence.
But listen! Another soft sound underlies
The tranquil scene by the shoreline.
A soft muffled throbbing, regular beat.
Two hearts punctuating a singular theme.

Enjoy and experience this unique creation!
A new love, a new life emerging,
Unlike anything else pre-existing
Our love, so different, beautifully new.

Would that this moment could last forever!
How to preserve the magic, the essence?
Where is our island where this never changes?
In our notes, in our minds, in our love everlasting.

MIW 28.x.92

Purple Book: 'A life's journey into a short walk by the lake.' This was the first reference to the lake that was to become their special place for assignations. But to me it was our lake, and he had written me poems about it. Thinking about it still brings an overwhelming sadness.

25 October

Linda: 'I could see in your eyes – FEAR – what if we might bump into someone who knows you or knows me. This is the real thing we have to hide.'

Purple Book: 'Hiding their relationship' – the first explicit mention either had made of having to do so. It will always be extraordinary to me that I had no inkling of this affair, which at this stage was in its early flourishing, nor any idea of

Michael's ability to keep secrets. To me he'd always seemed an honest man. He was obviously a good actor too – another characteristic of his that had never before seemed obvious.

On 26 October he made a comment about this: 'Our love is amazing – I want to jump and shout and burst out laughing. But I maintain my dignified demeanour so nobody suspects this senior academic has finally flipped and gone off his head. They would be close to a correct diagnosis. I am, at least inside, not recognisable as the person I was BL (before Linda), though hopefully not so different that the person Linda respected at first, and later loved, has not entirely gone.'

That night Michael wrote Linda another letter. They'd returned from an evening walk to find Lin waiting in Linda's room and it had stirred up mixed feelings all round:

It's been a big day with big mood swings – for all of us. So over the moon in the morning; so sad in the afternoon, with Lin so upset about our walk. He is a soul torn between respect and jealousy.

I wanted to hold you and make you feel safe. I wanted to give you assurance that what we did was clean and good, not dirty and shameful. Lin never said he was going to come back to the room to wait for you/us and had no right to hold you to a time, or to question what you did. It is insulting to your goodness and my first reaction was not fear for what he might do, but anger that either of us had to answer to him or explain anything.

Purple Book: 'Clean and good, not dirty or shameful.' It seems that this was the crux of it – as well as petty jealousies, defensiveness and a fear of being found out. I remember Lin as a nice, quiet little man, and it appeared Linda was fanning the rather immature crush he had on her.

Michael had a good explanation for Lin's jealousy – he was a lonely man looking for a cure for his loneliness and Linda might be able to provide it:

> And then he realises that you and I like each other a bit more than supervisor/student and that is a difficulty which he solves for himself in unusual ways. He always insists, if I call him on the telephone, that I talk to Linda too. He draws attention to the nice things Linda does for me. He even urged me to go on the walk with you.
>
> But now he is sure we got together more intimately than just two people going for an evening stroll. Trouble is, he's absolutely right!! But not in the way he sees it, a way neither of us intended or really wanted. Our minds did overcome our bodies and we were spiritually moved by the beautiful, uncomplicated sharing of each other's essence.

How he could say that their sharing was 'uncomplicated' seemed like a testimony to his growing delusions.

Towards the end of October Linda wrote that she was 'agonising and suffering' and asked if God was punishing her for something because she was not free to love him. Michael responded by telling her she was showing a child's understanding of a God who rewards the good girls and punishes the bad ones:

> No, my darling, you are not being punished. Whenever we reach for and attain great joy, we are in line for the possibility of sadness, misunderstanding and even persecution. Not from God, but from the cruellest animal in the world – humans . . .
>
> Continue to love God and share your joy with him. Thank him for it, and you will be reassured of his love for you. God came not to give us a Spirit of fear, but of Love, and a sound mind. It's in the Bible somewhere.

Purple Book: 'God, God . . . thanking God. God is creeping more and more into these letters and it is beginning to irritate me.'

Linda went on and on about Lin and worried about what he might think and do. Perhaps they should stop seeing each other. Not likely! Michael wrote on 28 October:

> Oh Linda, don't think I would just abandon you to Lin, whatever he might think of you . . . I don't want to hurt Lin and neither do you. But it is very far from my mind to stop seeing you so [Lin] could have a free go. Anyway how could I stop seeing you? I LOVE YOU! . . .
>
> The downside is the perceptions of other people. Not just Lin. People we love like husband/wife/family, and other people capable of drawing conclusions – other students, staff etc. We cannot even confide in our good friends – not yet anyway – because of the hurt of misunderstanding. We need only to continue to reinforce each other – to transmit energy and strength to each other . . .
>
> We kiss well, you and I. The whole range of beautiful kisses – the most delicate, barely touching kiss, the soft hold-your-breath, savour-the-moment kiss, the excited, greeting kiss after a separation, and the urgent, barely-controlled, passionate kiss. I love all your kisses and I long for many, many more. Oh Linda, I feel like taking a sickie with you!!!

Purple Book: 'A sickie! Oh, for goodness sake – has he lost his marbles?'

Michael's thoughts turned to Linda's husband, Roy, and to me. On 29 October he wrote:

> My thoughts ran to Roy, and were you thinking of him, protecting him, salving him in the light of the present situation? I have certainly had moments of assessment of just where I am at with Nola, and I know I love her as my life's

companion, my very good friend, the one to share children and grandchildren with, the house-builder and homemaker.

Our love – yours and mine for each other – is on another plane, another plateau would be better.

Purple Book: 'Nola – house-builder and good friend.' He talked about me as his life's companion, and of the sharing of our children and grandchildren. Had he ever reflected on his behaviour and wondered how all that would have been affected if any of us had found out about his affair while he was alive?

30 October

Michael: I am looking forward to you coming for lunch in my room. Don't bother about the intrusions; though I have many . . . don't get embarrassed. If we were really wanting to have a secret rendezvous, we wouldn't have it in my room. We'd take a 'sickie' and go somewhere else. What a great idea!

Purple Book: 'Another sickie.'

On the same day, Linda wrote a long series of anguished notes, starting with the fact she was too depressed to see Michael, even to get out of bed. Her relationship with Lin was troubling her. She had asked him for some help in the lab and she felt he'd overstepped the line and misinterpreted her actions. Whatever had happened she didn't like it and was 'pissed off'. She couldn't understand why Lin thought she was playing with him (though it was obvious that was exactly what she was doing) and she said, 'He is really dangerous. If I am not careful and strong enough to defend myself, I would likely be in big trouble. I thought he promised not to be naughty. I thought he cares.'

She said she pitied him and knew he needed attention, but felt he couldn't control himself. 'I might have gone beyond the boundary of bro and sis and gave him too much attention. Oh, dear what have I done to him? Can you be my father this time?'

Purple Book: 'Now she wants a father.' It wasn't just Lin who was immature in this threesome. There was a lot of childish game-playing going on.

31 October

Michael: What can I say? It is always easy to be wise after the event, and as I wrote earlier, I understand why you want to be friendly towards Lin, as I do. We both see how alone he is and he must feel it whether I was on the scene or not. But there is a difference between me being friendly. I am a supervisor; you are a fellow student. I am 56; you are 31. I am a man; you are a woman . . .

I feel like I want to say to Lin that the relationships among all three of us has to be professional without preventing us from doing it in a friendly way. But of course I know, you know and Lin suspects our relationship is far, far closer. What Lin doesn't understand is that the one way we are not being close is the carnal, sexual way. And, at the base of it all, that is the way he wants to be friendly. And there's no way he can be. You are not in any 'danger' so long as Lin knows we are not lovers in the physical sense. We are lovers in the Abelard and Heloise sense, though he probably doesn't understand that. It is the thought that I'm getting favours that he is denied that is eating him up.

Purple Book: 'They're not close in the "carnal, sexual way".' Interesting comment he made about the age difference not coming into it because their connection wasn't physical. Did Abelard and Heloise engage in deep kissing?

31 October

Michael: I've been a busy, respectable, middle-class, suburban-dwelling Canberra resident. I have been up since

5.45 am and for most of the day I have been helping at a church fete with many others.

While I was busy I did not think of you, except in brief flashes, but now I am relaxing with my Walkman clamped to my ears, I can think of nothing or no one else. You really have become like a heartbeat for me. Often you are unaware of your heartbeat, but in the quiet thoughtful times, you realise it is there and you realise how essential for your well-being it is to have a good heartbeat and you are grateful for it.

I'm glad you liked my poem. It was, maybe, not my best, but I can't remember being so excited before about anything I had written – probably because it was so personal. I felt a child-like excitement about it. You helped me rediscover the child in me, because you have never lost the child in you.

Purple Book: 'Respectable middle-class suburban-dwelling Canberra resident helping at the church fete!' More rampant hypocrisy. All the time he was lying to us all – his wonderful generous friends and family. Monday to Friday he was an adulterer, Saturday and Sunday he portrayed himself as a fine, upstanding member of the community. He was a parish councillor and warden. I will never be able to understand how he could reconcile his life as a Christian and his life as an adulterer.

The same day, Linda wrote about her mixed feelings in returning home for the Christmas break. While she was excited about seeing Roy and her children, she was also nervous about facing them because of the secret she was carrying, and she was sad at the thought of not seeing Michael for two months.

By now she had date-ordered Michael's letters in a folder because Michael in an earlier letter had promised he would write a book about their love. She reminded him that 'a promise is a promise' and said the notes would be a good reference for the book; a book in which she dreamt that the last chapter of her life would be covered and she and Michael would be together. 'If you always end your notes with "be beautiful for me" perhaps I should end with "be strong and handsome for me always." I hope you'll not forget me.'

In the last paragraph she suggested that Michael 'trim down his tummy a bit' by doing an hour's gardening in the morning while she was away. How rude. This extraordinary advice could probably only have been given by the brazenly young. Michael was a tall, well-built man and while he may have had a slightly bigger girth at fifty-six than when I married him when he was forty-six, he carried it well. I would never have said such a thing to him.

1 November

Michael: So how have you been for two days – three days by the time you read this? I will need to be more disciplined if I am to survive our separation Dec–Jan. And just imagine the state I'll be in if you stay until February! NOT POSSIBLE! I'm not strong enough yet. My love can't be turned off like a tap, or like switching channels on the TV. I hate TV most of the time. So phoney, so crass, so false, so low grade. I am a snob. I don't like low quality 'entertainment'. I don't like low quality emotion; if it's worth getting emotional about, then the emotions should run their course. And now that I have experienced superlative love I want nothing less to merit the label 'love' . . .

Church was good today and the Bishop preached well on the 'bit-players' in the Bible, who 'walked on' for a brief scene, said their lines, and left the scene forever. Few of us are stars and most of us are bit players in life, but we can all enrich the total experience if we realise one another.

Purple Book: 'Church was good and the Bishop preached well'. What more can I say about this?

In Linda's letter the next day she reminded Michael of 2 October – the day they had both declared their love for each other in Melbourne. She wondered how they'd still be able to write while she was away but, she said, 'Maybe we don't need to talk, to write or to act because just by thinking about anything, we can already send the message.' And then she wrote effusively that she'd never experienced this kind of perception. She told Michael that she wasn't getting the weakness she'd had before; maybe he was nourishing her with his strength and energy, and she thanked him for this.

Then, she went on, 'I noticed also that I do write legibly well – look at my letters – giving all the complete strokes and they seemed written uniformly ... I'm still an old-fashioned person because I prefer handwritten notes than computerised ones. It gives me the feeling that it is more intimate.'

She finished by imploring Michael to never stop writing to her: 'The only thing that I could give you as a memoir is my notes.'

Purple Book: 'She's in denial about her handwriting.' Michael's handwriting was uniform and neat. Linda's was often a childish scrawl. Her notes on this day stretched over the whole day and her handwriting was as erratic as her mood swings. I couldn't help wondering whether that last comment had been part of the reason Michael had kept the box I'd found.

Because Michael seemed to have had a lot of affairs, she also asked him about his experiences with other women – did they have anything in common; did he feel differently with her? 'Was it because each had a different style/character/peculiarities to fill up the different pockets/spaces in you? ... You said you are insatiable – will this make you search and search.'

She suggested that his admiration for women was because their 'complexity and uniqueness' challenged him. 'If that's the case, what are we living for; in a relationship, what are the spices to make it last or will it always end?'

This was the first time Linda had shown curiosity about Michael's relationships with other women. Of course, Michael had never talked to me about any relationships he might have had with other women, even with Margaret. I considered it an unspoken agreement between us that we did not discuss the very personal side of our previous marriages: I didn't want to know about his with Margaret and I assumed that he didn't want to know about mine with Des. Perhaps I was wrong in this assumption. That he did discuss with Linda certain personal details of *our* marriage was a disappointment to me. I'm not sure how I would have felt had he discussed his infidelities with me – maybe it would have made me more aware of the possibility. I honestly don't know.

3 November

Michael: It has been a mixed day – perhaps a mixed two days because I wrote no Monday notes. You were very hard on me about Monday's notes! I spent a lot of time in your company, enjoying a nice excitement with you and still you 'stood me in the corner' because I had no notes to share!

No more about no notes. You remain the focus of my life and I can do nothing to change that. You dominate my thoughts; my life; my whole being is only whole because you made it so. I didn't know I was incomplete until I knew you . . .

Our walk by the lake was a special, special time – better than the 2 October morning in Melbourne where we first confirmed our love, which we both knew was there but didn't have the courage to go further with it.

By 25 October, our very deep places had been explored by ourselves and each other. By then we knew even more certainly that this love was VERY SPECIAL, VERY DIFFERENT,

VERY NEW, VERY CREATIVE . . . I dreamed (eyes open dream) that *we* had created new lives, maybe the two more children you say you want . . . It was AWESOME!

Now I am down from my mountain top again . . . to talk to God, to peer into my own heart and soul, the place to do it is in the mountains . . . God give me strength and peace, faced with cruel, denying reality.

Purple Book: 'God gets a workout.' God was not the only thing that got a workout in this letter. Michael gave full rein to a type of cloying prose, a voice of his that I wasn't familiar with. And 'We didn't have the courage to go through with it' seemed a rather devious comment.

4 November
Michael: Before I get up I'll try to remember or recreate, a poem I thought of last night. I did not go to sleep quickly, but I imagined you asleep, beside me or away from me I'm not sure.

The Sleeper

She lies so still, her only motion
The waves of hair that round her sweep
Revolving to their hushed explosion
Of fragrance on the shores of sleep.
Is it my spirit or her flesh
That makes this breathless silver swoon?
Sleep with no darkness to enmesh
That lovely rival of the moon.
Her beauty, vigilant and white,
That wakeful through the long blue night
Watches, with my own sleepless eyes,
The darkness silver into day,

And through their sockets burns away
The sorrows that have made them wise.

MIW 4.xi.92

There, I've done it! When I thought about it earlier, I didn't know it would be a sonnet. Sonnets come very naturally to me, but I haven't written one for years and years. You are an inspiration! I feel great. Where are you? I want to pick you up and whirl you around. Where are you? Come soon and make me complete.

Purple Book: 'Hasn't written a sonnet for years and years!' How irksome this was. He'd been inspired enough to write one to me that January.

In the same letter, Michael talked about coping while Linda was away by looking forward to her return:

Don't tell me not to be sad. You might as well say stop being alive – stop being a sensitive, feeling person.

Your analysis of my relationships with women. You don't understand what you do to me when you give me some psychological explanation for what I have been through! Basically there are only two facts that are important:
1.   I married the wrong woman and tried to make it work by devotion, sacrifice and downgrading my career, and after 20 years of that, the marriage failed finally.
2.   I met and married Nola who shares many things with me, who is good company, a good friend (my closest), someone I can grow old with.

The other women, the 'lot of affairs' you called them, were punctuations during an unhappy time for me and for them presumably. They never in themselves threatened that marriage but they provided a dimension to my life I was missing – for the briefest of times in both cases – just twice!! In 20 years!!

You will have noticed that I omitted the fact of you, from my 'facts'. That is because, unlike you in your proposition, I don't see you, regard you in any way, as standing at the end of a long line of relationships, affairs, searches after the perfect woman i.e. my mother. You think I am Oedipus?? I really and truly hoped you saw us as something very, very different. Different from marriage, good or bad; different from relationships, brief or long . . .

The two of us have as good marriages now as human beings have a right to expect. We cherish those marriages and want to protect them. So our love has to be strong enough not to be a threat to those marriages, because our partners would misunderstand and we couldn't hurt them. But the operative word is STRONG. If we are weakened by insecurity and doubt, we could indeed be in trouble. Only if we are STRONG can we overcome our own selves, transcend the mundane practicalities of existence. The closeness I want with you is to make our love strong . . .

I urge you to banish fear! Let us just love. Forget the questions. Forget the guilt. Be free Linda. Take the fruit offered to you as a free gift – no strings, no conditions, no nasty comparisons, no substitutions. Just a beautiful free gift.

Purple Book: 'Downgraded to someone "to grow old with".' His defensive comment about seeking solace outside his marriage 'just twice' in 20 years – was very ingenious. So was the comment about their partners misunderstanding their affair: I found this letter to be extremely manipulative. Here was this literate and erudite man writing beautiful love letters and poems that urged his young lover not to be weak and to accept his beautiful 'free gift'. With his letters and poems he seemed to be slowly leading her beyond a 'spiritual bond' to the inevitable – sex. Was this part of his overall plot to seduce her? I thought back to his slow seduction of me. Our relationship had taken years to move from friendship and hand-holding to sex. He had written me beautiful love notes and poems too. And he'd added marriage to the mix. But he couldn't offer Linda marriage. They were both married to other people.

The following day Linda was in the lab writing yet another note to Michael. I wonder what a lot of those scientists would have thought if they'd known what this doctoral student was really writing. She'd been unable to see Michael and was mulling on her disappointment: 'I just feel so bad . . . I thought you'll ring me. Please ring me before I go home. God, I feel the beat of my heart – hoping that you'll ring and say something. Please ring, please ring . . .'

Meanwhile, Michael was putting down more of his own thoughts:

I have been privileged to know you deeply, perhaps more deeply than anyone in the world. I have never experienced this mystical sharing we have with one another. Not with Nola – not ever before. If no one has experienced what we have (i.e. most of the world population) then they are bound to interpret our closeness by their own limited knowledge.

I have also had your notes and they are really beautiful notes today. Did I say I loved you? Perhaps it's slipped my mind. So here goes again – I LOVE YOU love you, love you.

Purple Book: 'No mystical sharing with Nola.' This hypocrisy never failed to rankle with me. He was so dismissive of all we shared. It made a mockery of his love letters and poems to me. And, to make matters worse, it was a theme he returned to again and again.

10 November

Michael: It's not productive to compare our love with the love experienced and expressed in conventional relationships. When two young people go out together and make a marriage, they want to show off their loved ones and don't care who knows about their decision. It's open; it is for all to see.

If, against the background of two people with marriage, households and children, those two people discover a spiritual union like nothing ever achieved before, even with their 'loved ones', it is inevitably a new ball game. The marriages, households, children etc, do not just disappear, and we don't *want* them to. We have something new, something special, something we cannot share with husband or wife and it means something only to the participants. To protect the participants themselves and to save all sorts of misunderstandings by others, the natural tendency is to keep that special love to one's self, a special 'secret' if you like. But it should never be a guilty secret, a shameful secret, a treacherous secret. I am no real threat to Roy and our love does not put at risk my marriage to Nola, though there are inevitable distractions at times.

It is obviously the hiding, the goodbyes, the frustration, the enforced separation that gets to us at bad times. Some of these 'realities' cause us to devalue the beauty, the special quality of our love. I am responding to your reaction after we parted last Friday. It is hard, very hard, but it is not because our love is wrong, wicked, shameful. It is the down-side, the sacrificial side of something very beautiful.

The world's history is full of such examples, and I don't just mean the love stories. The greatest example of all of course is the sacrificial death of Jesus to bring life and forgiveness to all humankind . . .

11.30 am. Damn, she came to see me and I wasn't there. It's not fair! IT'S NOT FAIR! I need to see you as often as

possible and I don't need to miss any of the few opportunities I do have. Oh God – how I miss you when we are apart.

Purple Book: 'Their love is not wrong – the sacrificial side
of something very beautiful. Comparing it to the sacrificial
death of Jesus! Dear God.'

I could barely contain my rage when I read this odious
drivel. It was quite extraordinary coming from a religious
man, one who was a church-going Christian. Indeed,
Michael was asked to preach occasionally at our church and
he enjoyed it immensely. He delivered his well-researched
sermons with great aplomb. One he gave seems notable now
in light of his many sacrilegious declarations to Linda. It was
called 'Enlightenment' and one passage he wrote read:

As a young person, grappling with some of the claims made
on my life and considering also the numinous, the inherent,
spiritual dimensions to life, I used to think that it's all very well
for Jesus to be this perfect specimen of humanity. He had
very good connections. He was co-equal with God. Indeed
he was part of the triune Godhead – which I thought to be
a distinct advantage over my all too human limitations. But
Jesus was subject to a gradual preparation for this earthly
life and mission, and I was able myself to come to an appreciation that God's example to humankind was to allow for a
gradual process of acquiring wisdom. I was able to expect
that testing periods in life could not only be endured, but
could be real learning experiences from which I could emerge
stronger and closer to God. And I came to realise that light
and darkness may be seen as parts of the same process of
enlightenment.

Statements such as 'I am no real threat to Roy and our
love does not put at risk my marriage to Nola' were a
clear indication to me that, in the end, any wisdom he'd

acquired had disappeared with that knock on the door in Melbourne.

His selfishness and self-pity also took my breath away: 'It is hard, very hard' and 'It's not fair' – he sounded like a petulant child who wasn't getting what he wanted. The fact that he could continuously shut out so completely the implications for me of what he was doing was very hurtful and hard to come to terms with.

A couple of days later Michael must have used the word 'trick' in a conversation with Linda, because she wrote a long letter about how offended she was: 'I painstakingly trying to have as much time with you as possible but you changed with a not so nice sounding word "trick" . . . I feel as if you're telling me I'm not sincere, true and honest? . . . I love you. It's true and it's not a trick.'

> **Michael:** I just read your awful note about 'trick'. Why oh why do you think for one minute that I consider you insecure??? . . . Are you really prepared to question my deep, abiding love, strong love for you on the basis of a word you don't like and certainly misunderstood?
>
> Trouble is I don't even think I can remember what I said and how I said it but I was certainly trying to make a joke. Trying to say something funny. I was exuberant, in high spirits, happy, joking. *Not* judgemental, *not* sarcastic, *not* critical, *not* suspicious.

That tiff was obviously smoothed over, but a few days later Linda was thinking of the people close to them – one of her fears was that what they were doing might be 'felt' by their partners. She asked Michael if he could be displaying some unusual behaviour at home: 'Women have their sixth sense and you can be easily trapped. I don't want to hurt other people. I'd rather sacrifice myself than seeing them in misery.'

Purple Book: 'She doesn't want to see Roy and me in misery.' It was laughable for her to claim she didn't want to hurt other people. Her paranoia was also laughable, really: she talked about a 'sixth sense' that women have about unfaithful partners. Yet I had no such sixth sense about Michael's behaviour – I never questioned him. My trust in him was absolute.

18 November

Michael: We have two realities to face – one is our respective marriages; the second is our supervisor–student relationship. Anyway you look at it, these are complicating realities. But they were there from the beginning and have not just surfaced recently. Our love grows in spite of that . . .

In my clearer thinking moments, I have had no trouble separating relationship-love from our new kind of love augmenting the relationship love, adding to them, an extra, a bonus. But you seem to be saying . . . that there will be an effect on our partners and it will show . . .

But I have not felt that there was such a danger because of the wonderful difference. My expectations of OUR LOVE are different from expectations of my love for Nola. You talk of a sixth sense that women have – do men not possess it at all? Some men perhaps but you are probably right. The flow of your thoughts, from my viewpoint, is that we are not talking of competing relationships. One love is not being exchanged for another – not for me anyway. Trouble is we use the same language for very different experiences. We talk of love for relationship love and for our kind of love. But we both know they are NOT THE SAME.

I found this letter and his next one especially difficult to read. This was Michael's first description of his love for me as 'relationship love'. He had no trouble separating his love for Linda from his 'relationship love' for me. Their love was *augmenting* the relationship love. I couldn't imagine what he was thinking – the more I read the letter the more his differentiation seemed semantic rubbish and a pathetic defence for his unfaithfulness and lying.

19 November
Michael: I have been trying to string together some of your recent thoughts about US. There does seem to be more of a conflict raging within you than I previously suspected . . . I ask, if I am succeeding in living day by day, valuing each day as a gift, why are you having more problems than I am?

I keep coming back to the different kind of love. Relationship love is demanding. We both feel the demands and we both yield to them. We are both conscious about nurturing our spouses and our families. But the different kind of love we have created about ourselves is not demanding in that sense. It is the meeting of souls and minds that is not concerned with the rhythms of daily living. It can be experienced entirely on a spiritual plane, made tangible by shared thoughts, appreciation of the beauty of nature, of the arts, of science even, in the delight of new knowledge. I thank God for the way our love vitalises me, makes my heart beat faster and my spirit rejoice.

It does intensify, and it does have 'high', 'peaks' of experience . . . And as we share the experience of enhancement and renewal you feel you are being disloyal to Roy and betraying the love you share as marriage partners.

But my precious darling, while sympathising with some of your responses, and understanding your sense of danger (too strong a word but it will do for now), I do believe you overstate the threat our love poses for those we love. It really is a different kind of love. I think that the different kind of love could, if circumstances were different, be merged with the relationship love. I mean that if we met and forged this new kind of love and were free to marry, we could have the perfect union. To be as one on all levels, including the day to day realities of life, it would be bliss indeed. Because we are not free, and in a real sense do not want to be because we care so much for our families, that does not invalidate our new kind of love.

Purple Book: 'Outrageous! "We are both conscious of nurturing our spouses and our families." He's milking the "relationship love" for all its worth. God gets another mention.'

20 November

Linda: I would like to thank you for the wonderful time we had yesterday. I'd really like to have that in one of the chapters in our book – don't you think so?

Purple Book: 'The book again.' She seemed to be quite fixated on this book they were going to write.

23 November

Michael: Will she come or won't she? I feel a little foolish, like a teenager waiting/hoping for a boyfriend to ring. Well, why not? I'm in love and I can't really control my thoughts. I have enough trouble controlling my actions!

We do need time together away from my room. It is becoming a prison for us, with the prison guards checking on us every few minutes. We want to elope, and at the very least we have to have some time away from the department, from your room, from my room, from people who worry us. You are tired. You are under pressure. We are bravely facing up to our inevitable separation and we just want some quality time together.

The next day, Lucas, one of Michael's colleagues, came into his office while Michael was embracing Linda. Linda was

upset and worried: 'Do you think no one is suspecting us
. . . we are seen all the time. We may not notice sometime
people having a long ear'. She said she felt uncomfortable in
his room – she loved coming inside and being close to him,
'but when somebody's knocking we have to hurry – what a
ridiculous thing! We may appear very obvious and that will
jeopardise the situation. I think this is a warning signal.'

> Michael: Of course you were upset by Lucas coming into
> my room while we were embracing. As I said in my notes,
> my room is far from ideal regarding its susceptibility for inter-
> ruptions. I wish I could have taken you right away for the
> rest of the day to talk quietly and let all your hurts and fears
> come out. I curse the things that kept us apart today. I felt so
> useless. Unable to be there for the person I love more than
> anyone/anything else.

Linda wasn't reassured by this: 'I feel threatened, I feel so
scared and determined to isolate.' She was anxious that
Lucas might be telling people what he'd seen: 'Gee, I'm not
prepared to face these people. What will they say?'

She apologised to Michael for hurting him and said she
would keep away from the department that day because
she couldn't face him. She was now too scared to go to his
room or even pass it – she was taking another way round.

> Michael: Yesterday was the longest day of my life and I lay
> awake so long trying to restore my body, which is reacting in
> tune with my mind.
>
> Whatever else I do today, I hope to take one practical step
> – to see Lucas and explain that you, my student, came to me
> feeling upset, and I was comforting you when he came into
> my room. Weeping students have been to see me before.
> In any case, you were upset weren't you? You must tell me

when you feel you can. The incident with Lucas just capped off some thoughts you already had. And of course you are tired, tired, tired. You need a break. You need to see your husband and family. You need to resolve the mystery of the two different kinds of love.

10.18 pm. What a day. I did, as I told you, go to see Lucas and explained how upset you were about a lot of things and he came in just as I was embracing you. He was absolutely fine. He did not think anything bad about either of us. He thought it was something like that, but was a bit embarrassed himself because he had spoilt the moment by blundering in. I said you were doubly upset because he would think bad things about you and me and he assured me that wasn't so. He knows me and he knows I am *not* a predator (my words not his). He is my friend and we work together. He is not a gossip. It was unnecessary to approach him really, but I did it for your sake.

My dearest one I love you so very much. I can't bear to see you hurt. Oh, please help us get back to where we were. I love you.

Purple Book: 'The lies begin. Lucas was "absolutely fine" about it.'

I have since wondered what Lucas really thought was going on. Michael's behaviour was reckless, imprudent and downright stupid. Given the risks, he was already living dangerously in the early months of this affair. He had a lot to lose – his job, his reputation (not to mention me).

The date of 7 December was, of course, a special one for me and Michael – the date he'd proposed to me. That 7 December fell on a Monday and, because our normal restaurant was closed on a Monday, he cooked dinner for me at home, bought me flowers and gave me a lovely poem about our special passion, clouds.

To Nola on our special anniversary – 7 December
Above the Clouds

Though damp mists cling, and blanket mind and vision
Or splintering rain shaft body and soul alike –
Still sunshine lives above life's chill's and clouds.

Though tortured thoughts despoil our restful sleep
And phantasies raise doubts and lower spirits –
Till love remains to warm our hearts and lives.

O give us wings to soar above this world
To where God's sun and Son shed loving light
And be restored and heavenly energised.

With you who have so blessed and
honoured me
I mean to know, experience all there is
In life's love-chest and heaven's treasure store.
O radiant one, share with me all God's gifts
That so outdo, outshine the world's rewards,
Let us abide, and His sweet love reflect.

MIW 7.xii.92

Imagine my dismay when I found a love letter he'd written to Linda on the same day:

This is the man who loves you very, very much and for whom your happiness is paramount. This is the man who gives you to the love and appreciation of your family, and does so willingly though sacrificially. As I said today I practically feel like the father of a precious daughter giving her in marriage. Without retracting what has been said or written before. I am not really like your father. I have more in common with a true lover. I love you with my whole being – body, mind, soul and spirit – and my desires for you are at all levels 'rolled into one'.

Purple Book: 'A precious daughter he's giving in marriage.' This is such arrant nonsense it's hard to believe it was written by an intelligent man.

9 December

Michael: I have waited until the last minute to pen you the last notes before you leave for your Christmas home visit . . .

Looking back over the past months I still find it incredible that we have built in that short time the kind of love that is so profound, so immense and yet so rare in the experience of the world. It sounds boastful sometimes to keep saying that we have done what so many, the vast majority, fail to do. It is a sad truth that to want a love that is deep and satisfying does not in any way guarantee that it will happen. One can smooth out some of the bumps in life's path by the exercise of will and determination by sacrifice and goodwill, and build the best possible relationship love. But I believe God gives to some people, even unlikely couples like ourselves, not the gift of love itself, but the capacity to respond together to the beauties of life, to the joy of living, to share the energy of all creation and to ENJOY at all levels the essence of God's nature, which is LOVE.

And so my darling co-creator, co-enjoyer, co-inspirer – I salute you as my partner in the most tremendous experience I have ever enjoyed. With our hands outstretched to each other, our fingers just touching, we can generate more love energy than millions of couples making sexual love. I am the last one to downgrade sexual love, of bonding, of sharing, of practical outworking of a caring relationship. Ideally, as I see now, it would add some surface fizz to the deeper love, but the deeper love would still be very deep if sexual love is absent altogether . . .

You have immeasurably enriched my life, and while I will always love Nola and the children very much, nothing can compare to the love I have for you . . .

Our love is good and clean and pure. It can never be harmful if we appreciate it for what it is.

Till we meet again.

By the time I had read to the end of these first four months' worth of letters, I was exhausted. To end the year with more talk of the 'good clean love' and how 'nothing can compare to the love I have for you' left me once again with an overwhelming sadness.

When I look back on that December I remember we were preparing for our second Christmas in our new house with the family, and anyone we thought might otherwise spend Christmas alone. Michael, as usual, was planning the Christmas menu – he always cooked the big traditional dinner with all the trimmings. We had decorated the house with tinsel and a real pine tree with beautiful baubles. Marlana was still living with us and it was all very festive. As far I was concerned our fortunate life was going on as normal.

Apart from family and work, as a couple Michael and I talked a lot about the things that mattered to us. We were political junkies so we'd had a lot to discuss that year: Clinton had been elected president in the United States; South Africans had voted for political reforms to end apartheid; the United States had refused to sign the convention on climate change in Rio de Janeiro; the Australian Capital Territory had elected a Labor government by a small majority; and the High Court of Australia had recognised native title in the Mabo case.

And Michael was having an affair.

1993

Purple Book: 'A record 206 letters this year.' This was also the year the erotica started in the letters, which caused me a great deal of additional distress.

25 January

Michael: It would be difficult to describe the excitement and anticipation as I await your coming. I have coped very well during your absence. I took your advice and made sure I enjoyed my time with Nola and other members of the family. While never a day went by without at least an early morning (while you slept) and a late evening (while you ate probably) special time with you.

I have spoken to Annette a few times on the phone – firstly about returning library books and latterly to find out if she knew for sure when you were returning (she didn't). It occurred to me and to my antennae, what an incredibly nice person she is. I'd like to get to know her better – she is obviously intelligent, has a well-developed sense of humour and is generally interesting to talk to. But from what you have told me about her anti-male outlook, I am careful to be as business-like as possible and not to seem too close and friendly. Perhaps I misunderstood what you said about her – perhaps she has no room in her life for any *special* man, without being completely anti-male.

But enough of Annette. Even as nice as she is she pales into insignificance when compared with you.

Our love is not governed by rules but by shared awareness of itself. It is a subset of the love of God . . . the love shared between us encompasses the love of all nature, all Creation.

Purple Book: 'Their love is a sub-set of the love of God.' Reading this almost took my breath away. This comment took his profanity to a completely new level.

5 February

Michael: What has life been doing for me since we returned from our momentous Yanco trip . . .!

My gradual wind-down from our evening together has left me with a wonderful memory of an upwelling of passion and emotion, but tempered with the knowledge that we might get too close to the fire. I am aware that there is a fascination in doing things that are dangerous or forbidden, but I don't believe we were just giving in to wicked temptation. I am sure that the love was fully established and that the closeness was an exciting setting to give expression to our feelings.

I love you so very, very much and I am aware how privileged I am to have been so close and intimate with you. It was magical for our skin to touch like that and our energies to merge. Though I had the strongest possible feelings and urge to enter and come inside you, I would not have done it. It is only the last step but it is important that there are no doubts or inhibitions whatever when it happens. I would not ever hurt you or force you against your will. Trust me, please Linda. You're so precious to me.

Dearest, wonderful Linda. Love is so great! What a force! What a tremendous reservoir of life's energy! How could we resist the power of love? I don't blame you for thinking at times that I am just fascinated by you as an exotic, new experience and that the experience will pass away and lose its appeal. But I am going to enjoy proving how *wrong* that judgment is. My love for you is the most enduring element of my whole being. I am gradually ageing, my intellect will perhaps diminish. My health will probably get worse (even though I *will* reduce my belly for your sake!) but my love will endure because it is built on foundations and materials that last. It does not depend on physical beauty, physical capacity, proximity or shared experiences and responsibilities. You are my delight and I want to be very special to you. Physical bonding is a bonus, not an essential. But it can be beautiful too! Do you agree?

Purple Book: 'A momentous Yanco trip.' Michael slyly made another suggestion about moving to 'physical bonding'. It was hard for me to think about how far they'd gone at this stage.

11 February

Michael: As we parted yesterday we were discussing doubts and faith. I could go on for ages about doubts. My doubts over the years have been my truest friends. They have represented honesty in a world full of deception. They have gone to the core of the matter while so many were content to stay on a superficial level. They were the truth behind the façade. Oh yes Linda, I have lived with doubts for a long time and I expect to for a long time still.

But then there is faith. In my experience faith is a gift or it is a hard won capacity after many doubts. Some people have a gift of faith and by that I don't mean blind optimism supported by ignorance or lack of deep thought. But in my case, faith is a state, a plateau, reached after a process of doubt and testing, until a position is reached where doubt is no longer sustainable. So despite how I might feel *today*, my judgment is to trust the accumulated wisdom I had built up previously.

I don't believe there is any topic, any pattern of thought, any feeling, any secret in my life you would be unaware of or else I am willing to share if you are unaware now. I guess I was always of the opinion that each of us should be permitted their secrets, whether thoughts or events of the past, and I still do believe we all have that right. But I have also thought that God knows all those secrets anyway, and so they are not unshared . . .

So when I experienced the love of my life, an aspect of God's love breaking through all the barriers to impact you directly – YOU!! – then there is no more point of secrets with you than with secrets with God. How I rejoice in this oneness! To love you is no great virtue, though it is a great joy, because in a sense I am loving part of myself. We strive to be at peace with ourselves and to love ourselves in order to be able to love others. Oh God, I never tire of talking, writing, thinking of our love. It's GREAT!! It's almost TOO GREAT for my heart to hold in sometimes. I want to shout to laugh out loud I am so elated. Just as well I can control myself – most of the time anyway!

Purple Book: 'God, God, and the issue of faith again.' I was getting more and more irritated by all this sacrilegious talk of God. One of Michael's strongest Christian convictions was that nothing is so bad that it cannot be forgiven. In this letter he also said there was no point in having secrets from God. He considered that people who confessed secrets about bad or immoral behaviour needed to be assured of God's forgiveness and God was capable of forgiving and loving even the most flawed and imperfect of us. Did Michael's certainty of God's forgiveness encourage him to believe he had a licence to behave immorally? Perhaps he lost sight of the fact that God likes some repentance in return, and there was no talk of repentance – just a joyous belief that God sanctioned their love.

I had always thought Michael was quite devout in his beliefs. He liked to discuss religion, and early in our married life together we started an ecumenical study group, some- times referred to in its later existence as the 'heretics group' because its participants represented a mish-mash of religions and views – Anglicans, Catholics, Quakers, Uniting Church, anyone was welcome. The group was called, with great originality, the Tuesday Evening Group because we met on Tuesday evenings. When it was sometimes moved to other nights for the convenience of members, it was still called the Tuesday Evening Group.

We initially shared homes for our meetings, mainly to assist with babysitting, but in later years Michael and I were happy to host many of the meetings. People drifted in and out over the years, but there was a core group of about six or seven of us. We would choose a book and people had to read a section of that particular book and come to the next meeting prepared to discuss it.

We were always happy to suspend our discussion and talk out any issues members had, and we certainly discussed a wide range of subjects. The books we studied were the result of a consensus of choice. Sometimes they were hard-going but we persisted; sometimes we struck gold, such as discov- ering Rabbi Harold Kushner's book, *When Bad Things Happen to Good People* and its sequel, *When All You've Ever Wanted Isn't Enough*.

Nor did we shun controversy, freely discussing the chal- lenge set by the controversial American Episcopalian and former bishop John Shelby Spong in his book *Rescuing the Bible from Fundamentalism*. We worked our way through Morris West's memoir, agonising with him in his ques- tioning of church authority; we talked through Aboriginal spirituality as explained by Catholic priest, theologian and archaeologist Eugene Stockton in his book *The Aboriginal Gift*. Bruce Wilson, the author of another work we studied,

became a bishop and visited our group to discuss his provocatively named book *God, Sex and Language*.

They were wonderful, stimulating gatherings and they
went on for almost twenty years – and all through Michael's
affair with Linda. I'd always believed he had a strong moral
compass, and his wit and good humour made him an excel-
lent moderator. Now I saw him as a fraud.

On 22 February Linda wrote, 'Since I came back in January,
I didn't even give you a single letter. This time I must – maybe
the best therapy to ease longing, wanting, connectness.'
She claimed she needed his 'shoulders and ears', and asked
him to 'please feel me – contact me. Great love, fill me with
your love.'

After each contact Linda wrote that she wept tears of joy
and sometimes tears of sadness (she did a lot of weeping
and wailing in this relationship). 'Maybe this is the irony of
the things in this life – we must have the left and the right,
the happy and sad, the hot and the cold – to signify the
meaning.'

Her relationship with Lin had resurfaced; she knew he
liked her and would do anything to please her. But she
thought the way that she had 'cared' for him had led him
to believe she loved him as more than a friend. 'He believes
I belong to him and that upsets me. I love him as my friend,
there is not more to it than that.'

The next day Linda wrote that she'd had a lot on her
mind. She couldn't believe she was having this experience at
her age, and how excited she was by it. 'It must be the same
feelings as when you have discovered other special women
in your life.' Yet, she said, she didn't want Michael to think
that she *felt* like she was the other woman. If he thought
that was what she felt she was, then it was very insulting
because it put their love in the realms of a basic, ordinary
relationship. 'As a human being I will continue to live by the
Great Love [GL] and as a super human I will reach for the

magical, mystique and mystery of both of us. Let us nurture the GL forever.'

Purple Book: 'She doesn't want to be the other woman.' A rather naive wish – after all, she *was* the other woman. As I read this, I felt scorn for Linda. And I was deeply suspicious of her motives in pursuing this relationship. I couldn't help thinking that somewhere in there was a need to please her doctoral supervisor – she'd already fallen out with her previous one. She needed Michael's full attention for the purposes of her PhD.

23 February

Michael: What a wonderfully honest, healing time we had today. Our feelings were laid open, our fears were expressed, our love was affirmed and we could share it all without any self-consciousness. Dearest, loveliest Linda, it was a precious time for us. Plenty of passion in the looks we gave each other, without the complications of too much physical arousal. Not that I can ever see you without getting excited. Do I show it? Or do I hide it successfully? I think the former, but I'm working on being 'cool'.

As I said today, I feel my great love for you is the most fundamental reality, and much of the rest of life are the 'accidents' of life. But I know that the 'accidents' are also real, especially when we include in there Nola, Roy, our children, our colleagues, etc. So how do we feel about our love in the context of all those other bonds? At one level we feel frustrated certainly; even irritated at times . . .

I don't compare my love for you with my love for Nola – they are different, so different that even using the same word 'love' is probably invalid to describe the two. From everything we have said and written, you also understand that difference. So there is really no need to ask – are we simply justifying our actions?

Far from justifying – in the sense of saying something is OK when it really is not – everything new that I learn or experience of our love I find pure and beautiful and clean and honest. Not grubby and dirty and shameful and unworthy. My love for you is on the highest plane – well above this weak body of mine.

Purple Book: 'Pure, beautiful, clean and honest; not grubby, dirty or shameful.' This was becoming a recurring theme – who was he trying to convince? I loved Michael as a man of principle, and it saddened me to find he had sunk to being a cliché – a predatory, lustful older man.

24 February

Michael: Your yesterday notes about you and Lin, and our conversation about the same thing, seem still to be unresolved completely. We seem to have discussed around the subject without confronting it. Perhaps you assume I know or can detect more than I really do. Yes I know that Lin 'fancies' you. You work closely together, and he wants that to be not just a convenience but a desire on your part. Not just a friendship and partnership with common interests but an emotional and hopefully physical relationship.

As to 'physical' the only thing you have ever said to me was that on one of the Yanco trips you did together you held hands and that while you were being just friendly, Lin read far more into it. So now, I suppose, he feels the relationship should be developing further into greater intimacy and you are resisting strongly causing him to feel confused. How am I going? Have I left anything out so far?

Then there is the fact – the wonderful, mind-blowing fact of you and me. As you have often said, it is difficult for us to hide what we feel for each other, and Lin is not blind. So he thinks it is a contest for the commodity which is Linda, or Linda's emotional involvement or Linda's body – and he deserves to win more than I do. But he can't confront me with it because of our supervisor/student relationship, so he transfers his frustration to you – challenging you to choose and thus settle the matter.

As to fear of detection – we did talk about that more satisfactorily. We can only do our best to be circumspect and not do anything too obvious in public which will be taken the wrong way.

Purple Book: 'Linda is a "commodity"?' There was something disturbing about Michael's exhaustive analysis of Lin's crush on Linda. When he brought up the student/supervisor relationship, it sounded as if he was reminding her that it was a competition for her that only he could win.

There were no more letters from Michael until 5 March, when he assured Linda of his 'tenderest love' and his concern for her as a 'friend/father/supervisor/lifelong lover', which I thought was an interesting combination of roles. In this letter, in which he again referred to Linda as his Heloise, he accepted an invitation on behalf of him and me to attend 'dinner, lunch, after dinner, tea' or whatever, at 41 Nicols with Linda, Annette and Kaye. I do remember going there a couple of times for coffee and I must have still been on the invitation list in 1993. I found Annette an interesting person, although she seemed pallid, as though she didn't enjoy robust health. I also quite liked Kaye, who was tall and very attractive – and I think she was going through a divorce at that time.

They used to discuss feminism a lot and presented as 'man-haters', especially Annette. I had difficulty with this because over the years they were prepared to let Michael do all sorts of things for them and this irritated me. I felt, it's okay to be man-haters, but do your own work – don't then grab a willing male to do things for you. Anyway, my invitations eventually stopped coming, although I can't remember when. I never questioned why, but I now see that as the affair progressed, Michael would surely have been feeling a little uncomfortable with my presence at these gatherings.

In March Linda backed off writing notes for a bit and Michael, in a letter on 19 March, appeared to be in damage control. It was in this letter he first expanded on the Great Love, which they referred to as the GL:

> I'd like to say sorry for feeling hurt by your regrets which you were beginning to express coming home on Tuesday. My feelings were not so much for myself but for the GL. I had felt and I thought, and indeed I still think, that the GL had enlarged and expanded and confirmed its genuine, mind-blowing creation-affirming wonderfulness. It seemed almost like sacrilege for the GL to be compared with ordinary sexual liaisons, even by implication. We can stand on the Holy Ground, we can tremble on HG, we can gaze with awe on HG and the wonder of what we have created, but we should not trample the dewy grass which covers the HG.

He went on to say that having written about the GL he didn't want to sully the page with anything ordinary. Then he started talking about what they had already experienced – 'the incomparable, heart-pounding kisses, the caresses, the intimate touches' – after which he waffled on about looking out over 'the Promised Land which is covered with cloud or fog'.

> Occasionally the clouds shift or the fog lifts and there appears a brief but beautiful scene, sunlit and blooming, brief but full of promise of the glory of the whole. Our poor small minds can encompass only the part, but they long for the whole – to devour the full blessing. What we need to learn is that the full blessing, the whole of Paradise, the entire Promised Land is already the possession of the co-creators. We just haven't experienced it all yet.

That was really the nitty-gritty. The Promised Land of sex. Then he started on about morals. First hers:

> I hope I didn't sound too negative in my last notes, thinking about your questioning of what we did and where we went and where was it taking us. Darling, dearest Linda, I'm sorry if it sounded like I was leaving you. No, no – far from it! I knew you were trying to come to terms with 'the morals, the norms, the values' of the culture that shaped you.

Then his:

> You should know too that my moral upbringing was not far different and the values almost identical. It is a lifetime of experience that has broadened me and given me different expectations of *ordinary relationships*. But my point was that our GL was *not in any sense* an ordinary relationship, and I was reacting to it being judged by the standard of ordinary relationships. It is very, very different from the ordinary – it is greater in every way, it is sacramental, it is a holy love, given to only a very few . . .
>
>   Oh Linda, I ache for you. I want you near me, in my arms, my lips and yours touching, devouring each other, our bodies pressed hard on each other, our stimulation obvious to us both but beyond comment. It is so natural and so right for such a love as ours to seek expression, even though opportunities for expression are limited. While I remain a male human being, my love for you will at some time or other stimulate sexual desire for my great love who is all woman. I will not, cannot, run away from that, and I don't want to! This is not just a male justifying his actions.

Purple Book: 'Not just a male justifying his actions.' Of course, that's exactly what he was doing. Although I could hardly bear to read about their intimacy, by now I was starting to wonder exactly what they were doing. He talked about 'making love' but they obviously hadn't fully consummated the affair yet.

29 March
Michael: I have spoken to Annette twice in the last 4 days and once to your answering machine. If I ever get an answering machine, I want you to do the recorded message. What a wonderful voice! As always, it was nice talking to Annette. She obviously loves you very much, and that makes her my friend. She cares for and supports you in a very special way and I relate to that completely. Do not tell her I told you, but when I enquired after you I used three words 'How is Linda?' She replied in one word – 'transformed!' Brilliant!

Purple Book: '"Brilliant"!' What on earth did Annette think had transformed Linda? I can't imagine that Annette didn't, as she'd claimed in her email to me, suspect that *something* was going on. Possibly blind-eye syndrome.

2 April
Michael: I am sorry not to leave some really good notes. I have been so busy . . . you will have to make do with my ever-present thoughts and cling to the Great Love as I have been lately. I am dying to hold you and kiss you in our special way. I am wavering in my resolve to just rely on notes . . .

I very seldom get sick but I feel all churned up inside and I have a dull headache. Pray for me. Send me your wonderful healing thoughts. Give me the capacity to be good and helpful to my students.

Purple Book: 'His other students get a mention! About time he did some work for them.'

5 April

Michael: I am amazed how I have been able to carry on with so little contact with you, and then always with Lin around. He is like your chaperone. Watching to see if we get up to anything naughty, suspecting that we probably do when he isn't watching. He simply does not understand where we are with each other and where he is with both of us.

And that brings me to the other ever present factor for both of us; maintaining both a professional and a friendly relationship with Lin while knowing there are other emotions and forces present which make it difficult. The reality of the GL which is so easily misinterpreted. So much so we are afraid to expose the smallest part of it to others, a nearly impossible task. And the lustful desire Lin has for you which is almost as difficult to misinterpret as the GL is easy.

I am excited at the prospect of going to Yanco with you overnight Tuesday/Wednesday next week. Time to talk. But I am also worried that Lin is going to make trouble for you about it if you decide to go, but not with him. He will say that you are avoiding going with him and will want to come or else delay till he can go with you. I am saying I want to go alone with you and I guess I should freely admit that. Of course I want you to myself because I need, *we both need*, to have some time together somehow, somewhere.

Soon to see you again. Excitement grows. Anticipation heightens. Heartbeat quickens. This is LOVE. Yes I love you, yes I love you, yes I LOVE LINDA!!!

May there be many hugs and kisses to share in our lives. Remember I am supposed to last till I am 100.

Purple Book: 'Yanco again.' Whenever Michael went away on a field trip or on other academic business, I quite enjoyed the time to myself. Matthew was married and Claudine had moved interstate, but Marlana, who was by now at university, was still living with us. If she was home, I would prepare something light for us (I never liked cooking much, and Michael did most of the cooking anyway). I might watch a bit of TV, listen to music or read. My social activities were mainly based around the things that Michael and I did together.

21 April
Michael: I love you so very much that sometimes I feel physical pain at the sheer ecstasy of it. A curious paradox. Your beauty fills the vision of my minds' eye, and my meditations on our love fill my mind, monopolising my thoughts. Fortunately, other mundane matters manage somehow to slip around the sides of my consciousness sufficiently for me to fulfil my normal duties and live up to most of peoples' expectations of me.

Have you yet thought about a lunch hour (or so) up the hills drinking in the colours of autumn? Today? Tomorrow? SOON? I long for even the smallest touch from you, but mostly to be able to look into your eyes and feel the love that comes from within. We could make each other blush.

The next day Michael's letter went on and on with overblown prose about the GL, but he also introduced some different language:

I have never wanted you so much as I did today. I wanted you with an urgency that was near to panic. A craving, like that of an unfulfilled druggie. I wanted love to engulf us both. I wanted you to openly embrace me, to receive me and for us to become one flesh, one love, indivisible forever.

Purple Book: 'Unfulfilled druggie!' Like 'awesome', it sounded like the language of an ageing man trying to grasp the vernacular of a younger generation. In this letter he used more religious imagery – this time to express his sexual desires:

> I did not want the lovemaking to be frantic. I wanted it to be slow and delicious – not hot and sweaty. The kisses could be wild, but lovemaking is a true sacrament to be savoured and worshipfully respected right up to the dam-burst of scream-ing nerve-endings. I know this is very sensual stuff I am writing, and I haven't written this way before. But you should know my true feelings as they affect me. They also affect you I believe, but please let them be free as I have just done.

A month later, his letters were becoming increasingly urgent. On 20 May he wrote:

> You have just called in. Oh joy for me and such kisses too. Always wonderful! Never enough! I will *never* be satisfied with your kisses because I will always want more and more and more . . .
>
> I wonder only why we both feel so urgently for each other just lately. I have been controlled, I have been well-behaved, I have been brave (!) but inside I am wanting to be with you, to hold and to hug and to kiss. I feel I need to touch you often to dissipate some of the stored passion. Can I touch you often? Even for a moment each time?
>
> Sometimes I call out, 'Oh God, why is it that <u>our</u> love must always make the sacrifice? Why can't this sacrifice be shared around more equally? You have given us this Great Love. You have collaborated in its creation. Why then do we, the blessed co-creators have to limit the free expression of such great and different and wonderful eternal love? Am I so far from your grace that I don't deserve to love Linda freely and to share with her the full flood of my passionate feelings.

Purple Book: 'Bizarre.'

On 24 May, there were more tedious references to the glory of the great GL and its uniqueness:

> The Great Love has carried us both forward in a dimension of our own, part of the new creation, and it is in that new dimension, it is in that Great Love context that I want you, that I want to make love with you, that I want to create a serenity and an ecstasy with you. I am somewhat sickened and repelled by physical lust, but love . . . Oh that is *different*. And the Great Love is unique; unique to M and L, the Heloise and Abelard of the late twentieth century.

Purple Book: 'What utter nonsense.' I have often wondered if he really believed claims like this. I presume he thought he could get away with it because Linda was his student. After she'd read the book he gave her on Abelard and Heloise, she constantly referred to herself as Heloise, keenly encouraged by Michael.

29 May
Linda: I can't stop my pen from writing about erotic thoughts. It is causing a lot of embarrassment. What happened last Friday is like a new door to open my mind.

She was referring to 28 May, when she and Michael had driven up to Mount Ainslie, the highest vantage point overlooking Canberra. Michael and I sometimes used to walk or drive up to look at the view, but I don't think they went there to look at the view, however stunning. On 1 June Michael referred to an 'afterglow from the 28th, when he said they were very 'tangibly *within* each other's minds, hearts and anywhere else in the body we could think of'. Later in the day he wrote her another letter and a poem:

Today, at lunchtime, my poem said it was time to come out. As I write this I still don't know the words, but I know they will come as I write; so I'll say farewell for now and start a fresh page. I love you, beautiful one.

With the Flow

Buoyed and carried, borne along
In the swelling stream of love.
Sometimes floating, sometimes
   tumbling,
Sometimes fumbling for a
   branch above.

Calm still bays and foamy rapids,
Silent reaches, deep rock ponds.
Finally the free fall cascade,
Propels the love past filmy fronds.

Who can ever dam this passion?
Who can make this stream stand still?
Who reverse a great love's progress
And make the waterfall flow uphill?
On in triumph flows this love,
This energetic willing carrier,
Making light of each obstruction,
Whelming past each bump and barrier.

MIW1.vi.93

In her letter of 16 June, Linda's intuition was telling her she had done something wrong: 'I can see in your eyes how hurt you are . . . Maybe I wasn't sensitive enough last week. I'm really very sorry – I can't afford to hurt you . . . I have to punish myself by not seeing you.'

18 June

Michael: You are a smart lady. What advice do you have for a guy who has barely set eyes on his most wonderful beloved for over a week, even though she has never been far away, physically, in all that time?

Oh yes, they have been wonderfully connected in mind and thought, but he needs <u>MORE</u>. He needs to be there when she is upset by people and circumstances. He needs to look into those wonderful eyes and to feel the incredible warmth of her hand as she clasps his hand in hers . . . He misses the creativity she adds to his own to produce an incredible synergistic force, which enables them both to have unique insights into the nature of love, of eternity, of meaning, of the ability to see the God and the Good in everything.

I suppose, good, smart lady, what I am saying is – have you any advice for a guy who needs his beloved as much as this? You see, he really misses *HER*, not her attributes, not her personal characteristics. You have a big heart, dear lady . . . what do you suggest?

29 June

Michael: We truly do make love with each other just by sitting, talking, occasionally kissing (oh, those kisses!!!), and seeing things together. It is perhaps an irony that in our marriages we are free, and expected, to make sexual love, and in the GL we seem to be denied that freedom . . .

But I believe we will one day, maybe soon, maybe far in the future, make love in that way to complete the experience. Yes we will walk, we will talk, we will read poems, we will listen, swell and touch things and we will bring our senses our desires for each other to the very top of that high mountain and THEN . . . we will begin the Eros experience. It will be only then, as a culmination, that the all-over kissing, the soft massage, the hair stroking, the probing, the licking, the sucking, the nibbling, the urgent hugging, the trembling, and the waves of passion washing on our shore will finally join us.

Yes, my love, I *know* what we are capable of. I *know* that we can convince ourselves we *need* to express ourselves this way. But I can be amazingly patient, for I have been given that grace, and I can wait. It is to be completely consensual, never forced; mutually desired and embraced, never the result of persuasion. Yes, Linda, I do love you that much.

Purple Book: 'Extraordinary!' 'Never forced' and 'never the result of persuasion' – odd to have to spell this out, I thought.

In early July Michael and Linda went overseas for a conference together. On 8 July, while sitting in his room at the guesthouse where he was staying, he reflected in a note to Linda on the dramatic changes of the previous three days and when I read the comment 'From Canberra, where Nola dropped us off' a rather unpleasant memory was triggered.

I had accompanied the two of them to the Canberra Airport: Michael was driving and Linda was in the back seat. They were booked on a 6 am flight so it was dark, and there was a heavy fog. Michael, who had lived in Canberra for more than thirty years, took a wrong turn to the airport and we ended up on a road that we couldn't get off for some time. It was slow going in such thick fog.

'I think I've taken a wrong turn,' he said a bit distractedly, when it became apparent he had.

'Yes, you have,' I said calmly.

'Well, why didn't you say something – you normally would,' he said sharply. I was rather miffed by this comment and I did not think I deserved to be spoken to like that, but I was not about to have a 'domestic' about something so trivial, particularly when we had a student in the back seat.

But reading this letter now, I realised it was *because* she was in the back seat that he'd spoken to me like that. At the time I thought he was just a bit embarrassed to have taken a wrong turn, but of course he was embarrassed to have taken the wrong turn *in front of her*, and concerned about the implications if they missed the flight.

It was around this time that I noticed Michael was often short with me, making cutting, uncalled-for comments or criticisms. Once, I reacted quite strongly by telling him not to speak to me like that because I didn't deserve it. This was rather out of character for me and I think it must have given him cause to be more circumspect about how he spoke to me. He left the house and when he returned he had a big bunch of flowers and said he was very sorry. I now understand this behaviour was probably due to the stresses of his double life – he was not closing the door fully on his other compartment – and I am sure he became more careful at home after that.

19 July

Michael: I can share some of your thoughts and I do feel all the vibrations you have been transmitting. For a short while there I was feeling rather low. There was your obvious delight at being 'home' with all your family and friends. And I was so happy for you but my personal feelings were becoming distorted and I was feeling increasingly hollow and irrelevant to your life. It was nothing you said or did that made me feel that way – you were overwhelmingly kind and considerate to me all the time – to the point of overdoing concern for my dignity! You just were so obviously 'in your element' and I was silly enough to feel left out of your life, having no real part of it when it was so full with other things, other people.

But on the trip home you obviously *did* cling to me, you *did* need me, you *did* want me and I was completely reassured. But the experience taught me a lesson. Even in the most secure, firmly-founded love, there will always be some room for uncertainty, some doubts, some bad thoughts – if we allow them room in our lives. We need reassurance and must be prepared to give it. So I now see that 'the shoe is on the other foot'. I was feeling 'left out' in spite of all the positives surrounding me. So it is quite possible, even probable, that you would be feeling left out of things back in Canberra.

Purple Book: 'This is about control' – his insecurity, and his relief that she did 'cling to him' on the flight home. Even Linda seemed to have found his behaviour pathetic. She wrote on 20 July: 'I am in shock. I thought you were strong . . . [the Great Love is] telling me to set you free. I have given you back to where you belong.' But, she said, she wasn't setting aside the GL, 'maybe just having it intimately inside me while I'm busy with the real world'. And she generously conceded that they should share themselves with 'our loved ones. They need us'.

21 July

Michael: It's about an hour since you left. I really needed to see you and seemed to make a mess of explaining why, because you said (verbally and, by implication, in your notes) that you had *no* doubts but that *I* had doubts. I don't understand the doubts you mean.

How can I explain anymore clearly how I have been feeling? Perhaps because we have such high standards from the GL, simply missing one's loved one and wanting to be with her is too mundane a thought! Oh God, how I have missed you!

What I said in my last notes, and what you say you felt anyway was the honest reactions of the period 6–14 July. I was having some difficulty reconciling what we had already shared as co-creators of the GL, with what *you* were experiencing in your home surroundings. I felt some sense of being outside of your life rather than the integral part of it I had grown to feel. But I also said that the trip home reassured me and I *was* reassured. But again (and here my honesty with you seems only to get me into trouble) I did feel some empathy with you in the reverse situation. How were you feeling in *my* country, *my* context?

. . . You can depend on my resilience, my strength overall, without demanding that I never fail, never have a low day, a fearful thought, a moment of misgiving. Please forgive me those flaws in my solid dependability. Please don't demand perfection from me. All I know and all I want to know at this moment is that we share a GREAT LOVE that is beyond our human imaginings but which draws us into a oneness that must be experienced to know what it is like.

22 July

Michael: I have just re-read your notes. I am overwhelmed by the sadness of their tone. When you are upset your writing goes haywire, and your expressed thoughts are somewhat confusing. Not a criticism, just a fact! But it makes me sad and a bit desperate. I don't want to be released from the bonds of love – I don't even see them as bonds. I don't want to be 'given back' – given back to what, to whom, to where for heaven's sake. The GL is not some excursion that has to come to an end. It is integral to life itself and it *augments* life rather than detracting from it . . .

I hate it when you speak of our love in the past tense . . . far from comforting me with how great the love has been and what wonderful memories we both have, such talk of a love that is just a beautiful memory is a stake driven through my heart . . .

I am feeling pretty awful today – another bad night – and I need you more than ever. I want to hold you and feel your healing warmth seep into my soul. Then I can be strong as you want me to be, and maybe that strength will rebound to you and we will have that peace which conquers all that life dishes up to us. I love you Linda and I need you and your love so much.

Reading through all this, it struck me again just how analytical the two of them were about their Great Love, their GL. The time they spent combing over each other's words must have been quite draining and stressful. Linda certainly seemed to get quite stressed at times, and would attempt to make a move away, but she always caved in to the temptation of coming back.

My life with Michael never had this sort of intensity, even in the early joyous days when we fell in love. I am reserved by nature and not given to overt displays of emotion. Michael was far more gregarious than me but I thought we gelled – a nicely balanced couple. And yet, when I read these letters I was overcome with the thoughts that he must have found life with me boring in its comforting ordinariness. His home life had become routine, stability had become dull, and the hedonism of the early days was gone. His career had reached a plateau, with few or no challenges, and so he found this passionate love with Linda something new and exhilarating, something different to break the monotonous predictability of his life.

I suppose deep down I'd always feared I might not be good enough, not exciting enough, and not intelligent enough for my husband, but, despite these thoughts I was, in hindsight, rather naively never concerned about the possibility that Michael would have an affair. I was content with my life, but I failed to recognise the contentment I felt was mine alone and not Michael's. But how could I? He was a chameleon.

Did he feel suffocated in our marriage? He may have felt that way, but he had no right to – the very fact that he was able to have this long affair without my knowledge is an indication that he had unquestioned freedom; that unquestioned freedom was because I loved him and I trusted him completely.

August 1993 was where the erotica started. By now they were obviously ready to consummate the affair, which had been teetering on the edge of being sexual for many months. I never copied out in detail any of the erotic writings in the Purple Book because it was too painful to imagine him doing such things with her.

2 August

Michael: It all began [in Melbourne]. Well it didn't really, did it, because we had been exchanging special thoughts and insights before then. But the physical closeness did begin there. What was it that drove me to knock on your door late at night? It was such a dangerous thing to do – dangerous for its consequences for us both if we were discovered, and especially dangerous for me if my visit was unwelcome to you.

How crucial was that encounter! Our first embrace, almost our first real touch besides 'high fives' and the like. And our first kiss, the first of many. You kissed like someone freed from a lifetime of restraint. You were free to kiss how you wanted to kiss, not how others expected or permitted you to kiss, and you went for it! My joy of course knew no bounds, though I could still hardly believe that this beautiful young woman really did feel for me so strongly, in response to my expressed feelings and actions towards her. My rational mind kept saying how natural it was for me to feel such a strong attraction for a beautiful, young woman. It was harder to see a rational reason for her to show an attraction for me in response. Everything seemed against such a response – age, culture, marriage status and professional relationship – and yet here it was, already strong with an exciting blend of passion. Unbelievable but true.

Now we have these strong, strong desires for each other. Though we are still capable of sublimating our love to imaginings and spiritual oneness, we seem to want more and more to complete our journey to heaven in a lovers' embrace. My desire to stroke, caress, massage and kiss your whole body and my urge to suck and lick you in the most intimate way are not trivial sexual urges. They are the most powerful, passionate desires for *us* to experience those extras, those natural extensions of an established love. Always I am aware that such experiences are to be *mutually* developed, never imposed by one on another, never one being persuaded or pressured by the other. As we said last Friday, we seem to be ready, *both* of us. My only concern is that it is beautiful, not hurried or awkward or worrying . . .

How thankful I am that we allowed the GL to develop this far before we contemplated the joys of physical love seriously. But darling I am ready. I am very seriously overwhelmed with love for you. I need you. I hunger for you. How long . . . how long.

Purple Book: 'Yes, it began in Melbourne.' I have often agonised over what exactly *had* driven him to knock on her door that night and what was on his mind when he embarked on this affair with a young student. She was no femme fatale – what was the attraction? Was he driven by sexual desire? Where did he think it would end? I have heard the crude expression 'just a man who couldn't keep his dick in his pants'. But Michael worked above and beyond the call of 'duty' to persuade her to become sexually involved; all the outpourings of love and creating this Great Love. Surely if he'd wanted an affair, there would have been plenty of women he wouldn't have had to work so hard to get. But, then again, maybe it was the challenge – she was young, his student and married.

9 August

Michael: Thank you for coming in this morning, I needed to see you, to take in your beauty, to experience your fragrance, the softness of your lips, the sheen on your hair, the radiance of your smile. Above all, just to know your beautiful presence – it's like the sweetest of mind-bending drugs for me. After a long weekend absence I *had* to see you. After the delight of Friday's intimacy, the urgency of our bodies' responses, the fires in our loins and in our minds – oh my God, how I love you Linda!!!

. . . Oh my love, stop me, stop me – I'm getting dizzy with love. We seek only what is the most beautiful culmination of the build-up over the past year.

You speak of the absence of guilt, the freedom to go so far. Darling, we are not going through some diversion from our mainstream lives. We have developed in a love, moulded it, created it, been carried along by it, to the point where our love, our Great Love, *is the main thing*. If anything, the other aspects of our lives are the incidentals – our jobs, our science, our marriages and families, though each important, yield to the centrality of the GL. Because we are kind, because we care for others and their feelings, we are careful and protective. Such care is costly to us, sacrificial even, for we both know that the GL is at the very centre of our being.

At 'down' times, we may feel the GL to be a monster that has taken over all our principles, all our cultural background, and our consciences, but when we think clearly, we see the GL for what it is – a unique new creation incomparable with any other experience we have had or are ever likely to have, something that expands us beyond the confines of isolated, circumscribed human experience, and blesses us with all the rest of creation in an all-consuming love for each other and all that lie around us.

And when we finally merge our bodies when our love flows completely feely between us, everything intermingled, everything coalesced, everything becomes just a single mélange of tastes, aromas, feelings and breaths, an ecstatic climax of urgent, loving passion – we will be joined with all creation – with heaven and earth.

Purple Book: 'The explicitness . . .' After all the flowery euphemisms, finally reading the explicit descriptions of sexual activity this letter contained provoked a physical revulsion. It was impossible for me to read any of their letters containing descriptive sex without a gut reaction, no matter how many times I read them. As if that wasn't bad enough, to then have Michael call the other aspects of their lives – 'jobs, science, marriages and families' – *incidentals . . .*

Linda responded to Michael the same day, saying she'd 'lost touch with the world' after receiving his letter, one of the 'boldest' he had written her. She said it made her believe he was 'one of the great persons I have ever encountered'.

10 August

Michael: You have just recently been here. The air is rich with your fragrance. The taste of your lips lingers in my mouth. And the fire of love burns within me. My darling love, delight of my life, core of my being – how absolutely wonderful you are. How I delight in you! How I cherish the love we share! What a gift! What bliss! What serenity!

We truly own this love . . . We have progressed a long way and at a fast speed lately, and we have surmounted all obstacles without a single moment of doubt.

Amazingly as I muse about making love with you. I can really taste you and feel you. You are really there! Is this self hypnosis? Is this something paranormal? All I know is that I only have to think of you to feel your closeness. If this is a love-drug, don't ever take me off it! Hug me till you drug me!

16 August

Michael: I became *very* aroused just thinking of you several times these last two days. Usually I feel your warmth in me and a tingle of excitement as you come close. Often I lick my lips and recall your taste as we kiss. Always I imagine you and me in an embrace, holding and hugging and stroking and caressing. Running fingers through each other's hair, kissing each other's ears and neck. But this weekend I was really sexually aroused, hard and hot. It was almost to the point of embarrassment. I was especially hot when it was raining last night. The sound on the roof, chimney and windows was incredibly erotic and I responded accordingly. I had to take the bin out to try to cool down, and it didn't work! I became even more stimulated! See what an effect you have on me!

Oh my darling love, I'm frantic for you. I felt like kidnapping you this morning, I was so excited to see you. We'll have to make an appointment to talk *work* sometime because I can hardly think straight when I'm with you. I can only think of holding, kissing, making love with you. I'm obsessed! You'll have to throw a bucket of water over me pretty soon to cool my ardour.

All that remains for full, all-over integration is the total physical union. Is it any wonder we both desire it so much? Our deep kisses are a profoundly sexual act. Our longing to taste each other 'down there' is a palpable hunger. And the longing to give and receive each other sexually, genitally, in a fully erotic way is almost more than we can stand. Our senses cry out for relief from this anticipatory agony. I need to fill you up and you need to hold me in. We need to rise up and fly, fly, fly . . .

17 August

Michael: You must be speaking from the blindness of love to call me 'handsome'. I have never had any illusions about my looks. The best I can say is that my face is 'craggy' – like a rocky mountain with perhaps a worn, rugged, interesting beauty. One woman, only a friend, but someone who spoke frankly about what was on her mind, said I had a 'sensual mouth'! I think she would have liked to kiss me but I just played dumb and the moment passed.

Purple Book: 'What vanity!'

On 23 August Linda wrote that she was feeling the pressure of their secret. 'I . . . can't mix my work with love. It's hard to do anything, especially in your seminar – it's just too obvious. You just can't hide your feelings. You made mention of my name several times.'

His obvious attention to her was making her uncomfortable and when she was with her friends she felt she was betraying them. Her letter ranged in emotions and she said she was only just coping.

24 August

Michael: I cannot in any way blame you for feeling frustrated and a little bit fearful given our difficult situation. We would both much prefer that our love for each other was a love we could share with our friends, with the whole world in fact, and that they could all feel happy with us and for us. As it is, we have this secret love, tremendously powerful and life-altering, which we are forced to keep quiet about except with each other.

30 August

Michael: The taste of your kisses still lingers. The miss-you, hollow feelings have evaporated. I can look forward to your return in a short time. So why not put down some of my thoughts as they affect me *right now*. I feel great, I feel strong, I feel alive, I feel invincible. To pick up the word we have both used lately – I feel far more *alive*.

I am quite unable to bring you into my mind without also bringing to the surface my passionate desire for intimacy with you. It is part of that ALIVE feeling. My loins are stirred by you and I long to be close, close, close . . .

With that build up we can, as you put it, go to heaven together. We can hold and extend the ecstasy and not come down from the clouds for a long time. You need to feel me filling you and I need to feel you clasping me and we are actually as well as symbolically fully joined. Our one-ness is already a fact, fully established. The sexual union is an exquisite technicality, but not the essential one-ness itself.

At least you must realise now that I am no Superman, and that there are some practical problems in having the Great Love and having a full marriage with Nola. You should also realise my own limitations in not being able to just switch off or switch over. I cannot, for instance, come from an afternoon by the lake with you, and go straight home and spend the evening in wedded bliss as if nothing had happened.

At such times, though it may seem strange to say it, I have envied you your independent status, and your freedom just to be alone to contemplate the GL and all it means to you. Nola and I are the very best of friends and we share a great deal in our interests and our dealings. We have involved lives together, and we sleep in the same bed. We are affectionate with one another without being hot lovers. Nola does not initiate sex – never has – and responds only if in the mood. Nothing wrong or unusual in that, but in the present context, if I am not making it known that I want to make love, she accepts that and does not expect anything. She probably thinks that, at my age, I've lost a lot of my libido! And, to be honest, that is the way I am with her; I love her a lot and we are very good friends and companions and I *can* make love with her, but I seldom choose to.

So you see, the Great Love, the Grand Passion, does affect my life. I have no secret means of separating my life into compartments. The GL always helps me through difficult times and I certainly have some. The wisdom I have arrived at is that the GL is DIFFERENT from anything that has ever happened to me or to most people. It is not to be equated to a girlfriend on the side, a paramour, a replacement, a guilty, cheating relationship. It can't be compared with 'relationship love'. It really does not negate my marriage or my love for Nola – though occasionally it can affect my behaviour for a while.

Purple Book: 'This type of outrageous writing certainly has the capacity to raise my ire.' Again, how dismissive he was of his 'relationship love', and it astonished me that he denied being able to compartmentalise his life when I could now bear witness to his ability to do just that.

Michael's letter of 6 September was one of those I emailed to Annette to prove his and Linda's relationship had been sexual long before 1997. The interminable references to his pelvic congestion also gave Pru and me a bit of a dark laugh:

Back to last Friday. Oh God how we loved. How we came together rejoicing. How hungry we were to be together. We were so R-E-A-D-Y!! The best thing of all for me was that on this occasion I did not suffer the physical pain I often get, with aches in my testes and general pelvic congestion. It was almost as if we *had* made love, we had climbed the mountain and slid down the other side. I know I wanted more, more, more, but the effects of my wanting did not leave me with an unfulfilled body, just a mind filled with love and the knowledge that the love has no bounds, no limitations and that all things are possible for us.

Can I just say further how great it is for us to be uninhibited not only in our physical expression of love, but in what we *say* to each other. I want to *share* my beautiful sexual desires with you – not to impose them or demand them or even politely request them . . .

I like to tell you how I crave to kiss you in the crotch area and to lick and taste your 'love honey' – I want you to *know* how much I desire it, so we can share and affirm the desire. If you want to hold my penis to feel it, to expose it and to lick and suck it, it is wonderful for you to tell me of your desire so I can be your partner in desire and to go with you all the way into the experience. Our feelings of intimacy, of actual love-making experience, is augmented in our minds because we know we both desire the same things, and our communing and sharing times have an amazing reality about them.

Now, having congratulated myself earlier on not having aches in my loins last Friday, I now have, you guessed it, aches in my loins!! Would it be better or worse if we made love and expended some of this sexual energy? I rather think we would want more, and more, and more . . .

On 8 September Linda wrote Michael a note, again asking if he'd write their story 'when the right time comes along, especially all the details'. She suggested some chapter headings: 'Living Kisses', 'The Indescribable Senses', 'The Student' and 'The Supervisor'.

Purple Book: 'How helpful – chapter headings!'

10 September
Michael: What I experience in the GL is the complete absence of those boundaries and a feeling of infinity in every direction. Our love soars above the restrictions of Supervisor and Scholar, of 50 and 30, of craggy and beautiful. Our magnetism towards each other overrides all other considerations. But each one is not half a GL without the other. Only together do we make this new creation, but having made it, it has life of its own. It is a cosmic zygote!

In his letter of 14 September, Michael wondered if Linda feared that his love-making would be old-fashioned, conventional and restricted – fears founded on doubts about their age difference:

> Have you found me to be conventional so far? Do you think I am inhibited? Have I been hesitant to talk or to act up to date? Don't you believe that the GL will get its truly loving response from us, as has already happened? Trust the GL Linda. It will give us the best experience possible and appropriate.

He marked the day before as a significant date and wanted to give Linda some thoughts for the journal he would write to chronicle the GL:

> How can I begin writing after the past 18 hours, maybe a simple 'I love you' might be best, because those 8 letters really do say it all. But I guess I have never been able to just say that without expansion. I need to try, even if I fail, to set down in writing some of my feelings and reactions, insights, perceptions – for myself, for you, for our 'journal'.
>
> Early this morning, before 5.00 am, while I was lying in bed and marvelling for the zillionth time at the GL, I held my penis in my hand (I am naked after all!) and it wasn't just a play-ing-with-myself gesture. I had the strongest sensation that it wasn't me but *you* holding it, and I also felt that it was no longer mine but it belonged to you now. And my thoughts ran along the familiar paths of integration, one-ness, merging etc.
>
> What a lot of significant dates and places we now have! We'll have to get together to try to list them all – some of them are milestones in our coming together, some are times of special insight into beautiful places, things, perceptions. When did we first look at a dusk silhouette together? When did we first discover the transference of heat energy from your hand held about mine? When was our first experience of thinking the same things, using the same words, feeling

the same vibrations, even when we were large distances apart? And that is not to mention first touches, first kisses, first . . . other things! Oh my darling, I can hardly keep my composure. I am in a jumpy state. My body is nearly out of control and my love for you is oozing out of me, almost literally.

Can I descend from the mountains of these contemplations for a moment. I was serious about the possibility of going away next Monday/Monday night/come back Tuesday. If our island/mountain top experience has to wait until 1994, then so be it, but I *could* be away 20/21 Sept. I don't want to do anything you won't find comfortable or which would make you feel strange or guilty. The purpose would be to have our free-flowing day, our relaxed unhurried sharing with no agenda apart from being together. If we make love, and the way we are now it seems likely, we would have to be completely at one with that, not tense or guilty. Our merging should be complete and unrestrained. Please consider honestly what you want to do and, for once, think of yourself and not of others' expectations.

2.30 pm. You just called and confirmed all I have been thinking. I wondered where you were and whether you would call – and a few minutes later you did! Your call did nothing for my jumpy state, and my talk of squeezing thighs, which just came out of the blue, did not help either. The GL makes me bold and I get greedy for intimacy.

Yes two days is not long enough, but two weeks would not be long enough either, or two hundred years. O Linda, I *need* you and your love. I am a druggie. I am addicted to love – hungry, thirsty, overwhelmed by desire for you. I long to be with you when your body is free of clothes and free of tension. Relaxed. Open. Then I can kiss your tummy and your thighs and your lovely mountain of Venus with its lovely textured hairs and then . . . well then it's too precious to put into words. The Italians have a word for it . . . 'carezza'.

Purple Book: 'A significant letter'. I don't know where they spent the '18 hours' of 14 September – perhaps it was a Yanco trip. When Michael talked of going away with Linda, he was telling her he didn't want to do anything that would make her uncomfortable, and urging her to think of herself and not of the expectations of others. The 'spiritual love' they went on about endlessly seemed to have gone out the window; now the focus was sex.

Thirteenth Idyll

Pine needles brown bestrewing the lake bank,
Yielding to mould themselves to those lying.
Pine needles green, fluttering over,
Screening, protecting and sifting the light.
Peewits and Currawongs, visiting, perching,
Black and white angels, piping and squawking,
And blessing the lovers kissing, embracing,
With bodies love-warmed, ignoring the cold.

Waves rolling shorewards, bumping and splashing,
Joining the scene to the opposite shore.
Sentinel silhouettes standing so boldly,
On western horizons, textured, contrasting.

Breath comes but fleetingly in the lovers' embracing,
Hotly touching the skin where the kisses have passed.
Now life, love and joy are eternally founded,
In the gathering dusk and the faltering sunset.

MIW 15.ix.93

16 September
Michael: I do need to talk with you before noon tomorrow [Friday] about going away together. Please, please don't feel pressured to do this unless you are *absolutely sure*. There will

be other times and we can cope with the love at the level we have it now. But if you *are* sure, then let us be as relaxed and open as possible, and let whatever happens be an honest expression of where we are at the time. And if some things *don't* happen, it is because they were not right for the time and there is no cause for regret or disappointment. We must feel *free* and *be* free.

But going away together appeared to hit a snag – maybe Michael and I had a social commitment that put a spoke in the wheel, I really have no way of remembering. The cancellation of their trip had obviously disappointed Michael greatly; Linda wrote the next day: 'There was a sad tone and pitch in your words, in your eyes and in your mind. Honestly it made me feel so down. I thought we would never regret if something don't happen.' She sounded frustrated and hurt; she felt he was only thinking about what he wanted and that even though he was asking her not to feel pressure, she did feel pressure – 'because of you. Instead of support you showed me pain.'

She was also worried about lying to friends and colleagues about where she was going: 'Maybe I am no good at lying but it seems so easy for you.'

Purple Book: 'She's picked up that he's good at lying.'

The next day she apologised for starting to question Michael's sincerity and truthfulness in yesterday's notes. 'I started doubting the love and forming bad notions, and then I thought, Oh, my God, this will ruin the growth of the GL.'

21 September
Michael: Thank you so much for raising my spirits. I really felt down since last Friday because I despaired of ever having even a day's free-flowing time with you, let alone any really intimate opportunities. And with you returning to be with your family, things seemed even more remote. I guess my

disappointment got the better of me, but it wasn't *your* fault. The high I was on was bound to let me down some time, but I figured it might be after you go, not before. Anyway, you are giving me hope again that we might still spend some time together without too much pressure and rush before you go.

Their disagreement had blown over and didn't seem to cool their ardour. According to Linda's letter of 22 September there was a lot of trembling relating to events on 20 September (the Monday) and more proof that their relationship had been fully consummated long before late 1997, when Annette said they'd only had sex once. I also mailed Annette a copy of the following letter from Linda to prove this, in which she referred to Monday's liaison: 'I had my "heaven" with you, my very first . . . THANK YOU VERY MUCH! I never stopped trembling . . . GOD! Thank you for being inside me.'

This seven-page letter repeated words of overwhelming passion and love for Michael and the GL. One whole page was devoted to his wild kisses; another to the Venus he had 'awakened' in her. She seemed almost deranged with desire: 'The juices of love are too sweet to bear and we almost die testing the sweetness of it . . . Do you reckon this would be a wonderful part of the GREAT BOOK!'

24 September
Michael: Your notes were the best ever. The feeling of openness and the freedom to express one's self without guilt, questioning, rationalising etc is a wonderful expression of trust and surrender to the love that binds. You are a fantastic lover, *very* sensual and *very* responsive. 'Mind-blowing' is too weak an expression for what happened between us.

26 September

Linda: I went to heaven again – you don't believe me but you drove me towards the sky – I can hardly describe it – oh joy – such joy to be with you for an hour.

Linda was returning home for five months the following week and nowhere in her notes to Michael around this time could I find any reference to her looking forward to seeing Roy and her children. Everything she wrote in those long letters revolved around Michael and the GL: 'Our love for each other will endure. Could you still write to me if you can when you'll be 75? I'll be 50 by then but I'll still be beautiful for you'.

At the beginning of October Linda wrote that her passion was drowning her. They'd spent four hours making love at No. 41 and she said, 'I can't believe you're such a bloody good lover.'

5 October

Michael: You will be nearing home as I write and in a couple of hours will be reunited with the family. I feel the excitement in you and in them. My heart, my part of our heart, beats with yours as you pour out that special love of yours. One of the beauties and special blessings of the GL is the absence of jealousy, which can be so corrosive in ordinary relationship love. Because there is such a secure knowledge of shared love, the overflow of love to others is not perceived as a threat, or even as a serious distraction. This is a high plateau of wisdom we have attained. You attained it first but you reached down and helped me up to your level. My grateful thanks.

6 October

Michael: I went round to No. 41 about 11.15 yesterday morning to see Annette and it was nearly 1.30 when I left. We had a great talk, and only part of it was about our favourite person – my beautiful love and her dear one! She told me that when you were home over the long weekend you would go around saying, 'Oh Sir, I love you Sir etc, etc.' [Annette] thought [this reference to Michael] was rather sweet, a testimony to our good *working* relationship. I hope she continues to think that way. It is not that she is wrong. Just incomplete.

Michael, Annette, Kaye and Linda sometimes used endearments for each other which cropped up occasionally in correspondence. I thought it rather childish.

7 October

Michael: Whenever I have focused in on the special encounter of 1 October and recall the delicious pleasures of our four hours together, I can still think of that time in the broad context of the GL. 1 October could never have been without the GL. The realisation of our mind-union, the gathering conviction of a creative togetherness, the merging, the mélange, the simultaneous experiences and insights, the liberation of passion and sensuality and much more all preceded our coming together by the lake and at No. 41.

You wrote expressively and spontaneously later the same afternoon. Beautiful! For me, writing some 6 days later, the appreciation might be expected to be more a critical analysis at a distance. But that is not how my passion works. I recall, or better still, *relive* every moment with an immediacy that is astonishing. I feel my lips bruising and swelling from the fierce passion of our kisses. My eyes fill with the visual delight of your smooth skin, your belly button, your Venus mound with its black hairs, the moist red core of you. My senses of smell and taste go wild with the special smell and taste of your love juices. My tongue aches to taste you and my lips long to kiss and suck you. I see you in different positions – frontwards, backwards, arched up, bent over – all yielding to my passionate touch.

I feel you dealing lovingly with my penis, holding, stroking, licking, sucking and finally swallowing. I don't know how you do it but I want more. The intimate tastes which we share in our kisses along with orange pulp and our own saliva are with me as I write, and I have a wonderful erection! Talking of erections, it was particularly delicious to rub myself over your clitoris though it was very teasing not to come in after. And that's the special delight of it all. No matter how high we soared together, how many times we 'went to heaven', how much we immersed ourselves in lovemaking, there is always more. Not just more of the same on another occasion, but more that we can do, more exploration of our sexual bonding, no limit to our sensuality.

I will always be your love – your lover even – no matter what befalls us and however the years deal with us. I expect always, if only in vivid memory, to be your 'hell of a lover' and you will always be my 'hell of a woman'. Come to think of it, your first statement was 'you are a bloody good lover'. Well, I think I can be with you, even bloody better still entirely because we love so deeply. The deeper love penetrates our hearts, the deeper I want to penetrate and stimulate your body – I want the 'us' to be the ultimate reality. I want our love to be a part of divinely inspired wisdom.

I have an urgent desire to feel your complete embrace right now. Our hands clasping, our skin touching, our lips together sucking to the point of biting, and your lower lips clasping me in the ultimate, squeezing embrace. Your vaginal muscles are very strong – I long for them to grab, hold and suck me dry. You are a magnificent woman – how did I get so lucky to love and be loved by such a wonderful person.

Finally, for this session of writing, I want to recall how we both *looked* after our four hours together. You commented at the time, and later in your notes, what a special look I had, especially how my eyes looked. I also commented on how you looked, but, inadequately when I said you were a loved woman. What I meant was you had a beautiful serene, fulfilled, satisfied dreamy look that was still excited. Your eyes were sparkling and your lips were ruby red and your smile shone – you were absolutely *radiant*.

12 October
Michael: I have decided that now you are far away, my writing to you will be of two types. One is news – keeping you up-to-date with things going on here, with people you know, the local political scene etc. The other is the usual things we put into 'notes' about our feelings and our insights and everything two soul-mates would want to share with one another. I try to keep them separate so you can keep and perhaps even share the newsy ones and you can destroy the other because I will keep copies. Any notes you send to me will be added to the file.

27 October
Michael: Not much to add to yesterday's message except to say I had a 'miss you' panic last night but I'm over that now. It wasn't long-lasting but it was severe while it lasted. If I could have jumped on a plane I would have – that's how much I wanted to see you. Oh darling, I hope you are all right. I'd love to hear from you. Can you write?

On 2 November Michael wrote again that he was longing to hear from Linda. He wanted to discuss with her (by mail) his timetable for the next two months as he and I were going to Western Australia on 15 December to have Christmas with my family in Perth. He told her not to be nervous about addressing letters to Dr Michael Westfield at the university. 'Sir can handle that.'

He finally received a letter from her dated 15 November. She was embarrassed she hadn't written when she'd had so many letters from him. She told him she'd been sick and asked him to send her healing thoughts; she'd lost 5 kilos. 'I went skinny again.'

In his letter of 19 November he mentioned again going to Perth and that it would be 'especially nice for Nola who hasn't been home since 1983'. Yes, I had been looking forward to it. The last time I'd been there was for my father's funeral and I hadn't seen my family since then. Michael also wrote that the break would be good for him after a busy year at work. Frankly, I'm amazed he'd got any work done at all. He went on to write that it had been the most thrilling and significant year of his life. 'I have no bad feelings about 1993.'

1 December

Michael: It is sometime since I wrote notes for you in the evening. It is not always convenient, but my feelings in the evening are as powerful and often more powerful than they are at other times. Tonight I am alone with my thoughts and feelings and you are in the very centre of both . . . In my mind I bring us together, and the sweetness of our love is tangible. But, my darling love, I do find that my body's response is not as 'smiling' as my mind's. My body misses you in a quite inconsolable way.

My mind is made powerful by the Great Love, given capabilities undreamed of a year ago. But my body feels young, maybe even immature, and it can't get away from the joy of our so recent lovemaking. My body really does want MORE!! Oh darling, help me please. Is this going to be a difficulty for us? Are we condemned to a life of frustration and denial of the sensuality of our love.

You said in your last letter how you have felt lonely and your spirits can be given a boost by my notes and the memory of our four hours, and the times by the lake. It seems to me *your* body must feel like mine – indeed I *know* it does – I feel it so strongly as I write. Our bodies have given our love a special tangibility, a kind of focus for the heart and mind. It is like Jesus Christ – God the Creator of the Universe, far beyond and more powerful than the Creation, yet he came to earth as a baby who became a man.

We can focus on Jesus at times when focusing on the God is too much for the mind. Our Great Love is a mixture of Creator and Created. It has the capacity to develop and reveal more beauty, to become greater as time goes on. But it is also the Creation of the combined loving energy of the two of us. Our GL is Creator/Creation, it is both question and reply, it is both energy and translated force. Its matter is of the same paradoxical kind, being enormously powerful at the same time as being incredibly gentle. It is, or can be almost purely spiritual, ethereal, but retains the capacity to be utterly erotic and passionate.

Purple Book: '"It is like Jesus Christ – God the Creator of the Universe, far beyond and more powerful than the Creation, yet he came to earth as a baby who became a man . . ."' This letter is filled with the most incredible statements. 'Our Great Love is a mixture of Creator and Created'. I'm sure most right-thinking people would think Michael was not thinking right.

On 6 December Michael wrote that we'd had a lovely Sunday picnic at Black Mountain Peninsula with Annette, Kaye and three other friends of theirs. They were all women, but Michael added a small comment (with what now seems like a large amount of conceit) that he could 'handle' that. It was actually quite a pleasant day.

He mentioned that Annette had told him a couple of things about Linda and her family of which he was unaware. Reading between the lines I would say she must have told him Linda had been having some marital problems. He said it wasn't his business, but asked if she had any concerns about her family life.

We flew to Perth for Christmas and it was a happy home-coming for me. Michael even said this in his first letter to Linda in January: 'It was very enjoyable for Nola because it was a homecoming for her, and for us both an opportunity to get to know the spouses of Nola's nieces and nephews and the next generation of small children.'

Michael and I went to church with some family members on Christmas morning, and later, when we raised our glasses of fine Margaret River chardonnay and toasted 'the family' over a noisy Christmas lunch, I felt very happy. Michael was his usual charming self; no hints of the dark secret he'd brought along on our lovely holiday.

1994

Purple Book: '101 letters.'

This was a notable year in my marriage to Michael due to his serious illness.

4 January

Michael: The new year is with us. Happy New Year! My dearest darling, wonderful love, I have missed 'talking' to you by letter. I relied completely on the GL to comfort me in my cut-off state and to transfer my constant love to you.

When I was away, I went for long walks by myself but I was never alone because you were always with me. I (we) saw some magnificent sights – beautiful beaches and rocky capes along the Western Australia shoreline; enormous forest trees (80–100 m tall). Early one morning, I climbed a large Karri tree called the Gloucester tree in the forest of south western WA. This Karri tree (*Eucalyptus diversicolor*) was 87 m tall up to a small lookout cabin from which forest rangers could survey the surrounding area (360 degrees) for any signs of forest fires. It has been decommissioned as a fire lookout (they use aerial spotting now) but visitors can now climb up in the spikes in the trunk of the tree to the top if they want to. At the height of the tourist season, there are many visitors and long delays for those wishing to climb – often because people start the climb and then get stuck – unable to move up or down for fear. So that's what made it so special for me – there was no other person around. Just you and me.

I enjoyed my holiday. Nola and I hired a car for 8 days to go down to the south west corner of WA to see the sights.

I hope that you are not disturbed by what I am about to share with you. We have spoken often about how our love for each other is of such a special character that it is not a reason for guilt *vis a vis* our love for our marriage partners. Of course we love them and affirm our commitment to them and perhaps some of the abundance of our GL can overflow into those relationship loves and enrich them. Thus we have reasoned that the GL actually *benefits* our marriages and other close friendships. Well my darling the focus of my whole life and love, I sincerely *hoped* that was so, but I can only report that I often felt disloyal to Nola on our holiday.

As I was sharing experiences – sights, sounds, tastes and fragrances – with Nola, my mind was sharing them with you and wished many times for your physical as well as your spiritual presence. I don't think I was obviously distant to Nola, and we really did share a lot together, but as I said before, I felt disloyal at times; my secret desire, which had to remain secret, was for *you*, and the magic you bring to my life.

Why I said I hoped you were not disturbed, is that I don't want you to feel guilt now after such great blessings from the GL. Please don't worry about my feelings – they were real and I wanted to tell you honestly how I felt – but they were controllable. Perhaps my feelings, as so often seems to happen, are mirrored by those you too have experi-enced. Please share with me. I feel even more special when you clarify for me the instinctive vibrations I sometimes feel coming from you or your words.

One last piece of *specific* sharing. Our overall sharing is strong and secure. Along with my desires for your physical presence as well as your ever-present essence, I allowed myself a number of fantasies. Things I would have liked you and me to be doing together. Making love figured prominently in these fantasies and I thrilled to the erotic thoughts. I could really feel your nipples between my fingers. I could really feel your hair on my face. I could really taste your love juices as I drank from your vagina. I writhed in ecstasy as you sucked me. I imagined your head in my lap sucking my penis as I drove along the road.

I can't calm myself down from all that. Oh darling, feel my passion and hold it to your heart. There is where I truly live.

Purple Book: 'He felt disloyal "at times".' I found this letter quite devastating. He'd written that on our holiday he and I 'really did share a lot together' – yes, we did. I thought we'd had a lovely time. But to read that his thoughts were with her made me feel quite wretched, and reading all that disgusting sex further sullied my memories.

It appeared that Roy and their children were planning to join Linda in Canberra for a couple of years. The first mention of this was in Michael's 5 January letter. Roy had applied for a job in Canberra and Linda was arranging to put the children into school. I think Michael may have felt a bit threatened by this and his letter back was full of interrogations:

How are you coping my love? Anything that affects you affects me so there's no need to keep anything secret, good or bad, from me. I have shared some of the tensions in my marriage with Nola, and I am not shy about the love I have for her and my concern for her.

- How are arrangements going regarding bringing the children to Canberra?
- For how long do you intend to bring them?

- How does Roy feel about all this? Are there benefits for him to come and work for a time in Canberra?
- How does Roy feel about the Pill? How do you feel about more children?
- Can I have one with you? (Don't answer that! I just threw it in!!)

Well, these are incredibly nosey questions about your private life. In fact they are none of my bloody business. But there you are, I did ask them, and you may find that Michael, the faithful, caring friend is what you need right now, more even than Michael the eternal lover, boiling over with passion. Maybe you need Michael, the father, with a particularly soft spot for his beloved 'daughter'.

Well my beautiful love, this has been a 'different' letter, but not from a different person.

Purple Book: 'A baby with him?' By now, nothing much was surprising me. So the thrown-in baby comment I put down to wishful thinking. The thought was quite ludicrous because it would have blown their secrecy. I guessed this was where the question about the Pill came in. As a Catholic she should not have been using birth control, but maybe she was, hence the question about how Roy felt about it.

20 January
Michael: I have not heard from you. Is there something wrong? Is it something you don't want to tell me about? Are you simply too busy. You should know that a simple greeting on a jotting pad would be enough for me. Are you sick? Oh please God, I hope not. My messages in the morning are not warm, serene thoughts, but nervous, jumpy thoughts. Please fax me with *any* news whatsoever.

23 January

Linda: With your letters coming one after another, it's . . . useless for me not to reply. But anyway, I don't need to write what I'm thinking because you have written it all. It's amazing we connect so perfectly.

Linda was having problems in her marriage, which, apart from telling Annette and her sister, she'd kept to herself. From things she revealed in later letters, it seemed the problems pre-dated Michael. She told Michael that Roy and their children would be arriving in Canberra in the first week of April, and asked: 'Can you be my father now?' She said her and Roy's minds no longer met, and it made her heart ache. She didn't know why she couldn't be a friend to her husband and implored Michael, 'Oh father, just understand. Help me pray everything will be fine.'

Purple Book: 'Be her father? "Oh father".' Was she talking to God or to Michael? Or both!

28 January

Michael: You said a mouthful when you said that you were not, and perhaps never had been, best friends with Roy. If you had listened to me for the past two years, you surely know how important I feel that marriage partners should be the best of friends. There are so many other passion killers in marriage that deep friendships are often all that is left. Such friendships come with effort from *both* partners. One alone can seldom make up for the lack of effort from the other. So my prayer for you – an unselfish prayer as you would appreciate – is that you and Roy find a basis for a deep friendship.

The wise old counsellor who spoke with Margaret and me during our 'troubles' recognised the need to begin something new, not to try to patch up what already existed. That had demonstrably failed and would fail again if given another

chance. The only hope was to learn to love afresh. It was ultimately Margaret's refusal to concede or believe this need for
newness that ended our marriage. I was lucky that later I was
able to get a mate, a best friend, in Nola. What I didn't know
then, but do now, is that the kind of love you and I have is a
rarity indeed.

Purple Book: 'Best friend Nola!' To be subsumed to friend
status so he could feel free to lust after a young student was
soul-destroying.

Linda had arrived back in Canberra. She said the last six
months had been full of reflections, not on the GL but on
the practicalities and routines surrounding her. She had been
haunted by the ghosts 'hovering' in her mind and didn't
know how to separate her two worlds. She worried that her
family, mentors and friends would know she had a lover,
and said she felt her ghosts kept teasing her, although 'the
GL has become my angel, driving away all the ghosts that
were pestering me'.

29 March

Michael: You have evoked for me very powerfully the 'ghosts'
that beset you. Your background, of culture, of societal
expectations, of family relations, of hierarchy, all anchor you
to the past. But while you embrace and value the past and
thank God for the influences you have experienced, you have
moved on, matured, experienced other things in your mind
and, I dare say, your body.

I will always remember at age eighteen how I grieved over
the loss of my adolescent friends. It wasn't that I went far
away physically. It was that they matured with me only so far
then stopped and I went to a world of ideas and exploration
they would never know. There were times I cursed myself for
being different from them, but knew from experience it was
futile to deny my destiny. For a short while before I drifted

away I would pretend to be just like them, to try to blend with their pastimes, attitudes – but it was useless. Even if they didn't understand the changes I had undergone, they were not so stupid not to realise I was a phoney trying to stay like them. They hated that phoniness more than the actual changes. But I was sorry I could no longer share my deepest feelings with them.

I suppose we both know by now the joy and power of the GL, and how profoundly our lives have been moved by it. I suppose too we are discovering, reluctantly, the price, i.e. the secrecy. While we are both very honest about our feelings we regret very much not being able to share those feelings honestly with our other friends. You may be right when you say that the high we are on must be visible to others, I am not so sure as you.

Most people's suspicions are a fishing expedition, and we don't have to take the bait. I don't see that as deceiving our friends – because what we are denying is that we are having a sordid clandestine, tacky, adulterous affair or fling or a-bit-of-naughty-on-the-side. I have no difficulty in failing to agree to that interpretation utterly. Our difficulty is in knowing so few people who can know the GL for what it is. It's a powerful, wonderful creation, not a guilty secret and does not threaten those loves and friendships that surround us. We have to accept that a transcendent love is just that. It goes beyond the everyday world of emotions, insecurities, jealousies and phobias. We can live with that. We can live with exclusiveness.

Purple Book: 'Defining the affair.' This was a notable letter on several levels. First, for what I saw as the conceited way he talked about how he'd matured more than his adolescent friends and had had to move on because he didn't want to become a phoney – ironic considering the way he was behaving now. Then for the way he'd twisted the meaning of honesty, saying they were both being honest about their feelings, but regretted not being able to share those feelings 'honestly' with their friends. And I noted the use of the royal 'we' – '"we" can live with this exclusiveness'. From my reading of the letters, this was not so easy for her. Last but not least, there was another delusional denial that they were having a 'sordid clandestine, tacky, adulterous affair'.

5 April

Michael: It is so long since I have seen you – and then such a fleeting visit from you and Annette. But even that had its positive. Annette saw us in a context of friendship, but professional appropriateness also. But it was also *awful*. I wanted so much to embrace you, to express myself to you *directly*, to kiss and cuddle you, however briefly. Worst of all, I couldn't give you my daily notes. They were there on the desk and I hoped you would be there to retrieve them, but they were still there this morning. I found yours after you and Annette had left. They were *wonderful* – so expressive of what we both feel.

That day Linda and Michael had driven up to the hills in Linda's car, but lamented that they'd only had four hours together. Afterwards, Linda described how she felt 'very bold' dropping Michael off outside the science faculty. 'But I can see you so nervous and conscious of anybody seeing you get out of my car.'

Purple Book: 'Getting caught.' More reckless behaviour – this was one of the few references of concern about being caught in a compromising situation ascribed to Michael.

7 April

Michael: It was so lovely to spend a few hours with you on Tuesday. I think my students will forgive me! It was, I think, very necessary for us to spill over into some touches, some special kisses and some talk.

Are you OK physically my darling love. You have been worried I know and you would like an answer. Please always tell me straight how you feel – I feel with you, but sometimes I don't know why. Like the other night when I was breathing so shallowly – I couldn't understand from my own perspective, and I figured it must have something to do with you. But until you told me about your fluctuating blood pressure, I didn't have a clear focus. Please my love, tell me your concerns. You need a father as well as a lover.

Purple Book: 'Switching roles with ease.'

Roy and the children had now joined Linda in Canberra and she had moved out of 41 Nicols. On 19 April Michael wrote of lost opportunities for them to spend time together before Linda's family arrived and she had to take up responsibilities that would claim her time and attention. But he said he was not jealous or threatened by them as he would be in relationship love.

Linda was trying to stay away from Michael and hadn't seen him or written notes for two weeks, although they had talked on the phone. On 9 May she wrote that if she didn't see him she would be free of the fears she felt about their love: 'I fear this powerful longing . . . so deep like I am with you and sometimes inside you or I am you. I fear the great love.'

In a very long letter she tried to explain her feelings, but at the end of it she admitted she was missing him even more: ' I feel I have purposefully done a big mistake last week . . . trying to test my endurance . . . It was devastating . . . What a mess I have done. I am sorry I hurt you.'

The next day Michael was ecstatic when Linda suddenly appeared in his doorway:

We have both tried from time to time to live with what you once called 'realities' – but the new creation really takes no notice of such 'realities'. They are irrelevant to the GL and our most joyous times have been when we went with the flow of the GL and stopped trying to fight against the true reality of that irresistible force. When we fight the GL we get hurt – in our hearts, in our spirits.

He mentioned Melbourne: 'What a joy we discovered our kissing compatibility so early, in the room at the top of the stairs.'

20 May
Michael: In my (perhaps crazy) mind, life is just a day, from the moment we wake to the moment we fall asleep. In that day-life, one can fit hope, refection, ambition, perception, kindness, fear, activity, but all should be underpinned with the *joy* of just being.

Life is but a day, a fragile dewdrop
on its perilous way from a treetop

In its descent from the treetop that dewdrop can brush a leaf surface, satisfy the thirst of an insect, feel the floating freedom of the air and glisten in the sunlight refracting it into a rainbow spectrum of colour. In the eyes of the beholder it is an unremarkable event, or it is a rich and varied life invoking an emotional response at every stage. In one day, or four hours, the richness of creation can be experienced if we surrender our sensitivity to the duty of living.

By 25 May Michael was getting anxious because he hadn't seen Linda and she wasn't responding to his messages, and by 3 June he was even more concerned, though he said he was reluctant to tell Linda because it placed her in an awkward position and he didn't want her to feel responsible for his 'condition' (not that it did stop him from telling her, of course). He felt his health was suffering because of a lack of contact with her:

> I am partially healed when you come by just to say 'hello'. But unfortunately it is not enough. I do apologise for this longing, this need, this urgency. It is unfair on you when you have so much on your plate at the moment. I do wonder at times whether there will be any time when you will not have 'so much on your plate'. Just when you seem to be about to plunge over the border between coping and chaos, you raise your energy input level and become 'coping' again.
>
> Please care for yourself my love. A life devoted entirely to others, consumed, burnt out in unselfish service, is not always what it seems to be – the pinnacle of virtue. You must be careful to examine your motives. I know I have been guilty of 'self sacrificing love' only to discover dark motives of self-gratification, or enjoyment of the good things said about me, and worst of all, self-justification for not doing other things I was trying to avoid.

Purple Book: 'Guilty of 'self-sacrificing love.' I wondered which relationship he was referring to when he wrote this. Once more, his advice to Linda really couldn't be seen as anything more than self-serving.

When he talked about enjoying good things said about him, I reflected on the wonderful eulogies and memory-card comments made at his funeral. What will be their thoughts when they know the other side of Michael? Surely he must have known that after I found the letters I would not be able to keep them a secret, and it was, and remains, hard to believe he knowingly would bring such shame on himself.

I have gone over and over this in my mind, wondering what he expected me to do with the letters after they so cruelly revealed this sordid affair. Did he expect me to simply destroy them?

On 6 June, our thirteenth wedding anniversary, Michael wrote a passionate letter to Linda telling her his love for her was so great and powerful he thought he would explode. Linda had written saying the burden of the relationship was serious and affecting her health and she was trying to spend as much time as possible with him. He told her that *of course* he understood that she'd been so busy that seeing each other had been next to impossible and he didn't expect her to do the impossible:

> I really only wanted to say how *I* felt – longing to see you but I didn't want to blame anybody, least of all you. But you answered your own question – the GL is not like other relationship complications. It is truly unique and not really a threat or a burden.

On the same day, he wrote me a poem:

To my darling Nola Happy Anniversary

How such a simple touch those years ago
Became love's strong and passionate embrace
Is history now. Yet in that grassy place
We tapped the spring that made the blessings flow
So here's to us, who dared to hope for more
Our hearts now sing love's sweet eternal score
MIW 6.vi.94

Two days later, Linda mentioned that every time she thought about Michael on a Saturday afternoon, she saw him by the fireplace. I have thought quite a lot about this – we had a fireplace and I've wondered if he actually had her there. I suppose he had plenty of opportunity while I was at work, but not on a Saturday.

Michael wrote more about his erotic fantasies on 15 June:

My experience, with what are probably called fantasies by most people, is very powerful. They are more real than fantasies; they generate an almost tangible presence. The most urgent 'I want' is to want to feel your touch, bare skin to bare skin. I can feel your warm presence and the smooth, living outlines of your body against mine. I don't ever have to fantasise love-making at such times – the touches are delicious enough. But realistically I know that hands, lips, fingers and other things can never really keep still in such circumstances. My lips tremble at the thought of sucking on your nipples, driving you crazy. My tongue longs to trace your body's contours, earlobes, mouth, arms, belly buttons and toes, feet, thighs until your hot volcano draws it in with the warm slippery, fragrant and incredibly beautiful taste of your love juice.

My fingers also trace the same path and can't stop touching you everywhere – hair, face, neck, back, bottom, the lovely skin of your inner thigh and again finding your beautiful mountain of Venus. My body screams to be touched, but the touches are almost too much for my sensitive skin. I catch my breath as you kiss me and touch me at the same time. Your hands and fingers going over my belly, my bottom, under and in, and holding my penis in your lips – it is unbearable.

But unlike our lovely four hours, this time I want to take you over the top with my tongue and mouth from the outside and with my penis from the inside and repeat and repeat until temporary exhaustion takes over. We can then just kiss and kiss, deep, moist, juicy drinking kisses; lip-bruising kisses, feather light kisses, tasting kisses, round the lip kisses, inside the mouth kisses, tongue and teeth kisses until we have to lick and suck again, and again, and again . . .

On 17 June Michael left his office and wrote to Linda while he was sitting in his car. There had been no notes from her for two weeks:

> You have made it pretty clear . . . that you are burdened by the emotional drain you are experiencing at the moment. But you have so many other serious demands on your lovely nature – not 'demands' that are at all unwelcome, for caring for and loving your kids and Roy are real pleasures and delights. And they have rights and expectations only you can fulfil – and you are never going to disappoint them, because serving them is right at the top of your sweetest experiences.
>
> Back to me. Knowing what I do about your position and how you feel, do I have any right to complicate your life with my thoughts, needs and desires? Can I still be true to the GL and not sometimes by notes and by personal contact, tell you how I feel and how much our love means to me?
>
> . . . I give you my vow that I will not make any demands, other than professional ones, on you by normal persuasion or by open request. This may be hurtful to us both, but not if we both fully understand that it is an outward denial not an end of feeling.

Purple Book: 'No demands by normal persuasion – now that would be a change.' His persuasive tactics seemed far from normal.

Linda responded to his letter the next day in an emotional outpouring, which included crying tears on the paper and telling him that almost all love stories ended sadly. A few days later he told her she had insights into the power of the

GL and the 'wisdom of its holism' because her diagnosis that they were both feeling hurt was right:

> The pattern had to be broken because we were wallowing in a grieving self-centredness which wasn't doing us any good and was causing distress to each other. Trouble was, I was longing so much to see you that I went overboard and wrote all that sensual stuff which must have put you under terrible pressure. I'm very, very sorry! I suppose I was being honest about my thoughts and dreams, but I was also being insensitive to your position, your thoughts, your needs. I am truly sorry. But at least it did one thing for me. It focussed my attention back on the GL.

I could see a pattern emerging; he'd already broken his last promise about not putting her under pressure. But he was sorry – he was being honest. She caved in. The next day, she wrote about the big smile on her face because she felt like she had conquered 'the greatest mystery in the history of human love'. She said she felt like the richest person in the universe and that it was great to know it wasn't 'the sexual part' that bound them but 'all the other aspects'.

Michael hopped back into coercive suggestion in his letter of 27 July:

> About yesterday – ah, yesterday! It's amazing when it was so cold a day that we were so *hot*. Hot for each other. Desperate to make love with each other – fully. We know that we make love all the time with a glance, a touch, a kiss. But we also know from our 4 hours that given the right occasion, circumstances and state of being, we can ascend great heights of passion and the cascading release of passion. I am hungry and I am thirsty and my libido is taking a lot of punishment with its constant highs and lows, ups and downs . . .

In August, Michael was going to the US for a month's lecture tour and Linda wrote on 10 August that she wondered how she would survive when she could hardly manage a night and a day without seeing him. She was crying, knowing their time together was running out: 'I can't bear the thought. It's a "time sentence". I am in seriously in great love for you!'

After Michael had left for the US, Linda wrote about how much she was missing him. She hadn't been to his office because she was too afraid to go in. She knew Michael had been unwell before he left and that his flight schedule would be tiring for him. But instead of worrying, she decided to beam him the GL's healing energies, praying he would recover. She was panicking: 'Gee – you have to get stronger. Oh dear – please, please together with our power lets join and shake these bad energies . . . Please recover for the sake of the GL.'

9 September

Michael: As often happens on such occasions, there isn't all that much to say because there's such a lot you want to say. I am pretty upset by the state of my health. It is not good. I am just managing and that's all. Weak as a kitten, no energy, breathing difficulty. The slightest exertion leaves me feeling exhausted. I have heard of 'chronic fatigue syndrome' and 'post-viral fatigue' but I have no previous experience of it/them. So I am placing one foot after another and plodding my way through the days. If only you could transfer some of your energy to me, I could cope better.

I wish I felt better. All this could be very exciting. Instead, it's all practically too much to contemplate. I look forward to being back in Canberra and a more settled life.

11 September
Linda: It's a very hard weekend, full of messages from you . . .
I feel very weak – missing, longing, . . . We only have the GL
to cling to – what a hard life . . . Do take care. I'm waiting.

Michael's heart failed while he was on this collaborative
lecture tour of universities. He had not been well before he
went and thought a chest cold was causing his shortness of
breath. I was worried about him travelling, and a doctor
friend gave him a Ventolin puffer.

About two weeks into the tour, he started to deteriorate,
and because his heart wasn't working properly, fluid began
to build up in his body. By the time he arrived at Riverside
in California, where he was to stay with Dr Paul Radford, a
scientist colleague from the University of California, he was
puffed up like the Michelin Man.

Paul knew that Michael's heart was in trouble because
his father had suffered heart failure so he recognised the
symptoms. He called a doctor to have a look at Michael
and she confirmed Paul's diagnosis and told him he had to
go straight to hospital. Michael wanted to get on a plane
home, but Paul insisted he go to hospital and once it was
determined by the hospital that Michael had insurance, he
received the best of care. Later, I asked Paul what he would
have done if Michael had insisted on getting on a plane
home. Paul said he would have rung the airline and told
them Michael was too sick to travel. He knew he would
never have survived the journey without specialist medical
care.

Michael was placed in intensive care, but wanted to
be the one to make the call to tell me he was in hospital.
Unlike Linda, I had not been receiving any telephone calls
from Michael letting *me* know how he was feeling and I
was unaware of how quickly his health had deteriorated, so

when I did finally receive the call I thought he and Paul were having some kind of joke with me. Unfortunately it was not a joke.

The wonderful cardiologist who attended Michael had laid it on the line to the insurance company: 'If you don't give me instructions within twenty-four hours, I'm going to operate on this man.' Naturally, the insurance company saw huge dollar signs if Michael had surgery in the United States, so he was air-ambulanced home accompanied by a doctor and nurse. Qantas removed four rows of seats in first class for his stretcher and the area was curtained off for privacy.

In the meantime, I was advised to arrange a hospital bed and a specialist in Sydney and I had absolutely no idea how to go about this. I knew no one in Sydney and nothing about Sydney hospitals, nor did I know any doctors, let alone cardiologists. I did a lot of ringing around and talking to people and feeling rather desperate. Eventually I telephoned Michael's niece Jane in Melbourne, and asked if she could help. Through her contacts in the medical profession she was able to arrange for a cardiologist in Sydney and a bed in Royal Prince Alfred Hospital in Camperdown, an inner-Sydney suburb.

Anthony and I drove up to Sydney to meet the ambulance at the hospital and we were there waiting when it arrived. Michael was not in good shape physically, but he was quite alert. We stayed with him in Emergency while the over-stretched medical staff dealt with the drug addicts, alcoholics and deadbeats there.

When he was finally settled in the ward, we left. I had managed to get a room in the old nurses' quarters, which were used for family members like me, who lived outside Sydney; they were cheap – only eleven dollars a night – and beyond basic, but I was grateful because I could not have afforded to stay otherwise.

I went back to the ward early the next morning so that I was there when the cardiologist came. Having examined Michael, he announced, 'Goodness, this is much more serious than I thought.'

Another person who visited that morning was from the hospital administration office. He wanted Michael's private health insurance details. Michael might have been critically ill, but his brain was still functioning well. He told them he did not want to be a private patient, he wanted to be a public patient, and he rattled off his Medicare number, which of course they said was not good enough, they had to actually see his Medicare card. Fair enough, but he had, nevertheless, quoted the number correctly.

The first few days were busy with doctors, medications and the physiotherapist. Their objective was to get him sufficiently well to undergo major surgery, but even with intensive physiotherapy his lungs were starting to fill up and they couldn't wait any longer. At one stage I took the cardiologist aside and asked him just how serious this was. I knew it was serious but no one had told me exactly *how* serious. The doctor said, 'He could go at any time.' When you ask the question, you have to accept the answer. I felt a clammy cold claw around my own heart.

Shortly after this, Anthony and his wife, Laura, drove up to Sydney to visit Michael and took me out to dinner. Over dinner I lost my normal 'Nola composure' and burst into tears in the middle of the restaurant and told Anthony his father could 'go' at any time. Does anyone know what to do in such a circumstance?

During the long operation to replace Michael's aortic valve, I sat in the waiting room. While I was there, I thought about some of the lovely wine we had stashed away at home, including some Grange, and I declared to myself that if we got out of this, when we arrived home again we would start drinking some of it. Silly, some of the things you think about at times like that. It was about twenty-four hours before Michael could communicate with me and that was one of the first things I told him; when we were home again we would celebrate. He loved his wine.

Miraculously Michael didn't 'go', but he wasn't out of the woods. He showed signs of an infection, but they didn't know where or what it was. He was put on a range of anti-biotics and was taken back to the theatre to remove and replace every tube; each tube was then tested to isolate the strain of bacteria so they could give him the right antibiotic.

After he was moved out of intensive care, he had a transient stroke. I was with him and he was trying to get his watch on (I have no idea why he was putting his watch on) and I could see he was having difficulty; he was also attempting to talk to me but couldn't. I told a nurse that there was a problem; she looked at the monitor and said no, everything was fine and went back to doing whatever she was doing.

'Just a minute, everything's not fine,' I said.

She looked at the monitor again. 'Yes, it is.'

'Look at him! Look at him! He's having a stroke – get someone down here *now*!' I raised my voice to a yell. She raced off and then all hell broke loose. A neurologist arrived and they took Michael off for an MRI. A poor nurse who had been about to go off duty just prior to this had to accompany us through the underground tunnel to another part of the hospital for the MRI and back again. And it was very late when we returned. He then offered to take me to my car; I explained that it was okay, I was staying in the old nurses' quarters, but he still insisted on walking me there. I was pathetically grateful for this small kindness. But I was grateful to all the staff at RPA – they were so kind to me.

Michael was in hospital for six weeks and there was a lot of time to fill. The family gave him a radio and earphones and I had a radio in my room, and through the long nights when neither of us was sleeping very well we would listen to Radio National and the next day we would talk about the programs that we had heard the previous night; we also both listened to the radio during the day.

I would buy two newspapers and read to Michael until he was able to manage one himself. We would do the crosswords together. There were always comings and goings of medical people of one kind or another, and we talked about his progress. I went to all the rehabilitation lectures with Michael. There were often other interesting patients in his ward; they would come and they would go and we would talk to them and then, discreetly, about them. You have to get your entertainment where you can in hospital.

Mobile phones were not nearly so common in those days and there was only one public telephone in the nurses' quarters and many people who wanted to use it, so communication with the family in Canberra was limited. We enjoyed the many 'get well' cards that arrived. Some of the family came at the weekends and a couple of friends made the trip.

Anthony and Laura came up most weekends and I always looked forward to seeing them, as they usually took me out to dinner. After a week perambulating the hospital wards and the nurses' quarters, dinner out was magic. One night Anthony and Laura took me to a restaurant in Darlinghurst. I really didn't know Sydney or its environs at all, and we were walking along a narrow street with rows of old terraces when I noticed there were a number of women standing or sitting in open doorways. I remarked how strange it was because, although it was October, it really wasn't that warm.

'Don't you tell Dad we brought you up this street,' Anthony replied enigmatically. Of course, a red light district – how naive I must have seemed.

Pru came up to see Michael a number of times and stayed in a motel near the hospital. Although Pru had known Michael longer than I had, these visits were as much to support me as to visit Michael. She took me out driving around for a couple of days to get the wind in my hair. We shared a bottle of wine and sat on Bondi Beach chatting about this and that, and talk came around to the possibility of Michael dying and whom I would ask to do the eulogy. I mentioned that I had thought about asking his former colleague Bruce Graham, who had retired to the North Coast, but wondered if it would be an imposition to ask him to come all the way to Canberra to do that for us. Fortunately, it was not necessary to ask him in 1994.

During the first couple of weeks in Sydney, I'd found what felt like a small lump in my breast and had been to see a local doctor who confirmed that, yes, there was a lump. He had me make an appointment for an ultrasound. One of Pru's visits coincided with the breast-lump problem. I was so pleased to see her and relieved to have someone to talk to; obviously I wasn't going to worry Michael or the family with it, and in fact I never did tell Michael – my focus was entirely on getting him better. Pru offered to come with me to the appointment.

When I came out of the radiology clinic with an envelope containing the results of the ultrasound addressed to the doctor, Pru asked me what the report said.

'I haven't read it so I don't know.'

'Well, go on, read it,' she said, looking surprised that I hadn't already done so. At the bottom of the medical-jargon-filled letter were the words 'I consider Mrs Westfield's breasts to be quite unremarkable.'

Pru and I couldn't stop laughing – sheer relief combined with the baldness of the radiologist's words went to our heads. To this day Pru will still ask after my breasts. 'And how are your breasts today, Mrs Westfield – still unremarkable?'

Finally, Michael was able to come home. Anthony drove up to collect us. I had taken long-service leave to spend time in Sydney and when we got back to Canberra I went to see my doctor, hoping I might qualify for some sick leave to care for Michael at home. The doctor asked to see Michael's discharge papers and after he had read them he looked up at me and said, 'He's had everything, hasn't he?' and wrote the certificate for the leave that I required.

As the referring GP, Jane received the usual letter GPs receive from specialists about referred patients, and at the end of his report she told me that the specialist had written, 'The survival of this patient is nothing short of a miracle.' And it was.

Recalling all this, I remembered something Michael said to Anthony and me when he first saw us at the hospital: 'I can't think of two people I would rather see.' This was not true. It was *her* he wanted to see.

On 17 September, Linda was writing by the lake after hearing from university colleagues about Michael's emergency surgery in Sydney. She was distraught and crying. Her writing was barely legible and the paper tear-stained. 'Oh please – don't do this to me. This is not a joke . . . I am not happy with this. It leaves me hanging, waiting and it drains me. God, you're some kind of idiot . . . I'm turning mad.' She wrote in capital letters how 'UNFAIR' it was, and beseeched God to spare Michael, 'even just for a short while', saying she'd willingly give him several of her years, and even her life. She felt sure if he lived he would touch 'so many lives on this earth', pleading, as I had, 'Oh dear God, have pity. Send your miracle soon.'

1995

Purple Book: '84 letters this year.'

Michael's first letter of 1995 was almost too much to bear. Discovering he had resumed the affair as soon as he could after his heart failure compounded the agony of discovering the affair itself. I felt utter despair knowing that he'd been thinking about her while I'd spent an agonising six weeks by his hospital bed praying he wouldn't die.

10 January
Michael: It's hard to draw in the teeming thoughts in my brain (mind) and to subject them to the discipline of written communication. I find it tempting to leave it all to the unspoken, telepathic, empathetic means we have both relied on for these past months. But the written word has always previously been an integral part of our love, and though it was a blessing that we could fall back on the secure reality of our non-dimensional love, we both crave the tangible presence of each other . . .

I was, from a distance, very concerned for your day-to-day wellbeing. I somehow knew you were in trouble but I was vague as to what kind of trouble. No doubt you were a tower of strength to all around you, but at a great cost to your own physical and mental resources. I now wish I could have been more close to you at that time, but I guess I was fighting my own battle then.

My own battle was in many ways a wonderful experience. Perhaps hindsight has romanticised things, and I don't walk away from the seriousness, but I had some very deep confirmations of external truths. For instance, I cannot explain the sheer positiveness with which I viewed my life-threatening condition except by the appropriation of an unquenchable spirit. Spiritually I was able to contradict conventional wisdom in its view of how seriously ill I was and how small my chances of survival were.

I was quite simply convinced in my mind that I was not going to die, that my life here was not over, that I had a future that was not known in detail but it would be exciting! Further I had the comfort of that special love we share, a love that was affirmed and is affirmed every day of my life . . . At a deep level I am never apart from you, but of course the knowledge is richer and more powerful when we occupy the same space.

You told me that you had read the letters in the box under the bench. Quite honestly I cannot remember what letters were there, let alone what they said, but I can look back to them as expressions of 'relationship love'. There was some spiritual sharing and experiential overlapping, some physical attraction and some recollected embraces. But in the light of this new kind of love it is clear that those relationship love experiences are destined to decline and all but disappear however keenly felt at the time. A candle can provide a welcome illumination in times of darkness, but it pales into insignificance when the searchlight comes on. I am now not in the searchlight beam, but in the dazzling sunlight of a beautiful, different, enduring love that stretches to eternity.

In that condition, how can I view my candle-lit former relationships, except as a part of my past and of life's journey, with ups and downs, highs and lows. My current desire is to rekindle some of our chats, professional and private. And in every way more important still, I want to share your thoughts, products of your beautiful mind, your insights. I miss those very much and I miss the opportunity to share my own with you – on paper and in person.

I need to finish these notes now, knowing them to be no more than the first few words of the latest chapter in the story of our love. I am excited by the prospect of the unfolding of the rest of the story.

Purple Book: 'A wonderful experience for him!' When I read this I was appalled that he could be so self-centred and cruel. How could he so casually appear to have forgotten my love and care? For six weeks I'd lived in a cold and empty room, shared only with the odd cockroach, in the hospital's old nurses' quarters because it was all I could afford and it meant I could be near him. So fixated was I on nursing him back to health that I hadn't wanted to worry him with my breast cancer scare. Yet his only concern all that time had been about her day-to-day well-being.

30 January

Michael: My most pressing desire has been to see you well again and *feeling* able to get back into the swing of things. Your health problems of course have an effect on my other pressing desire which is to see you and spend some time with you. I want to reflect my thoughts and perceptions from you with the enhanced clarity and inspirational content you always seem to add . . .

My own health continues to improve and my outlook on life becomes ever more positive. Having had a reprieve from death has made me even more sensitive to the joy of living. Not just living, but enthusiastically alive, and more appreciative than ever of the joys of the creation and the limitless scope of the mind.

Ten days later Linda replied, 'I have missed the magic of writing notes to you. I hope you are . . . in tune with the beauty and essence of living . . . I miss you and always will.' But, she said, that didn't matter because she had the GL. She said that when she'd first heard about Michael's heart attack she'd felt that life was a joke, unfair; that he couldn't leave her. 'It was awful and what a tragedy for me to be caught in the middle of the story.' She berated God for being cruel and said she'd thought at that time that he should not have given her the GL when it would turn out 'very tragic and painful'. But, she realised now, 'life is great and God loved me after all'.

Purple Book: 'What a tragedy for her?' The self-absorption of this woman was detestable.

10 February

Michael: Our lack of opportunity to see each other except for rushed meetings between appointments is frustrating us. I agree with your comment when I suggested we spend a much longer time together – time to embrace, time to kiss, time to share unhurried thoughts. You said, 'Yes, we need that.'

Our love certainly dominates my thoughts and I feel the warmth through my whole body. For 'warmth' read 'hormonal surges and sexual stimulation' as well as the warm feelings of joy and comfort in the knowledge of shared passion. We are so very privileged to be added to that list of great love stories.

PS I felt very much how you felt when my heart crashed. Was this the end not just of me but of the GL? Almost as soon as I questioned that, the GL took me and showed me this was not to be the end, no matter what the doctors might say. The healing of my spirit preceded the healing of my body, but the process started then.

14 February

Michael: I would like to record for our story, what we said to each other yesterday. We were, in a way, worshipping the GL for always being there – an expression of God to us really. And we were being thankful that the GL sustained us and strengthened us during our times apart.

To Nola – a Valentine message

Some people may turn up their noses
At syndicated, sentimental signs,
Hearts and baskets, cards and roses
And especially commercial Valentines

But I, in these nostalgic days
Prefer to express desire
In personalised and passionate ways
To fan our loving fire

Your constant Lover

MIW 14.ii.95

On 27 February Linda told Michael about two academic colleagues, James and Beth, who were concerned about her. She believed they thought she was hiding something because she had been keeping to herself recently. This had made her feel very uncomfortable: 'Friday was a terrible day. I didn't mean to hurt you – what a sad day. It was the first time to see you in that mood . . . I have to be very careful not to hurt you because of your condition.' She told him what James and Beth had said had annoyed her, but she knew they were only trying to guide her. She scorned the small minds who would not understand their plight. 'We have to understand them instead. I wish I can bear their accusations – if only they knew but they will never, never know.'

I imagine Beth and James did suspect that something was going on and they were trying to step in on Linda's behalf to avoid a possible scandal. They both spent a fair amount of time around Linda and Michael, and I imagine it would not have been too difficult to pick up any vibes.

28 February

Michael: I have been reviewing the conversations you had with James and Beth. In James's case, I think two things have become merged. His own very proper and understandable concern for you, including your emotional state. If Beth spoke to him, asking questions about you (why you left my office, why are you not so visible anymore) and about me (once again, why you left my office, why did James find you another office, why I don't go to tea often anymore), she probably offered to speak privately to you, and put her own interpretation on events.

It is clear to me, now that my anger and frustration have subsided, that Beth wants to paint me as a sexual adventurer who encourages female colleagues into intimate relationships and then drops them. I know she felt that way when my marriage was in its final death throes. I did confide in her how I was feeling. She did listen to my troubles as a close friend, but she became very vengeful when I began to be close to Nola. She sowed the same doubts in her mind as she tried to do with you.

Truth, facts take now, and took then, a back seat. I guess she felt that I had encouraged her to think she was the one I would turn to after my final breakup. But I turned to no one. I crept into a shell of self-examination and occasionally, self-pity. Only after a time in the wilderness did I emerge and felt I could probably start living again. Miraculously Nola came on the scene and we became good friends. She still is my very, very good friend. It wasn't high romance, but it was (is) fulfilling.

The most important aspect of it all for me is that *you* protect yourself. It would not be a good thing for you to become a special close friend to Beth, share 'secrets' with her. She is clearly not a sensitive soul and would be the last to understand any unfolding of our special bond of mind-marriage. She would make something truly beautiful into something really dirty. I am not prepared to watch someone trample on my beautiful flowers . . .

Finally, I would stress once again that I believe James to be an innocent bystander who accidentally said things to Beth which she chose to misinterpret. James in turn accepted Beth's suggestion that she would have a talk to you, because he thought that might be helpful to you. Unfortunately that was wrong. We can draw something positive out of this, I know it. We can prove again that the GL is above and beyond this mundane world. It is strong; it is not fragile.

Purple Book: 'Weasel words.' His self-righteous comment that Beth might want to put her own interpretation on events, as if they were conducting a wholly innocent friendship and Beth was wrong to question it, was absurd. He hypothesised on what may or may not have happened; and who should be absolved for showing concern and who should not. If Beth wanted to paint him as a sexual adventurer, he obviously didn't want Linda to hear that.

If the lid had been blown on the true nature of their relationship, I'm sure it would not have been taken lightly by the university. It would certainly have been seen as a case of serious misconduct on Michael's part, and dismissal would have been a real possibility. Did he care about this possibility? He seemed more concerned with Beth's 'misinterpretation' and 'unkindness' about his relationship.

The eighteenth-century German writer and poet Johann Wolfgang von Goethe wrote in his drama 'Faust' about a man who sells his soul to the devil. Dr Faust was a middle-aged scholar and scientist who had just about given up hope that he would ever learn the true meaning of life. He had begun to fear he would come to the end of his life honoured and well-educated, but without ever having experienced what it meant to be 'truly alive'. So he made a desperate bargain with the devil, promising the devil his soul in the hereafter in exchange for just one moment on Earth so fulfilling that he would be moved to say, 'Let this moment linger, it is so good.' Is this what Michael was seeking in his grand passion with Linda? He often wrote in his letters that his love for her made him feel 'truly alive.'

It was disturbing to know that Michael, at his age and in his position, could not see past the passion and question his actions. Was there never even a superficial process of reflection on what the consequences could have been for his career had the relationship soured, or had the affair become known?

I'm not sure what the consequences for Linda might have been had the affair been revealed at this stage. She could have been seen as a victim of sexual harassment. Her scholarship may have been in jeopardy; a new supervisor would have had to be found (if anyone was prepared to take over the supervision, given the circumstances). It's possible that her whole thesis may have been called into question.

Linda seemed to have taken the turn of events over the previous two weeks very seriously. In her letter of 2 March she told Michael she was having 'strange thoughts and feelings' about his previous relationships. She had also become suspicious of his motives regarding what he'd said about Beth. She realised it wasn't healthy to doubt the 'sincerity and truthfulness of the other half' constantly telling her stories of his past. But it made her question things and become defensive. It was simple human nature to protect oneself, she said, and although she was trying not to equate Beth's story to how she felt, it had given her cause to doubt Michael.

She wrote that even if Beth's own behaviour was very 'unkind and unbecoming', she thought that Michael, at his age, would have known how to handle Beth better. She was surprised that Michael had never talked about his relationship with Beth before and wondered if Beth's caring attitude towards her was related to something he was hiding. Then again, she claimed, 'I don't really mind hearing all the negative things about you, about your life – they are only circumstances of your earthly life – nothing to do with the GL.'

Purple Book: 'Jealousy.' That's what I wrote on the first reading of this letter, but later I thought Linda was rather perceptive.

3 March

Michael: It was good for you to tell me about your 'bad thoughts' even if you were reluctant to tell me exactly what they were. But I was disturbed, off and on, by conflict in what you said to me. You *did* trust the GL, *nothing* can touch the GL, but also 'Michael, be kind to me' and 'please don't hurt me. I don't deserve that'. And on the one hand you say it's all been resolved this morning, and then your very last words of the call begged me not to hurt you. Oh Darling . . . I *hope* you resolve it SOON. Just saying it is resolved doesn't resolve it. You wouldn't continue to question if it really was resolved.

My dearest one, if you are still battling, I do understand and empathise. Because I am still battling with the hurts of this week. I don't like being cast in the role of a philanderer, someone who preys on innocent women and then casts them aside.

It is as cruel as it is dishonest. Even before the GL I wouldn't have done that. Those that came close to me I thought were dear friends who came on their own terms and often wanted more than I could give. I was married to only one of them, and I tried hard to make the most of that marriage, as I understood my obligations then. You have seen me distressed, but never as low as I was at the end of my marriage. It was inevitable, but it hurt and hurt.

What saddens me, and occasionally angers me, is to have stories told about me which are untrue, based on malice towards me. I thought at the time (late 70s) that it was natural to share my problems and feelings with Beth. The first time I realised she was hoping to be more than merely a close friend was when she made the savage attacks on the developing relationship I had with Nola. I tried to smooth things over by continuing to have a *professional* relationship with her and I am staggered, after 14 years of marriage to Nola, Beth still wants to believe I am a sexual adventurer.

What I can't comprehend is that *you* can question my motives and actions with the GL in the background. We are bound by the GL in a beautiful way, which has nothing at all to do with 'having an affair' . . . My darling, please tell me you don't believe me to be cruel and unfeeling, a user of others, particularly women. To use your own expression – I don't deserve that.

Purple Book: 'Pru will enjoy this letter.' That he was 'staggered' Beth still saw him as a sexual adventurer was quite laughable. Was he not aware of what he was up to? He *was* a sexual adventurer.

Linda continued to be upset by the stories she had heard about Michael. In her 4 March letter she admitted she felt disillusioned, although she had been unfair to him because he was not with her to defend his position. She had, she said, revisited his past, and was frustrated by his tendency to constantly justify his own actions and think only of himself. 'You can't see anymore the consequences to others,' she charged. 'Because you have two parts to you, you can't seem to be satisfied with having one part missing and the other part whole. You always fill both, and that's where the difficulty lies.' She told him that loving himself would be his 'ladder to fulfilment'.

This was an interesting way of looking at Michael. I had never thought of him as a man without self-love. He appeared genuinely warm and caring to everyone he met, which I would have thought reflected a man who was happy within. Maybe I'd been missing something. So much of what I was seeing in these letters reflected a level of selfishness and self-interest that I would never have believed Michael capable of.

Linda knew that talking about Michael this way was 'outside the boundaries of the GL', but her confusion lay in trying to relate the GL to her everyday life. It appeared that she had tried to explain the special feeling she had for Michael to Roy, and had had to justify those feelings. Later she wrote, 'If I love him, why am I loving you? Can I separate my mind from him because our love is a mind thing? He challenged me – he let me define what sort of love I have for you – but I wasn't able to answer because he has never seen or felt this kind of GL we have and it would be frustrating to him.'

Roy then asked Linda what kind of love Michael had for me. The letter didn't mention how she answered this question, but she suggested Michael could divert his whole 'heart, body and soul' to me and just 'live with the magic and beauty of the GL'.

Purple Book: 'So much twaddle.' If that's what she really thought, why hadn't she broken off the affair instead of merely pretending to every few weeks? Perhaps she believed that if she really did end it, her thesis would be in trouble.

10 March
Michael: Whether or not Roy fully understands or accepts your understanding [of the GL] is relevant only from the point of deep sharing. You will radiate a blessing to his life and

those of your family. You are a primary source of benediction, of benefaction, of beneficence. In the same way I have obtained insights which energise me and cause me to radiate to Nola and others close to me.

Purple Book: 'Radiating insights to me!' I wasn't sure I liked this idea of having insights obtained from the GL radiated to me. As for 'depleting the energy source' – I'd never heard him use this New Age terminology, except perhaps in jest.

28 March

Michael: O I love you Linda. I love to hear your quiet tap on my door and to see your brilliant smile when you come in, sometimes followed by a slightly embarrassed expression. It's like the look of a child who has persuaded a parent or grandparent to grant some favour and has just been given the treat.

Purple Book: 'Just a little patronising.'

31 March

Michael: I am sending you healing thoughts and warming thoughts. I am sorry you feel the need for a hot water bottle. I want to *be* your hot water bottle, with a far bigger surface for conduction, convection and radiation and far more interesting contours. O lovely Linda it is true – I crave to be beside you, around you and within you. My thoughts oscillate from serene love to eroticism. I can cope, I can manage, I can O WELL. But as you perceived, I also have some longings at times. I am aware that you do also. I would expect that since we are so intimately bound together, we belong.

Autumn Leaves

Linear wisps of cloud streak the east horizon.
They barely reflect the pure clean autumn sun.

But still enough for us to feast our eyes on,
a muted contrast to appreciate as one.

Enough to give the mirror of the lake
A clear reflection back towards the blue
as its waters kiss the silent shore and take
comfort from the touch, as strolling lovers do.

Senescing leaves cling and hang precariously down,
trembling first, then breaking free and flying,
giving the earth a new and brilliant crown
with each a gem, their end of life defying.

But autumn leaves live not for just a season.
They live to nourish life the coming spring.
New buds break and give their life a reason,
Perpetuate new growth and summer blessings bring.

MIW 31.iii.95

April proceeded in the same sickly, erotic vein. On 4 April Michael wrote, 'Sometimes I feel desperate to come into you and feel the delicious inside of you, hot and slippery.' And on 6 April: 'If we gave full expression to our power – mind, body and spirit – would we be able to be satisfied by loving thoughts, orgasms of the mind, and squeezing our thighs together to subdue the erotic congestion?'

Around this time Michael must have given Linda the impression that their story was not worth writing, as he then had to reassure her this was not the case:

What I was trying to say, and what I said today on the phone, is that having written it and shared with others, we have no guarantee our story will be interpreted, let alone experienced, as we interpret and experience.

We have both expressed the frustration in personally expressing to even our closest friends, the depth of
communion we experience. Annette was one such friend
who I thought would find our story literally incredible if you
or I told it to her personally. But she may be convinced of its
authenticity if told in a book. Oh I hope so – she is such a
dear friend.

Purple Book: 'The book again.' I found it unlikely that
Michael would seriously consider exposing his affair in a
book with 'no guarantee' of how the story would be interpreted by people who knew him – including his family. At
what stage was he planning to write this book? Did he tell
Linda these kinds of things as a sop to her? Or was this just
part of the fantasy world he seemed to be living in?

On 19 April he continued a conversation he'd been having
with Linda about 'all those women'. He told her about
Aggie, the woman he'd had the affair with in the mid-1970s
when he was on sabbatical in the UK with Margaret and
the children:

I suppose in a funny way I changed Aggie's life. She grew up
feeling somewhat isolated by the people around her and her
expectations were low. She married Doug, an OK guy dedicated to his career, and chose to work in London while the
family home was in Cambridge. Aggie supported herself and
lived an independent life, including, as I found out, seeking
to satisfy her sexual appetite through a long string of affairs
(most not even that – just brief encounters). Doug by his
long absences and inability to keep up with Aggie's libido,
proclaimed a lack of interest in sex and declared a sort of
open marriage.

When I came along, licking my own personal wounds,
Aggie thought I was a wise bloke, but basically all blokes
were the same. They were only nice because they wanted

to get into a girl's pants! I, on the other hand, treated her as a friend, easy to talk to, cynical about some of the same things, with a sense of humour that went right to the core of every subject. We enjoyed each other's company, and joint family outings had no undercurrents of anything special or different.

Then came that fateful day. I offered to drive her to her foster mother's funeral in the country and we had a not very serious accident on the way, in a snowstorm, but I was very cool in the crisis and Aggie was scared and impressed at the same time. When we drove back to Cambridge she invited me in for coffee. Well the record would show that I was offered, and accepted, more than coffee.

It was a time of great turmoil for me. I didn't want to hurt Margaret, though our marriage had been just going through the motions. And I didn't want to just treat it as if it meant something special between me and Aggie. But I did like her and I felt sorry for her. In subsequent weeks, before leaving to return to Australia, I learned about 'all those blokes', and I felt even sorrier for her. She was doomed to failure because all those casual relationships just gave the blokes a bit of fun and she was no better off except for momentary pleasure.

When Aggie discerned that I was not just a typical male who takes what he wants and then pushes off, she couldn't understand. This was a *friendship* not just a quick roll in the hay. She also taught me something I didn't know. Like you, after years of having just one sexual partner, I never knew how I rated as a lover. Now whether it was because I really liked her, compared with the no-nonsense physical experiences she had been used to, she told me I was great, I went on longer, I considered her responses as much as my own and she had never known anyone like me before. I guess that's all very flattering coming from such an experienced woman, but I was rather astonished.

But I put it down, in my blundering amateur psychology, to the emotion factor. If you *like* someone before you go to bed with them, it is more likely to be a better experience than if there is no feeling there. I may not have been any better than anyone else, but it felt better because I was a nice bloke and a friend.

There's not much more to say really. When we said goodbye the future was uncertain for both of us. I wished I could leave my job in Australia and try my luck in the UK. But I couldn't just up and leave. My family should not be made to pay for my desires.

I still count her as a special friend. She sent me a card last Christmas. She didn't know I had been sick. I don't know whether at 53 she still has casual affairs; I would never ask. The AIDS scare would probably be enough to make her cautious, and maybe she is no longer a sad sex addict.

It has been good to write all this down. I don't much like going over the past, preferring to leave it as the past. In particular I have experienced in my early old age a revelation in the GL. My perseverance in my marriage to Margaret until it finally died, my brief time-out with Aggie, my friendship with Aggie, and my happy marriage to Nola are all different from the GL. The GL has now liberated my past. *You* have liberated my past. I see now, thanks to you, that you love *me*, and my past is part of the me that you love. I know now that I can discuss the past, reveal the past, answer questions about the past, and not feel at all threatened by it, nor feel uncomfortable about doing it.

Needless to say, it was illuminating – if somewhat disturbing – to read the details of his affair with Aggie. It seemed ironic that he called Aggie a 'sad sex addict'. And there was the neat double standard when he wrote that his family should not have to pay for his desires. And of course he had to mention that Aggie had called him a 'great lover'.

By early May Michael had had no letters from Linda for
several weeks, although he saw her at the university and they
talked on the phone. She had called off the correspondence
while she worked through some personal issues. In earlier
letters she had indicated time was a problem for her. She did,
after all, have three children and a husband to look after,
although she rarely mentioned them.

Michael continued to write regular letters, pouring out his
undying love, sympathising with her situation and begging
for contact. On 9 May he wrote:

> Your decision to go into retreat for something like spiritual
> enlightenment was complicated by your back injury. Two
> quite separate conditions, one mental and one physical, but
> with some features in common – you and me. In the one case
> you seem to need reassurance that I truly care for you . . . You
> believe the GL is real and unchanging, but at the same time you
> question what that means in reality . . . In the other case, when
> you suffered your injury . . . you wouldn't let me do anything
> practical other than confirm who was a good chiropractor.
>
> Of course I respect your desire not to see me, but I have
> had a hard time knowing why. I am very concerned that
> in this chosen solitude you reach true enlightenment and
> not spurious convictions about the meanings, motives
> and morals of other people's actions and thoughts.

But of course it wasn't long before Linda returned. On
15 May Michael wrote a long letter welcoming her back
and laying out his feelings about a meeting in which they
discussed a few things. He did not want her to think he felt
she simply needed to come back to her senses (although that
is probably what he did think):

> I was lonely when you were 'away'. It was confirmed for me
> how much your physical presence heightens my already

strong feeling of our connectedness. The bond never weakened, nor did the sense of unity in *us*. But at the human level I was concerned by the knowledge that you were going through some personal questioning and turmoil that I was unable to participate in. You were somewhere else in mind and spirit, and I was lonely. Not too sorry for myself, but certainly wishing for your company, in the form of joining in the process. You did try to reassure me the GL was unaffected but I was feeling tested. I felt like some unfortunate complication in your life.

Linda apologised and asked for forgiveness – 'I'm sorry I made it so hard for you . . . Please take me and take care of me.' And Michael responded, as usual, that there should be no more apologies: 'I do not want them and I don't deserve them. Just let us *both* say that we have both learned from our retreat and meditation, and we have emerged much wiser, more certain of our need for each other, and more joyful (if that's possible) about the miracle of the GL.'

6 June

Michael: As I write, and maybe as you read, I have this deep longing to see you to look into your eyes, to watch the sparkle and the slight tremble in your lips – oh those lips! The softest, sweetest, most lovely lips in the whole universe. Lips whose loving kisses inspire and delight my very soul. I could die for those kisses – kisses like no other. They do not merely carry the exciting physical sensation, but they tap into the inexhaustible springs of love within us both and the fresh spring waters mingle, as our lips, our lives, our innermost beings mingle. Who can ever separate the waters when they merge? And who can ever separate the love of Linda and Michael?

Anniversary message for Nola

Thank you for sharing your life with me these last 14 years.
I think we made a really good decision.
Let us celebrate it every day.
Your happy partner, Michael

6.vi.95

Purple Book: 'Happy partner!' It was quite distressing to find that throughout his affair, in all but one year (1993), he'd written a love letter to Linda on our anniversary while also writing me an anniversary message. I guess it was part of this ability I was discovering he had to compartmentalise his life. When he was in his 'compartment' or 'room' at home, he displayed contentment; when he left that room, he closed the door and moved into a different compartment and became whatever he wanted to become in that new room. Thinking about what Michael became in his other compartment, outside his life with his family, was almost too hard for me to bear. Looking back on those anniversary messages to me, this would be one of the least loving he ever gave me.

8 June

Linda: Why do we kiss so wonderfully? You were right, the pleasure comes from the very core. But I can't help feeling guilty about our stolen kisses.

Michael responded on the same day: 'Guilt about "stolen kisses". Not likely! We deserve it. And they are so very special kisses. So special in every sense. True magic. No, no guilt.'

I was so exasperated when I read this – what a comment.

It appeared from Linda's letters that her marriage to Roy was under severe stress and the main issue was her 'special bond' with Michael. On 22 June she reported on the serious discussion that she and Roy had had about it: they'd come to some resolutions and she sounded more confident about their problems, and felt now that 'everything will be fine with the family'.

4 July

Michael: We are truly one, Linda. How we celebrate this oneness will always be moderated by circumstances and obligations, the nurture and love we have for others. It is not our nature to be completely selfish or willing to be hurtful to those close to us or who depend on us.

I suppose at the back of my mind, as I write this, is your sharing with me the discussions you have had with Roy about our special bond. I can't say how sorry I am that he doesn't trust me and thinks you are somehow being fooled into believing we are special to each other. I do not fit comfortably or happily into the role of sexual adventurer or predator on gullible women. But I am most particularly unhappy to think that *you* are not trusted to know your own mind or to exercise your own intellect and judgment. You have been blessed with a wonderful mind and a loving spirit, and many have had their lives enriched by both; not least Roy and the kids, and your wider circle of family and friends.

It is tempting to 'prove' the genuineness of my love for you by denying myself access to you, minimising my contact with you, separating myself by self-imposed exile, of the kind that was imposed on Abelard and Heloise. But I feel that would be as dishonest as it is unnecessary. I don't want Roy to feel threatened or to feel diminished in your eyes just because you and he do not have the same kind of bond that *we* have. He needs reassurance obviously, and I hope to prove his fears to be unfounded.

Purple Book: 'Roy doesn't trust him and he can't believe it.' His discomfort at being cast in the role of a sexual adventurer had resurfaced. He thought it would be *dishonest* to prove his love by denying himself access to her. Yet he didn't want Roy to feel threatened and hoped to prove his fears 'unfounded'. And I noticed that Heloise and Abelard had returned.

13 July

Michael: The powerful passions we have felt for each other have been surprising, astonishing, in their intensity. It is as if we would explode if we didn't touch, kiss, lick or suck each other. It was a spill over of the wonderful, mind-bending reality of our love, which grows with each contact, and the removal of inhibitions born of complete trust, finding ultimate expression in the intimacy of physical, erotic love. As it is for the whole history of the GL, the order of experience is all-important.

First comes the CONNECTING
Our realisation that we occupy
a dimension beyond ordinary experience.

Then comes the SHARING
Our freedom and comfortableness
in discussing and experiencing together
the connection we have to eternity

Then comes the TRUST
The removal of doubts, 'rocks in the head'

Finally the PASSION
We are whole, with each contributing to the whole,
and we bond in every way.

13 July

Linda: Are you okay now? I am worried about you. It's like I can't stop my heart from beating fast . . . What about your heart – I'm a little bit worried . . .'

She continued that 'it went to pieces'. More expressions of concern that she'd put a strain on his heart gushed forth: 'I don't mean any harm to your body. I didn't think of the consequences.' But she believed they had 'a God' inside them, and finished, 'It's like eating the body of Christ and drinking his blood.'

Purple Book: 'Good grief – what on earth went on here?' More appalling references to God. I was affronted when I read the reference to 'eating the body of Christ and drinking his blood'.

14 August

Michael: *Forgive me* for my insensitivity towards the feelings of Roy. I am sure he doesn't fully understand our feelings and our bond. All he knows is that we have a very close relationship and we like to see each other – *often*. He naturally feels aggrieved and threatened himself, and is worried about *your* welfare and doesn't want you to be hurt. He doesn't trust me very much and I hope he will receive assurance over time that I have no desire to exploit or hurt you either.

Forgive me for my insensitivity towards you and your feelings. I am so blinded by my desire to see you and to feel the warmth of your close presence that I have been forgetting your position as a wife and mother protecting the family from any outside threat. You are, of course, absolutely correct. We must express our love not only to each other directly, but also indirectly by our concern and protection of others close to us.

Can I also say how thrilling it is to express some of our erotic passion, as we have done lately. Tiny windows through which we can glimpse the paradise garden. When we kiss as only we can kiss, and when I caress your breasts and your 'down there' and when I suck and kiss and lick and taste and smell and drink – I go completely over the moon, and, best of all, you come with me. How sweet it is!

That Michael, a highly intelligent man, was able to ask why Roy didn't trust him was extraordinary – the man was having an affair with his wife! Michael's constant taking of the moral high ground in a morally corrupt situation was breathtaking. I understood that in all affairs the unfaithful partners strive to ensure their partners won't find out, but I found the way he expressed himself especially infuriating. He used a sanctimonious tone when talking about protecting Roy and me. And we were the very ones they were betraying.

19 August
Linda: What do you think and feel when you kiss my 'rose'? I couldn't explain the bliss of that moment when you touch me, let alone caress me in there . . .

30 October
Michael: Last Saturday was my leaving hospital anniversary and consequently the beginning of a new life. It is hard sometimes to know how many lives I've had. I do know that my life since we met and became a new entity it is fundamentally changed new and different. And it is full of real joy and real optimisms. Living beyond a threatening heart condition brings a changed outlook to be sure, but living in the knowledge of a shared, merged love with you is utterly transforming. No circumstances can equal the hugeness of that change.

Remembering Leaving Hospital

The sun so warm, so bright commended
Shades to protect me from the glare
But wafting breezes could be encouraged
To caress my grateful hair.

Without restraint to walk unmonitored
Gave a spring to my weakened step.
And looking, feeling almost normal
Encouraged me and gave me pep.

The climax of those loving prayers
Which gave my life another chance
Was sweet indeed. And in the moments
My spirit beckoned me to dance

No more to yield to life's misfortunes.
Not to let them grind or bore
While love is gratefully acknowledged
And experienced for evermore.

MIW 30.x.95

A year had gone by since the day Michael had been discharged from hospital and, although the time had not been without its difficulties, I was hugely grateful that he had survived. It took him months to recover fully and I had to take extra time off work to help with his rehabilitation. He wasn't able to drive for some time so I had to do all the driving. Then when he went back to work part-time we realised we would need a second car – I suppose this gave him a tremendous amount of freedom.

But we were mindful of his lucky escape and we did share a celebratory bottle of Grange when we got home, after our pact while he was in hospital to make the best of every day from then on. A couple of months after we returned home we had a big thank-you barbecue for all our supportive friends. Michael referred to it as a 'celebration of life'. After I read this poem, I reflected, sadly, on what these lovely friends and colleagues would think when they read what had really been on his mind that day.

On 10 November Linda wrote a very long letter. She and Michael hadn't talked much over the past few weeks, mainly due to the difficulties in her relationship with Roy, which was conflicting with her love and longing for Michael. She felt helpless in a situation that she couldn't do anything about: 'The pain is excruciating. But when we meet, all the pain vanishes and we have another chapter for the story.'

There were more tears from Linda on 13 November. Michael was sick and she was disappointed she wouldn't see him. She feared that he would go away again, as he had done when his heart had failed: 'I don't know if you really know how I coped last year. I guess it was the hardest part of my life. It was really hard given the situation – I had to keep it to myself.'

In Linda's letter of 17 November was the first overt reference to her coming to our home. Michael was unwell, I can't remember what was wrong with him, and no doubt I was at work. My thoughts have often turned to the idea that she came to the house to be with him more than once when I was at work. I picture them in front of the fireplace, but I will never know if they were there. On this occasion she wrote, 'Oh God, I cross boundaries. I honestly wanted to see you but I felt awkward visiting you in your place. What would Roy and Nola say? Oh God, my desire to see you came first and everything else in my head disappear.'

Five days later Linda met Michael at the lake to tell him she had again made a decision to stop seeing him, after another altercation with Roy over their relationship: 'I regretted being very honest – too damn honest. I think I pulled the string too hard for Roy. I guess if you were also this damned honest to Nola the same response is expected. I can't continue to hurt Roy. It's all my fault and I have to give way. He does not understand.'

She said she couldn't complicate her life at the moment (I can't imagine what she thought it had been like for the past months if not complicated) and urged him to 'stay sensible – given your condition you have to stay at your place – you need Nola even more.' She asked him to think of the GL as something that would keep him alive longer.

Purple Book: 'If he were "this damned honest to Nola".' What a dysfunctional couple they were; Linda was semi-honest with Roy and made attention-seeking attempts to end the affair, while Michael was completely silent about me with no apparent internal suffering at all.

On 28 November he wrote his first letter to Linda for a month. It wasn't clear why he'd been withholding from her, but perhaps he was waiting it out until she came back. She never stopped writing notes during her period of 'absence' and they talked on the phone.

Firstly I am very, very sorry you have had this trouble with Roy. It is possible for me to feel sorry for all three of us at the same time. I am especially sorry for Roy, not so much because he feels threatened or diminished by our special bond, but more because he has no way of understanding what is in our minds and in our hearts. I sometimes feel it would be easier (I am speaking ironically now) for him if we were having a plain, ordinary sexual affair. He could wrap his mind around that and he would have an easily defined target for his anger. But he is unable to comprehend the GL. It is sometimes hard, even for us, because the GL is bigger than we are and has a life of its own.

Secondly, I am naturally sorry for your special position, juggling the family wellbeing with those things that are very close to your heart. The realities of both family and the GL have definitely clashed. No longer can they be kept entirely separate. It may be thought, in retrospect, that you were over-ambitious in expecting total openness with Roy about your feelings for me would be fully understood. You felt comfortable only by being completely honest, but in the end you have caused misunderstanding.

My main worry is concerned with how you respond to this difficulty. By being the model wife whose life is dedicated to her husband and concerned to conform to his expectations and obedience to his wishes is, or can be, itself a serious form of dishonesty. The aims may be virtuous in showing a loving concern for Roy and his fears and hurts, but it is likely to leave you with unsatisfied needs. There is no doubt you can sustain such a behaviour pattern for a long time, but believe me, I know there will come a time when your energies and resolve will fail. You are not the same woman you were when you first married. Your intellect has been challenged by broader aspirations that need not be suppressed in conformity to societal expectations . . .

Which brings me to my third concern – being sorry for Michael. In all honesty, my main sorrow for myself is frustration in being unable or unavailable to help you. It goes without saying that you are never out of my thoughts and your wellbeing is my life's primary motivation.

When I reread this letter later it disturbed me greatly. He'd told Linda that by being a model wife she was being dishonest about her own needs and feelings. I felt this was where he began to try to instil real doubts in her mind about her marriage. Did he feel he was being honest with me by not being a model husband? With his comment that it was possible to feel sorry for 'all three of us', it appeared that I had been excised from the equation. And 'most of all, you have to accommodate the GL' sounded like an order. So often it seemed that this intelligent scientist had lost any vestiges of logic.

This was a long letter and spilt over to 1 December. There were no more letters from either of them in December. No doubt Linda was busy with her young family and preparations for Christmas. Michael and I had spent a few days in the country before we had Christmas at home with the family. I enjoyed the break immensely. It was a chance to unwind and do pleasant, relaxing things together. Michael had recovered his health, but I thought the break would be good for him too.

1996

Purple Book: '88 letters.'

There were fewer letters this year, but there was no reduction in their ardour – in fact, they ramped it up. I found many of this year's letters either too erotic, even pornographic, to comment on or reproduce.

2 January

Michael: Greetings! A happy New Year! I know it will be a wonderful year. I can feel it. Busy, yes but full of achievement. And not only in the academic, scientific part of our lives.

Well, the break affected me in several ways. The very necessary 'holiday' from departmental cares and concerns. The leaving behind of family tensions, none very serious, but sometimes time-consuming. Everyday concerns of the house, garden, pets, neighbours and community – all forgotten or pushed to the back of the mind for a brief few days. A time to rest, unwind, do something different.

But . . . and it was a powerful 'but' . . . I was never far away from you, except physically. I was always thinking of you if I was lying down resting, or walking by the river, or crossing shady parks, or looking out at the beautiful mountain views. You were in my thoughts as I watched families buying Christmas things. When we drove to the orchards to buy fresh berries, peaches, nectarines, apricots – I couldn't help thinking how you would enjoy them all. I wanted to discuss the books I was reading with you to get your unique insight. I never did or thought anything alone. So you see, you were always with me – my constant companion and influence.

Purple Book: '"When we drove to the orchards to buy fresh berries . . ."' These were such lovely memories for me; the enjoyment of doing these simple things together – tasting the fruit, bringing it home in the boot of the car to make jams and tarts. Memories of simple pleasures now rotten like discarded fruit. He'd even thrown in a comment about family tensions. Our children were all living independent lives and Michael and I never fought, so I have no idea what he meant by this. And I will never know.

9 January

Michael: I am so very lucky. Your beauty, internal and external, illuminates my whole life. So even when I'm feeling desperate, I feel lucky also. When I am almost overwhelmed with longing, we have the chance to share our kisses and caresses as we did last Friday. Of course I wanted to help you to orgasm after orgasm for as long as we could stay awake. Of course I wanted to kiss you forever and wherever. My whole body tingled. But it is so different from anything I have experienced before.

My tingle is not just a sexual congestion focusing on orgasm and relief. It is an acknowledgement of our *belonging* to each other. Everything is shared – everything belongs to us . . . The giving and receiving are indistinguishable – the perfect example of the double blessing.

Purple Book: 'Not just a sexual congestion.' I'm sure Linda was thrilled to read that.

On 29 January Linda wrote a very long letter that continued on 6 February and, bizarrely, included a letter to her

dead mother, which told her of her turmoil and confusion but
didn't say over what. But it became apparent in her letter to
Michael. She had determined to write down the thoughts and
words that 'aren't very good for both of us … that will destroy
us'. She felt she was in an impossible situation: she was trying
to put distance between her and Michael, yet having done so
couldn't cope with the lack of contact. She was tired by the
effort and pain it caused her. And the more she lost touch
with Michael, the more critical she found herself becoming
of the way they handled their situation – when she said she
wasn't coping, he described this as her 'overdoing' things,
which she found patronising. She said that she'd lost the GL,
and 'its essence, beauty and magic'. It was affecting her and
she believed it was affecting Michael. She was also baffled by
her thoughts about Michael and the GL:

> The more that I know you, the more that I don't know you
> anymore. The more we become closer, the more we are
> drifting apart. I feel alienated towards you. I can feel the
> distance growing between us but I don't know why.

Was it because of her 'limitations and weaknesses', she asked.
She now saw 'differences in our way of thinking, loving,
opinions and spiritual and intellectual needs'. She said she
was sad and lonely and the GL had become a paradox – 'a
pain and pleasure at the same time'. She felt conflicted and
trapped: to mix life and the GL seemed imperative; to be free
of the GL made her feel guilty.

She harked back to Michael's affair with Marie when
he'd still been married to Margaret – how Marie had only
wanted Michael physically. Yet, Linda said, 'I thought it
might be the other way round . . . aren't you grateful for
what these real persons have done for you.' She pointed out
that he seemed to have never learnt to be satisfied, and said
she didn't want to be like them – 'that one day you will tell

someone that Linda loves me because she is looking for a father image.'

Linda believed Michael's inability to be satisfied with one woman was a reflection on him. She could see how he compartmentalised his needs: one who could fill his mind, another, his heart; one to satisfy his soul and one his body. This, she said, was how she also felt now.

Certainly, compartmentalising his life seemed to have become second nature to Michael. How many men would have been able to carry on so blithely with their marriage while immersing themselves in a full-time affair for so long?

On 6 February Michael wrote:

I have had an awful time since we spoke yesterday. I have the deepest most heartfelt sorrow because I upset you . . .

It must be awful to feel that I (and Annette) don't understand how you are, how you feel, the work you must do at home and Uni, the taxiing you undertake for Roy. Perhaps I don't fully understand, and I really want to understand. It hurts me to see you hurt – the GL makes sure of that. My concern that you might be 'overdoing things' is not ignorant criticism; it is loving concern. It is not pressure to add to your already heavy burden; it is the expression of a desire to help ease your burden. And if I sounded offended that you hadn't come to see me, I was clumsily trying to indicate that my love for you was hoping you would come and talk about things . . .

13 February
Michael: I have been experiencing shivers of delight regularly and frequently since our windy few hours last Friday. I keep thinking of swans, cygnets, ducks, willows, tree-roots – even water rats! . . .

Most of all I recall touching you, feeling you, caressing you, kissing you and tasting your unique kisses. I regret not being able to kiss you 'down there', though stroking you was nearly as good. As you drove off I sucked the fingers that touched you there. I had to squeeze my legs together, so exciting was the taste, one I will never, ever forget.

After this letter, they must have had yet another verbal conflict – again, over what Linda saw as Michael's inability to appreciate how busy she really was. Michael didn't write to Linda for more than a week and she thought it might be the end of the GL. On 26 February she wrote telling him that, while putting the balance of the 1995–96 notes in date order, she had read some of her earlier letters and was embarrassed at how immature and 'unknowing' she appeared in the 1993–94 correspondence:

I am more convinced now that any minute you will disappear and I can't blame you for that. You've shown a lot of strength and sensibility, quite contrary to my actions and responses. I am so sorry for everything I have done . . .

She felt that she'd revealed her true nature (good and bad) in the first three years, and it was quite 'devastatingly bad' in 1995. She was probably referring to her frequent immature outbursts and the way she had blown hot and cold – one minute almost calling it off, the next frightened when she didn't hear from Michael. Not that her behaviour seemed to change during the duration of their affair. But he adapted very well to this pattern, and used it to manipulate her. She came back begging for forgiveness and he said there was nothing to forgive and that the GL had saved them!

Linda prayed that she would get an answer to his sudden silence. She said she held no personal grudge but they did need to talk. They obviously did talk when they saw each other at the university, and there was a copy of a letter she had sent to the registrar reminding her that her PhD course expired on 23 February. Then there were no more love notes until Linda wrote on 30 April, telling Michael she had difficulty coping with long periods between notes and meetings and was finding it increasingly hard to mix work, family and friends with the GL. She said she was very selfish to follow her wishes and desires, but that her intuition told her she would never find bliss in this current situation. She asked for his help, finishing, 'I am lost.'

They must have cleared the air on a few things, as Michael wrote her a long letter on 15 May. Much of it was his usual overblown erotic rubbish, which I won't repeat. But when he started on how his near-death trauma must have affected her, it was almost too much for me to bear.

> Your fears of losing me, such as you had late 1994 early 1995 are genuine and need to be understood. It is awful for you to relive that trauma, though I am sure the other terrible experiences must have made it so much worse. My collapse was unexpected and was nearly impossible to bear. For myself because I was directly experiencing the threat to my existence, it was somehow more bearable. I was not a spectator and I was not in the dark. I did not have to imagine how things were. I could focus.
>
> My poor darling, it must have been awful for you. But one thing I know now, death has no more fears for me, and I know I shall be able to face it confidently. When you have time for contemplation, you will also accept the beauty of having a soul mate who will never leave you except in the crass, mundane, accidental physical sense. Our shared life is immortal and our shared combination of essences is eternal. We can access each other at any time.

Purple Book: '"You poor darling. It must have been awful for you . . ." Poor darling!!' I found this comment most offensive and reread this letter many times, raging with hurt and anger over 'poor darling' as I recalled my bleak weeks of stress and worry that he might not survive; no poem or letter of appreciation from my husband, the prolific poet and letter-writer. I recalled Annette's email to me in which she said Michael was so grateful to me for the way I nursed him through his illness that he had tears in his eyes as he spoke about it. I simply do not believe he was sincere; talking about it through crocodile tears was all part of the act.

In Michael's letter of 17 May he revealed some frustration at Linda's momentary resistance to being bamboozled into falling for his semantic rubbish:

Who was it that said 'The path of true love never did run smooth'? Whoever it was, I could give him/her a case history of a true love journey with many a bump and pothole!

I'm keen to discuss with you the notes I wrote earlier which you said were full of paradoxes. I would love to hear your thoughts about that. I have no general opinion contrary to that, because life itself is full of paradoxes. But I'd like you to tell me which aspects of us/the GL are so paradoxical, and how they affect you.

For example, on the one hand you feel that being young, as you are, makes you want physical erotic expression more than an older person, as I am. On the other hand you express the opinion that I do not press for full physical expression because of my life's experience which has taught me self control. And clearly you are interested in how I feel, or at least how I used to feel, about 'all those women'. I sometimes wonder if, like Roy, you think you are just the latest addition to a string of flings or affairs. If I haven't convinced you yet of the vast difference between the GL and relationship love, I despair of ever doing so!

I am left with your statement 'Just leave me alone to finish my PhD, and then I'll be gone.' What a turmoil of emotions that suggestion can cause. I don't take it in a brutal way. I see there an appreciation that I understand your desire to minimise distraction so you can work most efficiently at this important time. I also see that you are suggesting that if you try to be strong and avoid closeness with me, I should respect that and not make it any more difficult for you.

I see too that you are struggling to accept that GL's 'are always like that'. They are filled with unsatisfied yearnings and desires and you are calling for help to accept that inevitability. That is, you are with Roy, and I am with Nola, and the GL, though real and deep, can never achieve full expression. You seem to feel we might as well go to our respective monasteries now and live out the GL in a disembodied, spiritual way. I can say that I *can* make whatever sacrifices you truly and genuinely request of me. I can say, with all passion, that I love you deeply and will respect you in whatever you desire for the sake of that love. I can withstand whatever the GL, through you, asks of me.

Linda responded on the same day to tell him that she'd sent him a message through the 'sunset, the skies, the bushes, the grasses and breezes' that said she loved him more, even, than life. But then she'd read his letter and it had chilled her 'to death'.

Before reading the letter she had concluded that hiding herself away from him was not only unfair to him but also to the GL. She thought she was unworthy of his love because of her emotional swings. She felt she had made a big mistake and had to pay the price for her words, actions and thoughts. She said she took responsibility for the 'bumps and potholes' Michael talked about, and that she still had to 'grow and learn'. She meekly accepted that Michael had been right when he had said that if he helped her, she must acknowledge his effort or she would still 'experience instability'. She apologised for pushing him too hard – 'you are already sick and tired'.

Originally I'd dismissed Linda and her rambling nonsense out of hand – she was a young hussy who'd had an affair with my husband. But rereading this letter I wondered what on earth had driven her to make comments like these? Was it Michael's powerful personality and his ability to manipulate her; or was she just emotionally immature and completely infatuated by him – despite the damage he was doing to her life and marriage?

21 May

Michael: Since your response to my notes written on Friday night, I have seen and touched you on Saturday and again yesterday (Monday). Much has been achieved in the quietness of reflection to quell the turmoil of confusion and questioning.

I must say I was a little surprised by your response, but on reflection it was good that you responded quickly and spontaneously. You were utterly sincere, and didn't try to polish the words, as I sometimes do after reflecting.

My darling one, your apologies, though heartfelt, were truly unnecessary. Your feelings of unworthiness certainly were. I fully understand these were instinctive reactions and were real to you at the time. I am labouring under a difficulty now in that I don't remember very clearly what I had written. I confuse the two sets of notes. But I do know that I conveyed a mood of frustration and disappointment which had dissipated when I saw you on Friday. Hence the warning to read the notes in context, and to let the GL interpret. What I really wanted to say was not my concern for my suffering self so much, but a concern for *you*.

Let us see the GL as the *positive force* that it is, one that greatly enriches us . . . one that can lift us on eagles' wings and carry us all the way to heaven . . . Perhaps we should allow ourselves the child-like pleasure of anticipation and suppress the adult-style capacities for doubt and mistrust.

Two weeks later, on 2 June, Linda wrote another long letter. It was one of those that had provoked my comment to Annette in my email to her in September 2011 that Linda had started to express her concern about Michael's silence to me about the affair, when she was being open with Roy. She asked Michael whether he had been as honest with me, and with Annette and Kaye, as she had been with Roy. She even said she was beginning to doubt both her own and his intentions. She then made an uncharacteristically perceptive judgement: she said she had started to doubt Michael's 'human dimension'. She went on to say she oscillated because they didn't talk much! A ridiculous statement when one considered the number of words they'd wasted on each other over the past four years. After that she had the cheek to complain that she didn't know of his whereabouts or where she stood 'in the personal, professional and social aspects of your life. I only know I am filling the spiritual void in your life.' A spiritual void? The Michael I knew was far more spiritually advanced than me (knowledge that I would have thought would have made him more content with our life, not less).

Linda also observed, as I had in the past, that it was in Michael's nature to love the company of women: 'You know women pretty well and you know how you charm them . . . When you like someone you make an effort to be a friend or even a lover. There's nothing wrong with that.'

Well, there is something wrong with that if you've pledged to be faithful and loyal to them! I found this a very strange thing to say. However, in retrospect, her next observation was prescient. Linda felt it would take 'a superwoman' to make Michael feel whole. She said he would never be fulfilled by one woman alone and she conceded she could never be all he was looking for in a woman.

She went on to say that she felt Michael had withheld from her his feelings about his special friendship with Annette and that she was sure he felt self-conscious about it. 'I saw you set your eyes on her when the three of us faced you . . . You felt so embarrassed – I hugged you and you pushed me away.'

Her jealousy had been aroused because she believed Michael was hiding the fact that he was seeing Annette, and was having difficulty in admitting his friendship was becoming deeper. She was also upset about Michael's embarrassed 'red face' when she'd revealed she had told Annette something of their GL. She told him not to be alarmed – she wouldn't tell Annette anything else. She seemed rather confused as to what she did want from the GL, provocatively writing that the GL wasn't exclusive and he was welcome to have 'a GL' with Annette – in fact, perhaps Annette could fill the 'big void' in him. Linda finished by almost urging him to see more of Annette: she prided herself on not being possessive and was therefore happy to share him in a 'leap from the bondage of possessive love'. She warmed to her theme, saying that perhaps Annette could provide him with the 'ultimate fulfillment' he seemed to be seeking.

3 June

Michael: I am glad we shared that time together before I read your notes. I felt embarrassed to think that the Annette and Michael friendship had assumed such significance, but fortunately you had elaborated in our talk about the gaps/voids which a variety of other people might fill.

I am so sorry to have caused you to swing, by not causing an informed understanding of some of my feelings for others, like Annette.

As I said last week, I really didn't know myself what I felt for Annette and I still don't. She is a good conversationalist and we can discourse on a number of subjects. But we have never really attempted really deep philosophical or spiritual topics. So I am not at all sure if we will become deep good friends or remain as interesting and likeable acquaintances. Most likely something in between. But you are right to tell me how you interpreted my silence on what Annette and I may have discussed and how I felt. But I really don't think I was being secretive; I just wasn't sure there was anything to tell of any consequence.

I am not really in the market for friends to fill my voids to any extent. My liking of the company of women has never been a secret. Not even those who may have become lovers. But the GL has changed me completely in my essence, in my core being. I may still prefer the company of women, but I utterly desire you at all levels – from the deeply spiritual to the frankly sensual. But if I can't/don't have you, I don't want the human needs you can fill to be filled by anyone else. Perhaps I am obsessive, though not possessive. The sharing of intellectual thoughts and ideas with others does not add up to sharing the GL. Only you and I can do that, so it is not in anyone's best interest to try.

You and I must help one another, and we can do that by sharing a lot, and *often*. Don't let the spaces get too big between contacts, because too much unhelpful stuff seems to get into the gaps. The GL can fill, and overfill, most of my gaps, but there is always room for growth.

Getting back to your notes, why are you so definite now about not telling Annette about the GL and us? When we talked last week I thought we were uncertain *how* to tell her but we both felt we wanted to tell her. I didn't want to be the first to tell her because I thought you should be the one. You and Annette share on a much deeper level than she and I do so far. We may go deeper sometime, but not yet. I guess we both would like to be sure the time was right, that Annette would not react with stereotyping but would trust us as close friends seeking to include her in an important, life-changing experience. But enough! We should talk again.

Purple Book: 'Not possessive?' Michael had proved thoroughly possessive in his many and varied questions about Linda's marriage.

Two days later Linda had turned her back on any doubts: 'If we could only have a simple ceremony, we could pledge to each other.'

I wondered what she was talking about now. I was soon to find out.

6 June

Michael: Gee, it's three days since I started these notes. In that time I have seen you only once, briefly, yesterday. We both wanted to be with each other so much. The atmosphere was electrically-charged. The desire we both felt was urgent and obvious. If anyone had seen us looking at each other they would have been in no doubt about the passion we felt. In the brief few minutes we had to talk, we seemed to confirm where we see our lives going. You seemed to be saying that the GL was always going to be present with us, blessing us with deep sharing and insights and helping us to live our ordinary human lives with gratitude and caring for others. I may not be able to share with you fully, but I shall never stop wanting to.

Purple Book: 'Gee'. This was a funny expression for Michael. Again, he seemed to be picking up her slang. His letters were getting more nonsensical – 'ordinary human lives with gratitude and caring for others'!

To my darling Nola
Happy Anniversary with all my love

Our happiness together and our
love for one another give today
a special meaning and fill tomorrow
with special promise.
I am so happy to be sharing my life with you.
From an ever-grateful Michael.
The next 15 years will be even better!

MIW 6.vi.96

Purple Book: 'Our anniversary. So what . . .'

Linda wrote back to Michael that same day. It was horrible to read what she'd been thinking on our anniversary: 'I will shower you with my juices . . . Can I take you into my mouth? You will beg for mercy and I will feel you to your very core.' She said she was high (adding, somewhat bizarrely, that she'd been drinking Penfolds port) and hoped 'we can go on like this forever – no more SWINGS'. 'Please help me' she finished.

7 June

Michael: I know you asked me to help you and I also asked for your help. That is a wonderful start to our life from here on – a trust in each other and the realisation that our love is mutual.

Perhaps the loveliest of all your ideas, all the more beautiful because it has never come into our conversations, was the one about some kind of 'ceremony' where we could pledge to each other. In a very real way, we have already done that over and over again, but I love the idea because of where we see ourselves now. As we come to terms with the mundane realities of our everyday lives with family bonds and commitments, we both feel the need to re-affirm *our* bond and commitment to love and care for each other forever.

Purple Book: 'A 'ceremony'. The hypocrisy and profanity of this whole idea was just so preposterous it took my breath away.

On 10 June, Michael's birthday, we had a lovely party at home with family and close friends. He seemed pleased to have us all there and was in high spirits. He was always a good host. We all toasted his good health, being genuinely happy that he was still with us and hopefully would be for many years to come. He made an eloquent and funny speech in response. Looking back that whole evening seems remarkable: the dual life that he was leading must surely have been quietly taking its toll – always being careful to never let anything slip, never giving anything away.

The day after his birthday, he received a letter from Linda, lamenting not being able to join in the celebrations, but saying she'd sent lots of nice thoughts and thanking God for giving him another year of life. Then she became morbid, asking if she was simply filler in his life. But she snapped herself out of her mood: 'It is really silly. Stop it Linda . . . we might as well get back to work . . . Help me professionally!!!'

The arrival of Roy and the children appeared to have nipped Lin's crush in the bud and Linda now mentioned him only in the context of their work. On 20 June Michael was writing notes to Linda while Lin was in his office using his phone, making him feel 'strangely self-conscious':

There is no need to worry because he can't see what I'm writing and there is no indication who is the recipient. But

I know how nervous you are sometimes when notes are left unattended. He's gone now so I can put down my thoughts with no inhibitions. How beautiful it has been to see you these last days. You are my beloved and my betrothed. We commit to each other and allow our lives to flow – sometimes colliding in a burst of passion, sometimes side by side gliding together towards a goal, sometimes separating but still in the same stream. We promise to remain in eternity, and we promise everlasting love.

Oh Linda, when can we have our ceremony?

They had the ceremony the next day. Linda wrote on 21 June, 'Our wedding day. The title of our book or film.' The 'soul marriage', as they referred to it, took place by the lake and they used bands of entwined pine needles as wedding rings. Later, Linda wrote notes to Michael listing the next chapter headings for their book: 'Smiling to eternity; From here on; Winter solstice; Made in heaven; Made for each other; 21 June; New wisdom and dedication; True mind's marriage; Everlasting GL and Marriage in the GL.' She said she couldn't stop shaking, had burst into tears when she waved goodbye to him, and claimed, 'From the moment we exchanged our vows, we were transformed. Thank you for marrying me, thank you for our marriage. Amen.'

Purple Book: 'Transformed by their "marriage".' I had thought it couldn't get any worse, then along came this 'marriage' folly.

26 July

Michael: How long is it since I put pen to paper! It's not that I haven't felt like it, but only now have I felt I had some time to express myself. Since our soul-marriage by the lake I have been really different inside. Some of my clouds have been transformed from storm clouds to soaring towers of shining, opulent clouds. Sure I still miss you when we are unable to meet, or accidentally find ourselves in different places at times when we could meet. Such is the reality in a marriage where there is not a common home base or a shared bed. But I have a sureness and a serenity, knowing it is a true marriage, and not just a marriage of minds.

My wonderful positive mood is matched by my delight in how you have been . . . I sense your delight when we meet . . . and our continuing love was the central purpose in my life. Forget my job, my responsibilities, my marriage to Nola – nothing means more to me than your love. It consumes and obsesses me.

Purple Book: 'Forget my job, my responsibilities, my marriage to Nola . . .' Another passage I read over and over with disbelief.

In her letter of 30 July Linda wrote with more frustrations about their circumstances. They may have had their soul marriage, but in reality they were not free to marry and display their love. The ever-present threat of discovery by their university colleagues was making her moody and causing her emotions to 'swing' again. Apparently Beth had walked in on a little tête-à-tête and Linda had had to leave the room. She accused Michael of pushing her away in front of other people:

Like when we were interrupted by Beth . . . I hated it when I had to make way for Beth. You acted as if you wanted to get rid of me and that I misinterpreted the scenario – you are a great actor.

She surmised that he must want to protect himself by denying her, and again sounded furious that he'd pushed her away from the hug she'd given him when they were at 41 Nicols with Annette and Kaye. 'Then in front of Beth

– and what about other people?' She had convinced herself that Beth and he had been lovers, and told him not to be afraid to tell her. 'Let me know where I stand so I know how to react.'

Purple Book: 'She thinks he's a great actor. She's right about that.' She couldn't get over being pushed away from that hug. Did she ever pause to wonder how I would have felt being entirely chopped out of his conscience and consciousness?

On 7 August there was more erotica from Linda. She and Michael had obviously been up to no good in his office, of all places. She'd 'tried to moan in passion but it was inside as I was so afraid someone might have heard us.' She said she shivered when she felt 'it so hard as if to tease me to death' and was 'so excited to play with you again'.

8 August

Michael: Those were very beautiful notes – so full to bursting with our shared passion. You were so hot yesterday. I wanted you to orgasm so much and I was so glad you did. How much more beautiful to do it with my penis and my tongue. And my nose and my hand and any part of me I can contact you with . . . Never stop Linda. Please share this passion always, wherever. I love you, want you, need you.

Linda's sister, Grace, who was apparently living with them in Canberra, was now posing a new threat to the GL. Together she and Roy had broached the subject of Linda's relationship with Michael. Linda felt she had already been open with them about her 'special love'. But Grace had suspicions and wanted to know the 'real score', and Roy had told Linda he could no longer tolerate her frankness about the GL with Michael. They felt it was impossible for them to be friendly with him anymore. Linda wrote on 24 August that she felt sorry for them and she planned not to be 'too open with them anymore'.

On 28 August, Michael had the temerity to blame the messengers for their interpretation of the truth:

> In a strange backhanded way, the attacks by Grace and Roy on you and the caricatures drawn about my actions and kind gestures were evidence of a concern for *you*. It was a strange way of showing it I know, but they may see your 'infatuation' with me as foolish and misguided and my affection for you as exploitative of that infatuation. I do try to understand the motives of others, and I feel kindly towards them if they cannot understand. But oh, if they only knew.
>
> I could understand jealousy; I have a curious kind of jealousy myself from my perspective of marriage to Nola. I realise that however much I love her as a wife and a friend, I can never approach the full multi-dimensional glory of the GL. It is not a matter of fault – not my fault, her fault, your fault or anybody else's fault. It is not a matter of diminishing commitment to our marriages, or the tossing out of our responsibilities; it is a completely different, but very powerful experience . . . we are ever conscious of the difference and you were right to identify 'different' as the key word describing our present state.

Purple Book: 'It seems clear that Michael had moved me into the friendship compartment of his life.'

He was describing to her the same old story – the words had just been rearranged. But his self-delusion never ceased to amaze me. Later, he had a phone call from Linda, telling him she had been encouraged to draw on the GL for strength. The GL had saved the day again! But all the energy he put into constantly putting out spot fires must have been exhausting.

Around this time Annette re-entered the picture. Linda had informed Michael that she was going to have a 'special chat' with Annette to give her a few details of the GL. In a PS, Michael told Linda that he had spoken to Annette on the phone and she confirmed the 'deep and meaningful' talk.

30 August

Michael: If you do get a chance to spend some time with Annette this weekend, you should know that she has received a note from me already. I wanted to set down just a few sentences to describe a little of the hugeness of our love. You will describe our love in your own way and I know you will speak from the heart on behalf of US. You will always be Annette's very special dear one.

This week has been truly momentous. Thank you for your beautiful notes – your dancing words. You are right – we do regard the GL as God. Everything we ever read about the nature of God, the love and care of God, the strength of God, the steadfastness of God – we have found in the GL.

Purple Book: 'God's busy.'

There was yet more angst from Linda a fortnight later, in a letter in which she apologised for causing Michael so much pain, and described her uneasiness with his definition of the GL or SM (soulmate), when her definition was the total surrender of one being to another. She thought they had both found the ultimate fulfilment and contentment in life in the GL but she now believed Michael's perception of the GL might be different to hers – she hoped she was wrong.

Michael responded with a long, verbose letter:

13 September

Michael: Your notes were very thoughtful, very searching and very careful. Never before have you written so deliberately or so circumspectly. It was obvious you had much more to say. What I missed, but I understand it wasn't the purpose of your notes, was any mention of a lightness of being or of being richly blessed . . .

What *seems* to be at the centre of your concern, and I repeat the obvious fact that it has to be *my* concern too, is the definition(s) of the GL and soul mate . . .

Oh my darling, how wonderful you are, but why the agony over the difficulty to define the indefinable? . . . we have experienced the most revolutionary change in our lives in the context of two marriages, two families, age difference and nationality difference.

I can only say, in concluding, that my trust in the GL is unshakeable . . . I want to go even deeper into the GL and be given new and closer bonds which will bind us together, strengthen us. I need help still to prepare me for [your departure in] 1997. Please don't say I'll be OK. You don't know that yet, about me or about yourself. And please don't say 'I hope so' when I declare my deeper love for you. The tears of grief for the GL are almost unbearable.

Again, I felt sorry for his other students. They couldn't have been getting much attention while he agonised over such weighty issues.

A few days later Linda had a hissy fit when she discovered an email on his computer addressed to a woman he called 'CP', saying he owed his life to her and he would talk to her again soon:

I went freak! What question is this? I went back to the time I came to your room and you responded in a funny way. You have a lot of parts in you . . . I already accepted your 'fondness' for women . . . you have a lot of secrets when you were still married to Margaret and I am a secret to Nola.

Purple Book: '"I am a secret to Nola".' She acknowledged that it was easy for Michael to 'make secrets', and he obviously did have an extraordinary ability to keep secrets. In this affair, he was a keeper of many secrets.

I was amused Linda thought CP was one of his other women. In fact, CP was a former student and the person who had given him the university insurance card when he was gravely ill in the US, and he was writing to tell her that's what had saved his life.

He must have explained this to Linda verbally because soon they were ecstatic again.

26 September

Michael: Can I remind you, one more time, how I love the very air you breathe, the space you occupy, wherever they are. Touching your breasts, sucking your nipples, having you fondle my parts is not just 'petting' or 'foreplay' or something. It's a sacrament when we do it. It's a *joy* not just arousal. It must be the spiritual dimension that underlies our desires and our sensitivities. Sex is OK, but THIS!

I crave the ultimate experience of merging our spirits, our wills, our physical bodies. I can taste you as I write. I need you Linda and I need you NOW! Oh GL, help us!

Loves Progress

Before Serenity
We Met
We respected
We explored and tested

We expanded our minds and our hearts sang
We created a great love from our separate beings
We basked in the beautiful sunshine of our great love
We, as creators, granted ourselves freedom to love fully.

So why?
Why did we think this way?
Why, when love is so wonderful, did we have pain?
Why did we ever doubt the truth of the great love?
Why did our bodies always envy our minds their
    contentment?
Why did we miss each other so very much when we
    were apart?

Finding Peace
We see
We accept our divine gift
We find so many things to be thankful for
We affirm the great love and gladly let it flow
We submerge ourselves in its invigorating, sparkling waters.

We abide
We know our blessings
We desire our dreams and know our realities
We enjoy our deep bond and know our endurance
We embrace the great love and are drenched with
    fulfilment
We are bound, protected and enriched by our love, and
    rejoice in its true beneficence

MIW 2.x 96

3 October

Linda: When you left, your smell shivered all over me . . . I wanted to grab you and kiss you but I promised myself I will not give you this virus, it's rather nasty.

Linda was impatient to make love, but she hoped they'd find the perfect time. 'Can you still wait? I'll have to finish writing my thesis first or else it's dangerous. I feel so close to you when we embrace. I love touching your sword. I feel excited how you will fit it in to me. I tremble with joy thinking about it.'

Michael told Linda he didn't have a problem hiding the affair. She responded by mentioning several people at the university whom she believed were suspicious of their relationship. I know the people she referred to and I would be surprised if they hadn't been suspicious. Because of this she was moving her work to another building. She asked him not to misunderstand why she was doing this and why she was unable to make time to see him. She said she wanted to use the little time she had left at the university to complete her PhD.

On 26 October Linda wrote asking why Michael was looking sad and lonely. Was he having 'difficulties at home' or 'personal trials'? She told him that she and Roy had decided to end the impasse, to 'go on living in a civilised way'. She said she had invoked Michael's name to help 'strengthen my faith . . . for the kids and for him . . . I must do my duty and go on with my responsibilities.'

This was the second reference to his 'difficulties at home' and I still have no idea what they were or what he might have told her. I suspect he was trying to elicit some sympathy for occasions when home duty interfered with his ability to see her.

On 29 October he wrote a significant letter – one that I mentioned in my first email to Annette. It was the one in which he told Linda what she wanted to hear regarding my knowledge and understanding of their affair. Had I known about their relationship, it would have been the end of our marriage, as Michael must have known. His solution was to lie, and on this occasion to Linda. And this he did effortlessly:

I am relieved you have broken the ice with Roy. Not because you should be the subservient wife who must be obedient to your husband's wishes and fulfil his (and perhaps society's or culture's) expectations. There will be other less fraught circumstances and occasions when you can take up the subject of independence and free choice. Breaking the deadlock was not really a surrender, but the exercise of love *and* control, aimed at a better outcome and as a small step towards a sustainable future.

While on the subject of spouses, I want you to know about Nola, me, and Linda. I know this is something that has clouded our lives in the GL. Perhaps it is the only cloud remaining. You have puzzled over the perceived discrepancy between our two domestic situations – how you have been very open with Roy (and others) and by comparison I have been very secretive with Nola, and about her. Well my darling one, I am in no position to question the proposition that we have handled the GL and our marriage partners differently. But the differences have been much less than you think and have more to do with differences in our spouses than differences between *us* – your honesty and openness and my secrecy and perhaps deception.

The fact is that I talk about you a lot to Nola, and she knows that I share a lot of things with you that she can't share. Take clouds for instance. Nola knows that I respond to clouds in all their forms and diversity. She knows my response goes to my very soul. She knows that you also respond as I do and that you and I have this kind of spiritual bond which is outside of the bond between me and her. She knows how I have changed since you came, how the dimensions of my spirituality have been inspired by you because you encouraged me to see things differently. She knows my religion has become more universal, encompassing small insignificant things as well as big concepts, and she knows I share that actively with you. She knows, in short, that you and I have this soul-mate status.

The difference in the situations of you and me is that Roy feels threatened and challenged by the bond between us, and Nola feels no threat. She knows and trusts me to be a loving husband to her, supportive in all ways and considerate in all ways. What Roy and Nola have in common is the inability to fully understand our special kind of love. Neither can understand the depths of experience we have, the experience of eternity, the reaching to heaven and the GL, and the centrality of that experience in our lives. But Linda, who *can* understand it???

Roy and Nola are not alone. None of our friends, our family members, our workmates, even the most special ones like Annette, can understand! So far as Nola is concerned she knows she hasn't the insights you and I have in common. But if I am made happy by that 'sharing', she is happy for me.

The concept of the GL in all its huge dimensions may be beyond her experience but her knowledge of our sharing of thoughts, philosophies and spirituality is well founded. So please Linda, give me some credit for honesty. I couldn't possibly hide from Nola my strong, strong feelings for you and your specialness to me. We call the bond different things, but the facts are known. She would not even express more than inability to fully understand if she were to read 'our book'.

Without knowing anything for sure, it would seem she and I are destined to move into old age together. My spirit will always be young and free but the package will get old and worn out. You and I have our precious soul marriage, and without exception that is the most important thing in my life and always will be.

Right now I pray for your healing and restoration. I would like to be the agent of your soothing and your comfort. Yes, in my mind's eye, your head is in my lap, your fingers touch and caress me as I stroke your hair, your forehead, your cheeks, I pause at your lips as you kiss my fingers. I am gentle and aroused at the same time. As you lie in my lap you feel me growing hard and you brush your lips against the hardness, as my hand discovers your breasts. Your nipples, your soft, lovely tummy skin. We bond we commune, we excite each other, and the cares and worries about health and work retreat to the background. Our senses are concentrated on giving pleasure to each other and expressing that deep love we share. So exciting and yet so tranquil.

Purple Book: '"I want you to know about Nola . . . I couldn't possibly hide from Nola my strong, strong feelings for you".' This was an outrageous statement and the whole letter offended me greatly. Assuring Linda she was not a secret from me, and all the things he was supposed to have shared with me about their relationship; that I didn't have the same 'insights' as they did; their soulmate status. It was clear he would say literally anything to serve his ends. Then he had the audacity to ask her to give him credit for his honesty! And capped off the letter with a bit of erotica.

A week later Linda wrote, 'You surprised me when you opened up yourself and Nola and you and me and me and Roy. I thought it was really the private part of you. I am pleased, thank-you very much.'

She went on to claim that it didn't matter to her whether Michael didn't share with her 'that private part of you and Nola'. But she did hope that I didn't start feeling threatened by their relationship in the way Roy was threatened. 'I guess it is expected of Roy because of the revelation I have given him. So perhaps it would be the same response if Nola was informed that deep.' She rather plaintively asked Michael how she could convince Roy, and finished by acknowledging that Roy could never understand their relationship, and 'wants me to choose and bloody hell, it's like I will be chopped in two'.

Purple Book: 'She's grateful that he opened up to her.' It was extraordinary that Linda believed I accepted his relationship with her. Still, she had another serious hissy fit on 7 November. She'd had a meeting with Michael in which he'd told her that he wanted her to finish her thesis by 10 January [1997] and she was upset because he knew she hadn't even completed the first draft. She asked him to help her get an extension, at least until May. She accused him of wanting her to complete it early so that it would not coincide with the start of his teaching semester in March, and asked, 'Why push it so hard to me, knowing my "bitter" condition with the family. If you are going abroad, or if you are taking another student or whatever reason, it is not my business anymore. You can do whatever you want. Just do not tell me I am your priority student because it doesn't make sense.'

Although Linda was prone to histrionics, mood swings and jealousy, she had rarely written in such an angry tone and it was the first time their relationship had very obviously clashed with her academic interests.

She had another talk with Michael and discovered she could have an extension until 28 February, but was still angry about the confusion over her request to extend until May. She wanted to know his real intentions for originally not supporting her extension, and asked if it was because it would make teaching more difficult for him, or if he was retiring. 'How can I trust you? You have to be frank and honest. Yes, even if it hurts – I can still take it. It is hard – your position, my position. It would have been easy if I am just a student. I can't explain and you can't understand.'

Two days later she backed down after getting verbal assurance from Michael that she had his full support and would get the extension she needed. In her letter of 11 November she questioned why she'd misunderstood him. She put it down to their lack of time together. The GL was resurrected.

By now Michael hadn't written Linda any notes for two weeks, and she begged him to write, even if they had already talked. 'Please, please, please. Oh dear, I never expect you will have this head attack so intensely. I'm sorry. Please tell me tomorrow what strategies to adopt to avoid more of my misunderstandings in the future.'

A few days later they patched things up with a visit to the lake to renew their vows. Michael wrote on 19 November:

The last two weeks have delivered many contrasts and still the GL remains triumphant! Returning to our marriage venue was very, very special. We are truly blessed and such occasions confirm that truth over and over. The pelicans and cormorants and ducks, the clouds, the pale blue glimpses of sky, the ruffling waters and the attentive magpies – everything was there to bless our love-sharing. We talk/think a lot about lovemaking lately and we both want that extra dimension which goes with our 'readiness'. But we also know we are lovemaking all the time in the true sense of the word, and we want the consummation to be as close to ideal as we can make it. I hope the perfect opportunity will come soon.

We know, at times like yesterday, that our love is pure and lovely. It is clean and profound. We are not wrestling with our

conscious moral feeling because we are convinced of its rightness. What we must also accept is that others, from those
closest to us, Roy and Nola, to those who observe from a
greater distance, will not understand the full nature of the GL.
Let us, from now to forever, accept this fact and not fret about it.

Purple Book: 'Conscious moral feeling.' That he seemed so
convinced of the 'rightness' of what they were doing was,
yet again, breathtakingly delusional.

On 19 November Linda returned to her ever-present fear
of discovery. 'I fear the knock on the door like yesterday. I
trembled because it was really obvious. The risk is so high
but I wish we try not to get caught as we know the consequences already.' But she couldn't stop herself from writing
the notes: 'I thought I'd . . . concentrate on writing my thesis.
It will not happen. The hand that writes the living book is
far more powerful.'

6 December

Michael: The paper delivery on Saturday mornings I will
never forget, as long as I live.

My subsiding to the floor on Tuesday 26 November and
inviting you to lie on me. We were so high. Oh what elation;
what dreams! When I was sick and we wanted to kiss but
you suggested we kiss in the mind. I said I wanted kisses
on the lips, not in the mind. Seeing you today. How lovely
you looked and you already knew, just from eye contact, that
Kaye and I had talked about *us*.

When I read the bit about the paper delivery on Saturday
morning, I realised something else. Michael always did the
shopping on Saturday mornings. I used to wonder why he
chose Saturday mornings when he could have done it any
time on his way home from work. Now I knew why – he
was her paperboy.

On 6 December Linda told Michael he'd been brave to tell Kaye about the GL, and she wasn't sure that Kaye would understand. She thought Kaye knew from Annette that their relationship had gone beyond friendship, and was waiting to hear it from Linda. Linda realised Kaye and Annette were disappointed that she hadn't had the courage to open up to them the last time they'd all been together, and that Annette had not accepted the reality of the affair, but she hoped Annette would change her mind and come to accept it with time.

Of course, I knew none of this. The year was drawing to a close and I was looking forward to another holiday with Michael in Western Australia in January. I was also looking forward to Michael's retirement. Sixty-three may have seemed a little young to retire a brain like Michael's, but he was keen on pursuing other interests, such as researching his family history and writing his memoirs. He would also be staying on at the university part-time to look after his students who were yet to complete their PhDs. He seemed well, but the heart failure was always at the back of my mind. And even though I was not retiring myself for another three years, Michael being at home more would mean we could spend more time together, and I was looking forward to this next stage in our life.

1997

Purple Book: '147 letters this year.'

Roy and the children returned home in early February, and Linda was busy with family matters before they went and hadn't had time to spend with Michael. She left to join them in July but they continued to write and email. Reading many of the 1997 letters was particularly difficult because they were so sexually explicit; some were those spilling from the top of the box when I opened it and therefore the ones I read first.

13 January

Michael: Oh Linda, I know you are out there. I know that you love me and I love you so very much. I know how busy you are and what a lot of demands you are striving to meet. Most of all I know how much I miss you and you miss me. I feel it and I know it and I cope with it. Sunday morning was the first time since before our soul-marriage that I woke up weeping softly. No particular reason. No special thoughts or problems at the surface. But somewhere deeper inside I was sad.

Linda responded on the same day by saying that the only way she knew how to cope with her conflicting commitments was to pull back from Michael. It was the 'best remedy' to avoid imbalance in her life but it caused her great sadness.

14 January

Michael: I want to say how desperate I am to see you before I fly to Perth on Friday. I will be away for twelve days my love and I will leave some classic quotes for you to refer to each day. It will be very hard to be in touch while I am in Western Australia because much of the time I will be travelling or recovering from travelling.

Purple Book: 'Classic quotes.' This made me sad. It reminded me of the times Michael had written me notes, quotes and poems for each day when he went away.

15 January

Linda: The time is past to grieve for the past's difficult experiences, the trials, the traumas and tragedy. I guess 1997 is a letting go year; 1995, 1996 were given to us to heal and to have quality time (soul marriage).

By the last page Linda was crying so hard that her tears had smudged the ink and her writing was erratic. The reality of letting go had 'hit me right through my heart. The bitterness of my imbalances is knowing how good it would have been to be with you all my life but I can't.' She finished by saying she had to stop writing and crying because Roy would be home in a couple of minutes.

In her next letter she said she couldn't decide what to do about storing Michael's notes: 'Should I leave them in your office carefully sealed and labelled? But what if some unexpected event results in them being thrown in the bin. I have decided to take them with me when I go back to Annette's until May.'

She also made a request: he should write a letter to Roy, and to each of her children, explaining the GL, and she would write one to Nola.

I was amazed by this idea. Of course, I never did get a letter, and I'm sure Michael never wrote to Roy – what on earth would he have said!

Perhaps Michael wasn't sure either, since he didn't respond directly to this particular idea. Instead he was focusing on the day that Roy and the children would be leaving Canberra. He seemed to think the GL would make up for Linda's temporary loss of her family. On 3 February he wrote:

> I am very conscious of how you will be feeling today. So very different from the family days you have spent in Canberra for the last two years and nine months. And although long anticipated, the departure of the family and the move back to Annette's would still be a shock. The tunnel you now feel you are in does have an opening at its end and the world outside is still there to be observed, absorbed and constructively celebrated. And among the unchanging truths and beauties is the GL and its many manifestations.

A week later Michael described to her a trip he and I had taken to an antiques exhibition at Old Parliament House. As the capital city, Canberra had many exhibitions, particularly art exhibitions, which we always enjoyed going to. We liked antiques and that exhibition would have been a 'must' for us to visit. Not that we could have afforded to buy, but it was fun to look. He observed:

> I was surprised to find myself looking at the women there and thinking how attractive many of them were. Sort of animal attraction. But my emotional core was also speaking to me, and telling me how different from these superficial observations was my love for you, and for Nola. Oh my dearest Linda, how many more dimensions, how deeper than deep, is my love for you, my precious soul-mate. And how lucky I am to have such a best friend as Nola. I tell you, inside my

tired body, I was jumpy as a young foal or a bull calf. Alive!
I haven't felt exactly like that for a long time.

In the same letter he told her the news that his eldest son,
Anthony, and his wife, Laura, had told us some days before.
We were overjoyed to hear they were expecting their first
baby in September. We'd had a happy celebratory dinner
with them; it coincided with Chinese New Year so we went
to our favourite Chinese restaurant, and Michael's description of part of the event really annoyed me:

> I have to say I was pretty emotional. When Laura asked
> me things about my mother, I told her how she didn't so
> much *teach* me things as provide an atmosphere in which I
> absorbed things – values, precepts, philosophies, attitudes,
> questions – and I ventured that in many ways it was the same
> as that with Anthony and me. I think we were both feeling a
> bit choked up for a few moments.

Given the way he was behaving, I found the comments
he made about his mother offensive. If she had imparted
all these values – well, he certainly didn't seem to have
absorbed them.

On 9 February Linda started writing a series of notes that
she finally gave Michael ten days later. She began by going
over all the reasons that she could no longer visit him or
hug him, and reiterated her love for him and the GL and
how she missed him. She said she was grateful to Annette
for having listened to her heartbreak over the past month
– 'Annette and I didn't have this closeness before – until I
revealed everything to her about the GL. EVERYTHING.'
(Although that was of course untrue – Annette had no idea
of the sex they were having, and in her house.) 'Don't worry
Michael, Annette is here and Annette will help you. I asked
her to take care of you and one night when we had a long

night sharing about the GL I told her that I would tell you that she would be the one to tell me when you finally go.'

At this, I'd written in the Purple Book: 'Annette got the job of telling Linda when Michael "finally went".'

I did send Annette an email advising her of Michael's death and as she had been designated by Linda to be the one to tell her, I'm sure she would have done so. Thinking about this now, I realise I never did receive a condolence message or telephone call from any of the three women, Annette, Kaye or Linda, who had such a prominent place in Michael's life over these many years.

Linda then turned to their cache of letters: 'She offered to keep the notes for us. Because she is so special to me, please take care of her. I love you both very much. Annette knows I want to make love with you. Don't worry Michael I'll soon go and I'll take you with me.'

She also explained that when Roy and the children had left earlier in the month she had felt very alone, but couldn't go to him for comfort. 'I was so helpless. You go on vacation – did you think of me and consider what I might feel? Many times in the past it is like this. Did you ever ask yourself "How is Linda when I leave her for awhile" . . . Did you know how difficult it is for her when Roy and the kids left?'

We had indeed gone away for ten days and it was a lovely holiday. How dare she berate him for going away with his wife. Michael resorted to his powers of persuasion in response to this. On 20 February he wrote:

Your approach and resolution are commendable as well as consistent. But I would ask for your understanding, also of how I miss you, and how I don't fully believe in the virtue of deprivation as a character-building, strengthening way to behave. Not even monks can sustain that, if you read the history of monasteries. A hug now and then, when it is available is a positive and beautiful experience which can be affirmed and embraced (literally in this case) as a part of life's flow.

Purple Book: 'Outrageous! "The virtue of deprivation as character-building"?' Not for Michael. Michael was known to love the good life. We had a wonderful cellar of wine never saved just for 'special occasions' and, as I have mentioned, he was quite a gourmet cook.

A couple of weeks later he was in an ebullient mood:

12 March
Michael: It's hard to write when you feel so fizzy! I can't seem to come down from this high. These last few days I have been above the clouds. It's uncanny – you just called me to tell me of the *clouds*! Just as I had written the word 'clouds'! I ran out to the front of the building (heaven knows what people thought I was doing) and I just caught a glimpse of the gold tinge. Oh Linda, it's great to be alive! I feel so very much alive. I can walk on air on water. I am in a drug-induced ecstatic state. High as a kite. Drunk with GL.

Purple Book: 'Fizzy! High as a kite. Drunk with GL. Talk about a love-struck loon.' I wondered about his sanity. I also began to think that his writing had deteriorated.

14 March
Linda: Seeing you today I couldn't believe the prolonged longing and orgasm. Oh God, my doorways are always so excited to welcome you, please don't let them wait any longer.

Three days later, knowing that it was too risky to ML in his office or her office, Linda suggested they do it at 41 Nicols Street on 18 March, when she knew Annette would not be home until late. It had been difficult to arrange due to her program and Michael's professed 'concern for Nola'. There was no mention of what his concern might be and I have no idea what he might have meant by it at that particular time. Linda continued in a remarkable vein: 'We know we do not want to hurt our dearest loved ones. It is easier for me now because Roy is physically away . . . Oh God we are moving fast . . . We are now ready to be vulnerable and risk once again. We are now ready to touch the holy ground we talked about in '92.'

18 March

Linda: <u>18 MARCH 97 18 MARCH 97 18 MARCH 97</u>. I am flying like a bird in heaven. I am obsessed with you. We truly have visited the heavens . . . Poor big one, it must be difficult for you because you have to go home.

Linda went on to badger Michael with many intimate questions: had she treated him well; did he think she'd responded well; had he liked it deep inside her; was he satisfied; had he gone to the heavens too? 'I can do more and more until I milk you dry . . . I like how you grind me to ecstasy . . . the way you thrust me to death. I keep coming and coming.'

She had a rush of sentiment for 41 Nicols, and said she would buy the house if she ever won Lotto.

In Michael's letter of 20 March there were more delusions and moral-high-ground-taking in how *thoughtful* they'd been in conducting this affair:

What I like/love/celebrate most about our GL is its genuine unselfishness . . . we both know we have been very, very considerate of our relative positions and our loved ones – those whom Annette was at great pains to protect from 'hurt'. We didn't need Annette to tell us we should be careful not to bring hurt to 'others'. We have been living that consideration for five years now, and in that time the GL has become the most wonderful force in both our lives.

We have truly just begun our future life. Our beginning may have ended with our first ML, but our new life, now fully begun, is before us. And once having ML, are we to feel satisfied to reach such a culmination? NO again. It may be surprising to some, considering my age and stage of life, but I feel like ML several times a day, 7 days a week!

I was puzzled by references to a new and 'future life' before them. Could Michael possibly have thought that they had a future? Especially as she only had another four months in the country. Did he want her to leave her family and come and live with him? He hated the heat so he would certainly not have been prepared to move too far north of Canberra.

24 March
Michael: Oh my precious one – where can I start? Your notes were so disturbed – you had not only the troubled experience of coming down from the wonderful, wonderful Tuesday, but you plummeted to the depths of feeling helpless and alone . . . And now – we have had another afternoon of liberated lovemaking. We have given our passionate natures free rein. We have surrendered fully to each other and we have merged our whole selves not just our bodies. We have brought delicious pleasure to each other and we could go on and on. So how does that make us feel? Well I do feel *better* right now. I'm still tingling with the knowledge that we can scale even greater heights together.

4 April
Michael: Lunch with Annette was very pleasant and relaxed. We did talk a little about you, but not all the time, and there are not any special insights to pass on to you. We

both love you so much. Though it is inevitable that 'love' means more to me than to Annette. We are in such different positions regarding you. How do you compare the GL and its marvellous depths, with the special relationship of a dear friend, who nevertheless has her own way of doing, seeing and thinking? To get the ultimate out of a relationship with Annette, one feels that you become more and more like her in your thinking and being. It is curious how much I like her, because though we have similar intellectual and cultural values our approaches are completely different. She will always be a friend, but I will always regret that she has time and energy only for those she has declared to be 'OK', and gives little attention to what makes some others tick. Please don't think I am being harsh on Annette. As I say, I like her a lot.

9 April

Linda: How can I describe when you bury your face on my bosom? Why do my breasts know you? They are so tender and responsive when you are near them.

She asked him to promise to kiss her breasts again and again and again and 'more and more until I beg you to stop'.

The following day she wrote to tell Michael she'd be in the lab for the whole weekend, 'But given the choice I would like to calm down ... my groin is starting to get tender'. She thoughtfully finished by informing him 'while the lactic acid will stay in my muscles for 3–5 days I wouldn't mind squeezing them again'.

Her next letter sounded petulant, as she complained about Michael's double standards – pretending that they hadn't made love when they had – several times – at No. 41. She was hurt by this. She understood the rationale for the pretence but didn't know why she accepted it. Was he afraid of Annette? Linda urged him to believe that Annette wouldn't mind – 'she knows everything and she can understand'. But Annette obviously didn't know 'everything', because then Linda taunted him that perhaps she had told Annette that they had 'ML'. 'Would you think bad of me because I didn't ask your approval', she asked. 'Will you be embarrassed because you'll lose your "good straight image"?'

She *hadn't* revealed all to Annette, she went on to assure him. Indeed, they had always told Annette they weren't having an affair when they were actually having sex under her roof. On the one hand Linda claimed Annette knew 'everything' and on the other hand she said she hadn't told Annette yet – another example of their loose definitions of words and values.

Linda began May by thanking Michael for the last two days of making love. 'We won't ever forget how special these days have been. They have healed the pain of 1994. When you come to this part of our story when writing the book I want you to say you made these two days the happiest days of our lives.'

She started on about the book again: 'Please write our story soon. Make it tangible in its true sense. Make it your priority after retirement. You will do it more justice than others and it is also the only living gift you can give me. We do not know what will happen in our lives – who goes first. It would be so good to see copies of the book in front of my eyes. The Great Love Story – probably a good title for our book, well that it suits us.'

If this wasn't enough to make me seethe, I then came to her postscript. She'd been sorting through the notes she had found in a box in Michael's office and had found an envelope containing family letters, and those of Edith and Aggie: 'I thought Anthony's card should be the only one to be preserved. Tell me what to do with the rest. I guess I will decide to burn them and bury the past – what do you reckon?' They were, she continued, all the 1978–1984 letters that were not worth keeping, including Edith and Aggie's. She asked if she should also throw those in the bin.

I found the idea that she would burn his personal letters an extraordinary cheek. Did she have no sensitivity at all? There were many moments when reading their letters became an entirely surreal experience, and this was one of them.

Four days later, more bizarre prose from Linda: 'I shiver to death how perfect we fit. We even discovered the wonders of the G-spot. Once you discover it I soar like a dove, fierce like a tiger, romantic as the Venus'.

More sex followed, as she told him how she had 'this tiger feeling . . . Your hard is so gorgeous, didn't they tell you that?' She ended – rather bathetically, I couldn't help observe: 'Is it OK to ML every day with your heart – didn't you have a muscle pain last weekend?'

Purple Book: 'She's worried about his heart!'

7 May

Michael: After your phone call and notes!! My dearest, my most wonderful, my darlingest, my most beautiful little one, my hot tigress.

Like 18 March. I can't take it anymore – I HAVE TO WRITE. Your today's notes from the HOT room were so very hot. Even if I am busy today, I can't wait to say what's on my mind, in my heart, transforming my energy into a maelstrom of love force . . .

What an amazing voyage of discovery we have been on these last weeks. Our vessel (our GL) has moved on from the abiding in each other's depth to the out-pouring of the thrilling, exciting, endlessly driven spirit. The 'can't take it anymore' joining with the short sweet episodes of touching, holding, brief orgasms of the past when we sucked and licked and stroked each other to trembling comings. Ordinarily it would be hard to make the 18th sound special or romantic with the mess, the scratchy carpet, the awkward space, but all the inconvenience and ordinariness are totally overwhelmed by the dam-break. The bloodstains were totally lost in the elation, the mind-blowing realisation in answer to the questions: Is it really true? Is it really happening? Is it REAL?

But even with the dam-break, our finite minds were still not prepared fully for the later times when we stretched out towards infinity. Our integration is complete but our experience of the infinite is limitless.

And so from the floor in the hallway to the floor in the kitchen, to the bedroom, the bed, the shower, always hungry to gorge ourselves on love we wallowed in the sheer delight of it. Can it really be a surprise that you loved to be kissed and licked and sucked – your lips top and bottom, your clitoris, vagina, even fingers, toes, belly button, everything, Is it any wonder I loved so much to be sucked and caressed, tasted and smelled, and finally sucked dry by your lovely mouth. We should know that anything we did was going to be wonderful – not just OK, but surpassingly beautiful.

I wanted what you wanted and always felt totally free to express our love spontaneously. But *everything* about us is joyous, whether me on you, you on me, front ways, front to back, legs tangled, legs stiffened like logs, tasting each other's juices, directly at first and then shared in deep kisses. It's all overwhelmingly amazing, hugely exciting, thrilling, and unbelievably beautiful. Everything is painted bright gold and flavoured with the sweetness of big, big love. Transformation, transfiguration. Ultimate experience.

Purple Book: 'Scratchy carpet? Mess? Bloodstains?' Obviously no one else home at No. 41.

9 May
Linda: 'You do not look very well. Are you OK? Please . . . be fit. Dearest take care of yourself. You might forget to take

care of your tummy – it's becoming yorkee. I'm afraid when you grow that big – you were that size when you went to the States. Are you sure ML is good for you? Do check, please do check. '

Purple Book: '"Yorkee".'

A few weeks later Linda wrote asking Michael, 'AREN'T WE GREAT LOVERS? The best ones!!!' and thanking him profusely. She thought he could kill people with the ecstasy he gave her; she wanted him to kill her with it. 'We were sprinting we want to come all the time. How many times did you come – you were so sweaty.' She couldn't bring herself to wash her hands or face, so she could still taste and smell him, and feel his face buried between her legs, his tongue inside her, and 'a hose squirting hot lava'. More thanks followed, and professions of desire, and how lovely it was 'to fuck, sometimes it's nice to say these words'.

Michael had told Linda he would book a room at a hotel for an overnight stay and she asked if he was sure. 'You don't mind wasting your money? I would love to have our space, especially with a fireplace, only once in a fireplace.'

They appeared to be doing a lot of ML at No. 41, in his room and down by the lake. Michael was the one to suggest an exclusive, heritage-listed hotel with function facilities. I wondered about the mention of a fireplace again – I became a bit obsessed wondering if they ML in front of our fireplace.

30 May

Linda: We will never be able to ML as we do with anyone else and we will never KISS as we do with anyone else. We are truly unique and our ways of expressing love are also unique. We will never expect to have them with Roy and Nola and it would be unfair to make comparisons.

Their letters were full of the way they kissed. In one letter Linda devoted a whole page to it. And Michael waxed lyrical about kissing in hundreds of letters.

On 13 June there was a second hotel mention, but I could not find any reference to them actually spending a night there. It would have been very risky. But of course, as they'd demonstrated, they were not averse to taking risks.

The next letter from Michael was truly awful – he was bemoaning his miserable weekends and complained about a party I was trying to organise to celebrate his impending retirement. What an ungrateful sod he had become.

18 June

Michael: Another bloody weekend over. Weekends are the absolute nadir of my life these days and I am torn apart by them. I know I am missing you terribly – really terribly – and yet weekends should be happy times. Relaxing from work, doing things around the home, seeing the family, having time to talk and make plans. Poor Nola is making plans for a big party on 2 August to celebrate my retirement. Lots of family and close friends to be invited. Catering arrangements. She's doing all this for me, and my enthusiasm is at rock bottom. I feel mean.

But I can't help my longing to be with you; like you say, just to look into your eyes and know what's in your head and heart. And if I think it's only a few more weeks (less now!) where this terrible inner conflict is going on, it makes it all so much worse. At least you understand how it is, how it was for you when the family were all here – the legiti- mate desires the family have to spend time with you, and you with them, and the deep emotional visceral need for *us* to be together. And since our ML it's a thousand times more powerful. And the tears we shed for the parting – how are we to survive a long weekend that stretches out till heaven knows when. I honestly can't think about it. I am trusting God as never before to give me the Grace to endure.

You often say how strong I am and how I will survive. Well, maybe, but I'll need a lot of help and I will be awful company for a lot of people for a long time. O God, renew my spirit, my optimism, my ability to count my blessings. I need to be strong for Linda. I need to give her strength and security.

On a more cheerful topic, I think the thesis is going/coming well. Tight in time frame, but what's new? So long as the deadline doesn't mean lots of mistakes, misspellings etc, being busy at the end is not surprising.

Yes, what a mean comment indeed about the party I was organising for him. It was a big affair, which I chose to have catered, and, apart from family and friends, we invited his university colleagues. It was actually a lovely party. He appeared to enjoy himself – I guess he liked the attention.

It was hard to believe he could describe weekends as 'the nadir of his life'. We had such a lovely, cosy home and there was so much to enjoy after our busy working week: I have memories of a warming fire, soup on the stove and homemade bread in the oven through the long, cold winters. When we were not busy working in the garden we loved sharing our home with family and friends, particularly on Sundays. Sorting through his poems I found 'Sunday After-noon', which Michael wrote sometime in the last years of his life, but is undated, which was uncommon for him. Reading it now, I understand its true meaning.

Sunday Afternoon

Outside the restless breezes fuss and swirl
and stress my sore condition –
a lonely lover longing for his girl
and cursing his position.

While rustling leaves express their discontent
I inwardly decry
This separation from my love, god-sent
Resentments flare – and die.

Soul-soothing music leaves my troubled mind
In its still wounded state.
The peace I so desire I cannot find
I try to concentrate

on hours to come, the gentle hours of healing,
so necessary now,
when I can show my love my deepest feeling
and when this burdened brow

will lose its furrows, and my eyes will smile,
rejoicing at your sight,
and I can even bear to part a while
without an inner fight.

You are, my love, both solace and relief,
The very sweetest balm,
whose presence brings such joy, tho' absence grief.
You, only you, bring calm

to make all things come right in every way,
and all life fits in place.
My heart ascends and love grows more each day,
God bless your lovely face.

MIW

Finally, on 6 July 1997, Linda returned home permanently. But before she left, Michael had the nerve to invite her to our home for dinner. As I recall, the talk was friendly – about what she was going to do after she got her PhD and how she was looking forward to seeing her family, especially her children. I remember her speaking of her love for Australia and how she was looking forward to coming back for her graduation the following year. I racked my memory for any hint of sadness or unusual behaviour from either of them that night, and there was none. But if you don't know, you don't know what you are looking for.

The email she had sent him the day before was curiously casual: 'Dear Michael, thank-you very much for being kind and good to me . . . take care, live and be alive! Cheers Linda'.

Michael did not write to her the week before she left. But once she had gone, they continued to exchange letters and send emails. By the end of the year, the number of Michael's letters (of which he kept copies) had outstripped Linda's three to one. They would refer to their letters using number codes written on the envelope, which seemed to me to be another example of how compulsive their correspondence was. When I reread the poems Michael had written for me, I discovered he'd written 'Awakening' three weeks before Linda left and it took on a different meaning altogether. It was also interesting in the light of a comment in his 30 August 1993 letter: 'In the present context, if I am not making it known that I want to make love [to Nola], she accepts that and does not expect anything. She probably thinks that, at my age, I've lost a lot

of my libido! And, to be honest, that is the way I am with her;
I love her a lot and we are very good friends and companions
and I *can* make love with her, but I seldom choose to.'

Awakening

Early lid opening, still dark morning.
Slower than normal stirring, squirming.
Distant traffic heralds the soon-to-be-dawn.

Was that a flash? A turning headlight?
A sputtering street lamp? Lightening even?
Can't be lightening. No thunder. No forecast.
Long weeks of 'fine and cool', 'dry with morning frosts'.

Still, outside the window, pavers glisten.
Probably heavy dew. Maybe frost. Not rain.
Another flash. A pause. A growling non-traffic rumble.
Unmistakable. Undeniable this time. Thunder.

Rain comes quietly, muttering under its breath.
Softly, softly. The new soft sound somehow
Making the doona seem even cosier.
And body warmth even more worth celebrating.

My hand in a guided, practiced wander
Finds familiar skin, smooth, thrilling,
And warm desire unfolds, envelops me.
My heart, steady till now, jumps with rekindled joy.

Each raindrop spatters the dried window grime.
But the gathered dust of passion also spreads.
And oh, if only I could freeze this moment.

MIW 11.vi.97

Linda left the box of their notes at Annette's for Michael to collect. On 31 July she wrote: 'I wept for days knowing how devastated I was when I left you and I thought you would have come to my rescue – notes would have comforted me . . . Even I do not believe you were too busy to even drop a line or two . . . Life is tough but I guess I made it tough for me.'

12 August

Michael: My very dearest Linda. I promise to write regularly from now on to assure you of my prayers, my deepest thoughts, my yearnings and longings. But above everything, just to let the two halves rejoin and rebound, recreate and rejoice. The hollow in my life can be refilled again and again by contact with you.

Your latest letters came today – they confirmed that we were both facing some similar difficulties. Nola and I were both home on leave for two weeks, and finding time when I could write to you *properly* was almost impossible. As I said in the last letter, my vow is to write often and regularly, even if it is only short, just to get something to you.

All my life I have known the word 'heartache' in its figurative meaning. During my illness, I was grateful I never had angina or heart pains. But now, when I am physically very well really, I feel heart pain. Not, I hasten to say because of constriction to arteries, but the psychological but real pain which grabs me till I cry to be released from my feeling of desolation and loss. I KNOW I haven't *lost* you; it is the FEELING I am describing. I need you so much, and I must practise the presence of you, just as the mystics used to practise the presence of God. God for me now is all rolled up in the GL, the accumulated insights into all aspects of love, and the physical Linda.

Purple Book: 'Poor God.'

13 August

Michael: Dearest, wonderfullest Linda. I hope by now you will have forgiven me for my late start in writing letters . . . What I do recognise is that we won't be able to maintain a one-to-one letter regime. I'll always want to write at least twice a week and at that rate I'll be three letters ahead before I get replies. Maybe our letters will be more observations, discussions, descriptions and perceptions. Once we are both settled, our question-and-answer matters will be better by email. I have the notes locked away at work for my (our!) PhD, and I am adding copies of letters to those I receive from you.

I know you haven't said anything, but by your silence on the subject I infer that no Heloise of M-L parentage is currently *in utero*. I have very mixed feelings about that. Relief that a complication of massive proportions has been removed from your family life. Slight disappointment that this very special life has not begun. The spirit must await its fleshly home for some time yet, and maybe even one not of our making.

Purple Book: '"M-L parentage *in utero*?"' Linda must have thought she might be pregnant when she left. Michael said he was a bit disappointed, and of course it was safe to say that now she was out of the country – but what would have happened if she had indeed been pregnant? What would his adult children have thought about that? She was a Catholic, too. Again, I realised that he had lost all sense of reality. Yet in the meantime – somehow – all appeared normal on the home front.

14 August

Michael: My dearest, lovely, wonderful Linda. I didn't intend to write again today, but I feel the urge very, very strongly . . .

I have been contacted recently by Lu, Lin's wife, asking about his movements, specifically when he is coming back from China. What she had to say made me very angry about Lin. I wasn't judgmental about his affairs or his deciding he wanted a divorce. What upset me so much was the evident lies he has told everyone about almost everything for the last seven years. I always wanted to help him, with all his weaknesses and faults, but I must say I had no idea of the extent of them. Your very mixed experiences with him were really the tip of the iceberg. Lin has taken up with a woman in China and he wants to bring her to Australia eventually. I don't judge him for his relationships but he has not been honest with us or with almost everyone else. I know that you, with your big heart, will not want to hurt Lin anymore, and neither do I. But I do resent the deceptions of those who were his closest supporters and helpers. It makes me lose heart a little. You have some idea of the extent that I helped him, but I doubt that you know it all.

Purple Book: 'Not judgemental about Lin's affair?' I thought all this sanctimonious bleating about Lin's affair and dishonesty when Michael was himself having an affair and indulging in his own dishonest behaviour was the ultimate in hypocrisy. It really was as if he had lost his mind; he had certainly lost his moral compass.

27 August

Michael: This is indeed a lucky day for me. An email message from the newly online Linda AND the first letter for a long time. You will know, as I write, that I have already written 8 letters over the past 2 ½ weeks. Your letter confirmed what I already knew – how excited you were about my call. You sounded so alive and special. Not for the first time, and certainly not for the last, I felt the combination of exultation and a lump in the throat. Joy and longing.

How unfair I feel it is to have the most precious person in all the world snatched away from me and I feel desperately lonely and bereft for those moments but dear Linda I am not a saint but I sometimes give in to self pity.

Dearest love, I am looking after myself very well. I have undertaken a fitness program for my body so I can be trim for you when we meet again. I eat and live very healthily. I also treat myself very gently when I recall the sweetest moments we shared. I practically have to hold my breath as I tread on that holy ground of which we have been aware for so long; the sweetness brings silent tears of joy, but I recall too the excitement and passion of our ML times.

Purple Book: 'Giving in to self-pity.' I don't recall Michael being particularly subdued around this time. There were obvious changes in his life with his retirement but if anything had seemed to be preoccupying him, I would have assumed he was merely adjusting to a new phase in his life.

29 August

Michael: Dearest Linda. Oh God, how I want to touch you, in a physical way. You were right about the wonderful kisses and the way you reacted to touching, rubbing sucking your nipples was supreme joy. And the look in your eyes and the rich redness of your lips after we kissed or made love or you sucked me. As you can tell, my thoughts today are very sensual, and my body vibrates at the very recollection of the magic love we shared. My lips tingle, my fingers itch to stroke you, outside and inside and my rod-down-there wants both sets of lips to enfold it. I am ultra-horny I know what you are capable of and I know you feel the same way. You want me time after time after time and I want us to lie wet and perspiring, sticky and smelling of love, kissing, and exchanging each other's juices, lying together, enjoying the afterglow embracing the tiredness as a friend who shared the beautiful experience.

Dearest, darling and delicious Linda. Our love transcends the whole of creation. It goes back to the very source and inspires us to worship. Oh mighty GL, give us love everlasting and give us unquenchable, insatiable passion.

5 September

Michael: Dear love – dearest love – dearest most wonderful love. Is it really just 2 months since I said goodbye at Canberra Airport? Hair uncombed and whiskers unshaven. And you without sleep for the umpteenth day. We kissed just the once before your friends burst onto the scene. How brave you were and gracious to your friends who all had the sweetest, kindest thoughts for you on your return 'home'. Everything they said and thought was right except for one thing. The omission of the home in my heart where you will live forever. They were not to know, and like me, they watched your small retreating figure going along the tube walkway to the plane – we all knew you would be crying, but I knew more. I had to be brave too, piling them all into my car and dropping them off, while all the time I was sobbing inconsolably inside. At that moment I felt the loss so desperately – only later could I recognize the truth of your indwelling spirit mingled with mine in my heart.

By mid-September Michael's letters had taken on a repetitive pattern. He was pleased they were getting through as they were more confidential than emails and allowed him to pour out his love and relive some erotica. At the end of September he spoke to Linda on the phone a couple of times – a 'choking-up' experience. He told her he was coping.

On 29 September he wrote, 'You may have thought, in your low times, that the absolute importance of the GL in my life would wane or fade a little once you were gone. Nothing is further from the truth. Not a single day have I not awakened with you on my mind, your name on my lips and a longing for you in my loins.' He then went on to urge her to share 'honestly' if anything at work or home was bothering her. He wanted her to have no inhibitions in what she told him and, as if to give her an idea, he launched into some sexual reminiscing:

> So, my love, I hunger for you now; I have your special aroma in my nostrils, I have the softness and taste of your lips tingling me as I picture our deep open-mouth kisses. I have the touch, taste and quiver of your nipples as I nibble and lick and suck. And I recall everything about your love opening. Its response to finger-touching and finally to contacting, sliding and entering my penis. Once joined we are truly one. Rocking, holding, folding, writhing and rejoicing to the point almost of pain as we go deeper and deeper into the core of our hot love. I know what we can do together, and I am convinced we can and will do much more – someday.

By October, his letters appeared to be getting increasingly over the top. On 7 October he addressed Linda as 'My sweetest, wonderfullest, excitingest, dearest, darlingest, specialest, beautifullest Linda.' He went on to probe her marriage situation and how it related to him:

> I have not commented on your [previous] letter NN6 very much . . . however, I will just comment on a couple of things. I'd like to ask if you can say a little more about your 'fights with Roy' especially when 'he gets jealous of (me)'. Are these fights brought on by the fact of receiving so many letters from me, or by your reactions to receiving them and possibly to what is contained in them? I guess he knows they are truly love letters and he finds it hard to accept that you want to be his wife and mother to his children when someone else is so much part of your life, especially your inner life and thoughts.

I know what I am now going to ask is very intimate and perhaps I have no right even to frame the question. But I have ringing in my ears the apprehension you expressed in the last days of June, about the physical side of going home. The marriage bed, the rejoining, the expectations, the comparisons. You were really torn apart by it, and the deliciousness of our ultimate surrender to making love only made it worse.

I knew your ambivalence when, on the one hand, we were absolutely desperate to ML and to let our love spill over and immerse us, but on the other hand, we knew that making love with our partners would never measure up. Neither of us was/is equipped very well to pretend, and neither of us can fantasise ourselves through a situation. In any case it would be unfair of us to spoil any ML with Nola or Roy by imagining what it was/is would be like to ML with each other. And I know it is easier for me. If I don't seek to ML with Nola, she can just put it down to being older, not so passionate, not as strong or fit as I used to be. But you my darling 36-year-old, are in your prime years, so your level of passionate activity can be related directly to desire and less to physical health.

Oh Linda, ridiculous as it may sound, the old cliché about being 'made for each other' surely, surely applies to us. We really did prove the truth of that didn't we! I *know* my love is forever and it seems often unfair not to be with you to have and to hold. Even as I go about my daily life, doing things within and for the family, making plans with Nola, reviewing my own future etc., I never, not ever, lose my conviction that the GL I share with you is always with me and is, in fact the most deeply important part of my life-force and reason for living at all.

Purple Book: 'Making love with our partners will never measure up.' The letter was very cruel. After his heart failure in 1994, I had deliberately avoided making any sexual overtures as I was worried about stresses on his heart. I used menopause as an excuse.

15 October

Michael: Darling Linda – my tears flowed so copiously as I read your notes. Your very serious telling of the economic realities, and your inability to plan further ahead than meeting everyday demands and anticipated school expenses. You are right to suggest I would have difficulty grasping the full reality, but my understanding is not completely lacking. I do know what it is like to have my entire income committed, to have debts, and to have no possibility of saving. I know it is OK, but wears you down because there is no relief. Like you, my desire was to give those things that didn't require money – love and support and, above all, availability. For many years, apart from nourishment, they were all the resources I had to give my family.

I know you have wondered and have discussed with others why I did not rise further up the academic scale than I did. I was a good academic teacher, I had a good brain, I had good abilities – I had all that one could ask for to have a successful career. The question boiled down to – what kind of success? Like you, I lacked the ambition to acquire power and I knew I was a superior intellectual than many who were more 'successful' in their careers. It was enough for me and I refused to play the game, to kiss the bums of people who could further my progress. Having made that decision, i.e. not to go after positions in the system, my only challenge became to maintain my integrity with consistency and never to waste time regretting opportunities either lost or never pursued. Mentoring other people, like students, became a satisfying fulfilling career goal, though it meant that I was going to miss out on getting a mentor of my own.

And as you say, doing research for your own satisfaction and for the good it might bring to others, is a noble ambition even if it is not materially rewarding. Providing you have enough for everyday needs of housing, schooling, nourishing the intangible aspects of living are the most important. Imagine you know your life is almost done, what are you going to look back on as the most significant and important aspects of the life you have lived. Will it be the car, the furniture, the clothes you have owned. No! Like me, you will cherish the GL above all, and all other aspects of love for family and friends. Your satisfaction will come from the knowledge that you have contributed to the happiness of so many people by giving your love generously and receiving their response.

His explanation about why he did not ride further up the academic scale was interesting. Very early in my time in the department, I was introduced to a technical officer, who was in charge of the nursery. He liked to invite people there when his azaleas were in flower – almost, but not quite, like asking someone to come and see his etchings. I received such an invitation one day and found that not only was he brilliant with plants, he was also a little bit of a gossip – he asked me if I knew who was the smartest person in the department. I said I didn't know (I had not been in the department long enough for that kind of assessment). 'Michael Westfield,' he said. 'But he's lazy.'

This was a very perceptive comment as I think Michael was lazy. I know he believed his devotion to his family had affected his career. He probably could have gone a lot further than he did but he made choices and as a result of those choices we struggled financially for most of our married life; an academic's pay was not huge and for two years I worked two jobs to help make ends meet. Money was a problem, but we managed.

I had a good life with Michael – a very happy and fulfilling life. I never doubted the choice I had made when I married him. I was sure in my own mind that he would be good to my children and that was very important to me. He was the embodiment of everything I thought a man should be and throughout our twenty-nine-year marriage he fulfilled all my expectations; he was my ideal companion and I thought I was his. Many of our friends seemed to recognise that what we had together was something special and I used to delight in that recognition. Michael was seen by others as a responsible person, a wise person, a person to whom people could turn to for help and advice. I think he found this quite satisfying and it is so difficult to understand how he could have abandoned such attributes in having this affair.

On 22 October, Michael responded to an angry, disillusioned email from Linda in which she asked if she could publish some research on her own, which they had done together with two other academics, without breaching a confidentiality agreement.

> While I am quite uncertain what the agreement contained, I am quite sure that you *could* publish without the others or myself. And perhaps you should, though it would be nice for the department if you did it jointly with me. I would be the one to edit drafts and discuss what went in, what is left out, and the form of presentations appropriate to the journal chosen. Any aspect you wanted to submit independently, such as bits not covered in the main paper, you could certainly publish on your own. We should discuss all these ideas *very soon*.

On 4 November Michael wrote that as he hadn't had any firm direction from her about her thesis amendments, he had gone ahead and begun the process. He reported that he had spoken to Annette; Kaye had returned from a visit to see Linda and mentioned to Annette that Linda was having tensions in her marriage directly due to her bond with Michael.

Darling, I feel pretty helpless and would value your thoughts on so serious a matter. For me, I feel I have no choice and no desire but to hold you at the very centre of my being. Whatever may happen, I shall love you with everything forever . . . We can acknowledge that physically we will not be able to spend our lives in each other's direct company. No holding, no kissing, no ML ever again . . . We fulfil all our responsibilities to our families and friends and work places. Alternatively, we can accept that for now the realities are as stated above, but cherish the hope that our burning love will never be quenched and that someday, somehow we will come together again and rejoin the two halves of the GL, physically as well as spiritually.

Michael then talked about arrangements for Linda's graduation – he had gathered from Annette via Kaye that Linda would not be coming back for the ceremony, in April of the following year.

The reason is not the cost though that is important I know, but once again it is an ultimatum of a kind to you to commit yourself to Roy and his 'needs' and to sacrifice any desires of your own or of mine, perhaps especially mine. Precious love, I wish you were not in this position, and I truly understand. No pressure will come from me, and I will do nothing to destabilise your marriage or your family commitment.

Finally, and again I relate what I am about to say and ask what has already been raised. I really want to know from *you* what I should do about writing to you. Given Roy's sensitivities, I must be a constant reminder to him that we truly love each other every time a letter from Australia hits your PO Box. At worst, this must keep open any wounds he is suffering from. At another level he must feel that while you constantly demonstrate loyalty to family concerns your true heart is elsewhere.

As an intelligent man, he has got it right as we both know! I hope you may be able, and I pray earnestly for this, to negotiate with Roy that you may receive regular letters from me, that you will not have to ask me to stop writing. It is our only contact outside of the intangible telepathies and our shared experience of eternity and our vision of meeting on the ridges. Oh please Linda (I am crying now, I'm sorry) help me. I must write to you and I long for you to write to me, so we can more fully share this marvellous love of ours.

Purple Book: 'Another disturbing letter.' I couldn't help wondering what he had hoped to achieve by asking her to negotiate with Roy so that she could still receive his love letters. Did he *want* their marriage to fail?

17 November
Michael: My dearest and greatly-missed Linda. I have read and re-read your last letter. I took pages 3, 4 and 5 round to Annette's place on Friday so she could read the news and comment about the family. In doing so she also read your comments about your longings for me, the pain, the sadness, and your concern to know my secret of survival.

Annette opened up to a more significant extent than ever before about you and me and the GL. I guess I encouraged her to feel free to comment and that I wouldn't dissolve with embarrassment or resentment whatever she wanted to say to me. It was a friend-to-friend thing, not an advice or coun-selling thing.

Annette 'fleshed out' for me the discussions she had had with you about the GL. Annette said that you went into one of your withdrawals for a while, culminating with a 3-hour discussion on Great Love. She said she was shown some of my notes to illustrate what you and I shared (details unknown). Her claim is that she has no particular interest about peoples' love lives, but that you wanted desperately for her to understand.

What Annette doesn't do very much is to give her opinions or moral position. She gives strong opinions and adopts moral stances on almost everything else, but rarely on what she would still call 'relationships', unless she was convinced they were exploitative. I guess I can take comfort, after all that, to feel that Annette doesn't think my love for you is exploitative. I think, between us, we have convinced her of the specialness of the GL, and the purely loving intentions we have in our feelings and expressions.

Also, and I don't believe any confidences are broken here, Annette told me, in more detail than you told me, of your conversations with Roy – was it all right to 'make love with Michael' etc and the purchase of a vibrator. It was all rather light-hearted as a conversation during which we were both confirmed anew in our knowledge that you are utterly and oh-so-lovably unique. The only thing that still furrows my brow (gives me concern) is your ongoing relationship with Roy. I admire him greatly and appreciate his politics. I commend his honesty as an unbeliever. There is so much that is admirable about him, and I know he loves his family unit and wants to preserve it. It is very hard for me to have the knowledge that the GL threatens him, that your honesty about 'us' probably does not improve matters and could put you in an unjustified unfavourable light.

I have said, and thought often, how much I felt for Roy. How aggrieved he must be when you receive so many letters from me – personal letters, not 'official' ones. It would be natural for me, feeling as I do about the situation, that I would stop writing so often so as not to provoke him unnecessarily. But against that is your need for a lifeline, a release from so many everyday realities and restraints and, let's face it, the potential disasters you have had to face since you got back.

Apropos of what I have been writing about, Roy, you and me, I would like you to be free and, if necessary, courageous and frank and tell me how things are. I have respected your silence on this matter for quite some time now, feeling that the time would eventually come when you felt free to 'talk'. But I feel bold enough to ask now because we need not fear any reaction from each other.

As I said before, I admire Roy so much, and wish I could know him better and discuss some of his views. But I wish sometimes that, good and admirable man that he is, he was not married to you. Foremost in my mind is the knowledge that you may conform to these restraints for the greater good of others, your spirit is free and your mind is not shackled. You could survive with your thoughts and the unshakeable GL intact. I just don't want you to suffer any hardship as a result of others' actions, including Roy's actions.

So I guess, if you want to be superficial about it, you could see me acting in a fatherly role here, rather than that of a lover. But let me assure you that the lover role, the abiding life-giving experience of my life, is the dominant one.

Purple Book: 'Breathtaking insincerity.' It was so devious to talk about 'feeling for Roy' when he really just wanted him to skedaddle out of the picture. I do believe Michael was making mischief in this letter.

The following day Linda replied. She didn't know whether it had been a mistake to tell Roy, but she felt that with all the letters arriving from Michael, it was obvious something was going on. Roy was bitter and felt betrayed, she said. Remarkably, she then had the nerve to tell Michael that such a betrayal was 'only in [Roy's] mind'. Her confession – however frank it was – had, however, convinced her to clam up again; she said she didn't know if she would keep on being honest, and had been shaken up when Roy had told her she must stop the affair to show her loyalty to him – her husband. She wrote that she couldn't stop, she thought the whole world was against her and she asked Michael, 'Please tell me what to do.'

The next letter was probably one of the most outrageous of all of them. In it Michael talked about how his failure to disclose to me details of his and Linda's sexual lovemaking did not detract from his honesty in acknowledging to me his love for her. This constant talk about honesty was extremely galling. I suppose Michael never specifically lied to me because he never told me what he was doing and I didn't ask, but he lied repeatedly to Linda. He even talked of the 'unbearable restraint' they'd exercised for five years!

26 November

Michael. My failure to disclose to Nola details of sexual love-making does not detract from my honesty in acknowledging my love for you. Nor would it have been harmful to your honesty to have withheld the full details from Roy. I know how you might have been put on the spot with direct yes/no questions, so I am not condemning you – far from it. I know you, and what your idealism constrains you to do, I do understand. The problem is that not everyone can pigeon-hole knowledge in the same way as you do. They are not in tune with your eternal values and feel threatened. All of which is essentially irrelevant now . . .

You and I will never get from Roy a gold star on the forehead or a big tick on our assignment, for the almost unbearable restraint we exercised for five years. We were *very* consider-ate and responsible in the face of the strongest temptation. We did not ever think that ML was wrong for us just unwise or potentially hurtful to others. That we finally could not contain our love any longer and felt that full expression just had to come is irrelevant to those outside the GL.

Perhaps we could have accessed the grace to continue our celibacy but what we did was never wrong, always right, and we know fully what is possible and what might still be, if only life's circumstances were different. What we did was pure and clean and miraculously lovely. But we can't expect anyone else to see it that way. To them it was unnecessary, ungrateful, deceitful and opportunistic. It only makes it worse to seek forgiveness, because for you there is nothing wrong to forgive, and for Roy forgiveness seems like condoning, and he cannot do that.

Where from here? Well you are probably right when you say a letter from me to Roy may only make matters worse. If it were very, very difficult for him to forgive you it would be quite impossible to forgive me. So what next? I believe you will have to raise the touchy subject with him once again perhaps in the context of receiving my letters. Tell him you have discussed the future with me, and received from me assurances we would never be physical lovers again, no matter what the circumstances but that neither of us can deny the other the contact through letters in particular, and the occasional phone call.

Our promise of fidelity is the continuation of our correspondence. As I have said repeatedly before by far the greatest part of the GL is in the sharing of our minds and the sharing of our genitalia is of minor importance however exquisite.

1/2 December
Michael: Dearest love. You will have had #31 hand-delivered and you will have #30 in the mail by now. So you will have read quite a lot of reaction to your [letter] concerning you and me, you and Roy, honesty and loyalty, understanding and forgiveness, openness and trust, love and something else. Is GL the only sort of love? If it were, 99.9% of the world population would never, experience love. So love is an intangible resource or force in the universe, outside of all of us but also impacting on all of us. The measure of love

we experience depends on many practical factors in each of our lives.

People who form close and intimate partnerships kiss, cuddle, make love and share their thoughts, plans, and dreams. Partners in a GL also share their minds, perceptions, instincts, insights, and they kiss, hug, ML etc if they are lucky. It is I believe, impossible, for anyone not part of a GL (and that's nearly everybody) to be able to distinguish the difference.

For us GL and marriage to another can co-exist. For relationship couples without a GL, it is an either/or thing. So I feel for Roy, and I am grateful to Nola for the level of understanding she shows – but Nola does not know the full, bedroom details, though she just might suspect it. Roy and Nola are our closest friends in everything except those spiritual dimensions where only the GL elements live. O God how I would love to have you here so we could make love as we felt like it. But it is so much more fundamental and deeply embedded in my soul that our love is so powerful so uninjurable, so independent of the accidents of history or of society that it can never be quenched.

Purple Book: 'Here it was again – blatant rubbish.' And plain lies. Although he was right in saying, 'Nola does not know the full, bedroom details', he was wrong in saying that I 'just might suspect it', as I did not suspect it; it did not occur to me to suspect him of anything.

5 December

Michael: Annette is OK. I see her a couple of times a week if the times we are available coincide. I pass on to her any news but I keep the intimate bits to myself. I think she just feels we are slushy and emotional and over-romantic. How could she know the reality of a GL.? I didn't for 56 years!! I told

Kaye once that you had 'utterly transformed my life', and she at least listened to that assessment, but you can practically SEE Annette's brain working out and *reassessing* the facts of the GL and coming up with very pedestrian and ordinary explanations. It is not that she doesn't have a true affection for us – she does very genuinely love us in the only way she can. But as for appreciating the cosmic force and spiritual dimensions of a GL, she's out of her depth. But we love her to bits just the same.

I can't help thinking that Annette must have thought all this GL talk to be no more than slushy and over-romantic nonsense. Surely she must have thought it bizarre. She wasn't an unintelligent person.

8 December

Michael: Hello! Hello! my precious one, How much in my thoughts you have been DAY AND NIGHT these last two weeks . . .

I often give myself a good talking to and ask myself many questions. And the usual questions emerge when considering a decision is to be made. You know . . . Is it right, or is it wrong? Is it expedient or will it cause problems? Is it justified or not? Is it natural or is it contrived? But often the question that resolves all the other uncertainties or dilemmas is the one – is it kind? So many things can be sorted out in the mind, given time, but when faced with an on-the-spot decision or course of action, the 'is it kind' test can often solve an immediate concern and buy some time to wrestle with the deeper implications.

Purple Book: 'Is it kind?' Michael spoke about the 'kind test' often. He certainly did not pass his own 'kind test' in relation to his betrayal of me.

14 December

Michael: Dearest lovely precious darling Linda. As this is the last letter I'll write before Christmas (and you won't receive it until well into the New Year) I am feeling very, very emotional. It's not so much that I am particularly sentimental about Christmas itself, because I am not but it represents another punctuation in the story of our life together.

It has been a very full year. What with so many PhD students completing, my own 'retirement', your very special thesis, and the climax of our own lovemaking – long overdue! I can't fully overlook the times when there were misunderstandings misinterpretations and even some real unhappiness because of them. But even at these low times, I know that their poignancy came from the deep love underlying. The saddest times were when you were feeling so stressed by trying to finish the thesis and having to wrestle with the issue of the ownership of your work, the cuts made or suggested to your thesis, you doubted my commitment and questioned my helpfulness and, all in all, it was a tough time for all. Without the honesty and specialness of the ML times, it may have taken even longer to get over.

1998

Purple Book: '17 letters this year – only two of them Linda's.'

Michael wrote fifteen letters and many emails to Linda in 1998; she wrote two letters and many emails to Michael. Her tone to him seemed to cool somewhat. Her emails became quite demanding, continually seeking his help on various matters – the completion of her thesis, publication of research papers in academic journals, her graduation, financial problems, family illness and relationship difficulties with Roy.

In the meantime, now that Michael was retired, we were looking forward to our first visit to the Adelaide Festival in March. The festival had always coincided with the beginning of the academic year, so we had never been able to go before.

7 January
Michael: Dearest love – my life-transforming, life-affirming, life-validating, life-beautifying and oh so life-enriching Linda. Your explanation and revelation contained mixed messages which probably mirrored the mixed emotion and mixed motives that have surrounded the whole business. You down played the importance to Roy of our physically making love, saying he was more unforgiving about my position in your heart which he sees as supplanting him. But you also report

that should you make it to Australia to graduate, you are forbidden to meet with me.

From my own reading of the signs, Roy was very, very hurt indeed by both the ML and the GL. The combination was more than he could bear – almost. I was encouraged by your account of a tender time you had with him where you emphasised his importance in your life and the satisfying ML you shared with him at that time. I continue to hope for continued happiness for you and Roy and your beautiful family. What about me. I'm afraid my miss-feelings are a little better than they ever were since you left. I miss all the tangible things dreadfully, to the extent that my behaviour is affected, even if others don't really know the reason why. I say to Nola how much I miss you, but I don't go into details. She generally leaves me to my thoughts at such times, but generally we have so much we do together that, superficially, our lives are not perceptively affected – on the outside at least. But my inner life, my soul my true self is Linda-obsessed and I have a mixture of ecstasy and agony in my communing.

Dear Linda, not a day's awakening goes by but I am aware of my erection and I dream awake and fantasise that you are taking me into your warm moist places – so beautiful in their slipperiness so tantalising to the senses. My lips tingle from the remembrance and the imagined kisses. Dear Linda, by the time I get up in the morning I have been comprehensively made love to and have given everything in return. I wonder sometimes will this fade. Do I have to wait for the ageing process to be so far advanced that only my failing memory can recall the beauty?

Purple Book: '"I say to Nola how much I miss you".' What rubbish! I'm not sure what my reaction would have been if he had really told me he missed her. It would certainly have raised a lot of questions.

The next day Linda emailed, sounding cheerful but anxious about how much she had to do. I presume she meant in terms of administration, since in a PS she said she must ask her funding agency for travel money for her graduation in September. She signed off 'Warm regards to Nola and Marlana.'

Purple Book: 'Warm regards to me and Marlana?' Sending regards to me was one thing, but to Marlana, whom she hardly knew, was truly bizarre.

In Michael's letter of the same day he confessed to something relating to his present state. Again, it was about me as his very dear 'best friend' and how we didn't make love anymore:

And when we do make love, on those rare occasions, it is more like a kind gesture to a good friend. Like a hug and a kiss, though obviously closer. And yet I want you every day and my dream and fantasies are very, very passionate and very, very real. No kiss on the cheek stuff! I am amazed that the passion in my mind, with my love physically so far away, is so powerful and yet making love with my beautiful partner and closest friend in bed with me is nice but not in any way mind-blowing. I don't seem to fit into the male stereotype. Sex without love has never been possible for me. I would be instantly impotent in such a situation. But amazingly when love is present, I can enjoy sex, as with Nola, and then there is the big one! Love with a capital 'L' as in the GL, makes all the difference in the world.

I am excited as I write, tingling all over and thrilled all the way down. I can taste your wetness and I see you squeezing your thighs together. Oh dear, if only my head was there, drinking thirstily at your love fountain as you held me with those beautiful thighs. I absolutely adore you Linda. I didn't set out to write all this – it just happened. See the effect you have on me. My body is so jumpy at the moment. I am useless for anything!

I haven't heard from you yet, as I write, so I am wondering if your travel plans worked out as you expected. Anyway I'll hear from you soon I hope. Love you so very much.

In another letter he wrote the following day, he talked about Annette and how he saw her most working days and they shared messages from Linda. He told Linda he would chase up the university's notification about her graduation, which she was now planning to undertake in September. He also told her the box of books he'd sent her and the children in December for Christmas should arrive soon.

On 12 January Linda finally responded by letter: 'Happy New Year!' She mostly talked of family news. When she talked about herself she did so, in part, in the third person: 'Linda is okay, enjoying every weekend with Roy and the kids. She is doing fine.' With the GL's strength and guidance she believed she would 'survive'.

Michael raised the topic of Roy again in his letter of 16 January: 'In loving you as I do, I mean him no harm, and I accept that your marriage to him will be full, involved and complete within all human expectations and commitments. I have even considered the sacrifice of not contacting you anymore . . . But you have begged me not to stop, and I can't deny your wishes, especially as I don't want to stop anyway. But I was willing for Roy's sake to back off if it helped . . . I only wish there was a way for me to convince him of the "otherness" of the GL, but I fear that any such attempt would only make matters worse.'

In an email a few days later, Linda sounded demanding, asking 'Where are you?' She wondered if Michael had gone on holiday, and told him to 'please answer me' if he'd got the manuscript she'd sent him. She wanted to hear from him soon, she said.

Purple Book: 'Hop to it, Michael!'

21 January email

Michael: The answer is 'right here'. I'm very sorry to have disappointed you when you expected emails and they didn't arrive. Yes, I did get the paper but the instructions to me were not clear. I also have some questions:

Firstly, you had just your name as author under the title, but in the acknowledgements you referred to the 'senior author'. Did you mean to include me as 'junior author'? If not you should perhaps give me an acknowledgement at the end. In the interests of responsibility and historical accuracy, I see no difficulty in claiming a slice of the authorship of that paper, but honestly, YOU have to decide.

In his letter of 4 February Michael's tone became a little patronising as he expanded on what he had (apparently) told me about their relationship:

It is certainly true to say you have involved Roy much more closely with the GL than I have with Nola. It is not deception or infidelity. She accepts your specialness to me and sees me as someone with a capacity for a BIG love a capacity she doesn't have. She loves our close, supportive friendship and concern for each other, and she wants our life together to be a sharing, enjoyable one. But she doesn't aspire to the heights of GL passion or the depths of the GL current energy.

I get concerned though about you and Roy, because I admire him tremendously for his willingness to try to understand. But unlike Nola, he does aspire to be No. 1 and feels you should grant him top spot and that breeds tension.

I have no pleasure in knowing your GL for me, deep and unchallengeable as it is, is the cause for marital stress.

In recent months I have become very close to Annette and I enjoy her company, brief though it usually is. But it is clear she still has no idea what the GL is all about. She says she loves us both dearly and she means it. But she has no understanding of the GL. She can understand your attractiveness. She can appreciate your thirst for knowledge at every level. Like me, she loves your specialness. But the GL, or anything like it, is beyond her experience and therefore beyond her capacity to understand or believe or accept it. I think she still thinks I have a straightforward, normal heterosexual urge towards an undoubtedly attractive young woman who set my hormones racing, despite my age!

This was yet another letter that I found deeply offensive in its dishonesty and dismissiveness. How had Michael managed to arrogantly delude himself for so many years that he and Linda were several levels above everyone else?

As planned, we went to the Adelaide Festival for five days in March. We stayed with Michael's oldest friend, who had also been his best man at his marriage to Margaret. We travelled into the city on the bus every day and mostly went to the book events. Then we'd have dinner and go to a show and do the whole thing all over again the next day. We had a wonderful time. Well, I had a wonderful time and I thought he had too. But it turns out he was such a good actor, who knows.

1 April email
Michael: I called the home number at about 7.30 your time and spoke to Roy. I of course asked about you, how you were etc. He reported that you still had pain and he would pass on

my concerns about your health and well-being. If I call again, I'll have to give you warning the day before by email, but you should suggest the time.

I expect you got my last email . . . it was a little bold of me to say what I did, as I'm not sure how secure your email is, but of course I expected you to read MUCH MORE into the actual words used. Please tell me if I must be very careful in my messages.

2 April

Michael: Dearest, oh-so-very-much-missed, lovely, lovely Linda. Some nights – early mornings actually – I do get episodes of panic. Will I ever see you again? I have always held to the vision that we *will* be together again this side of the ridges. We *will* gaze directly into the love pools of each other's eyes. We will embrace, hug, kiss and stroke. And we *will* make love again – tenderly, passionately or frantically – however it comes. But always <u>deeply</u>.

I am not sure if you know a lot about 'waking up erections'; in my rude early youth, boys used to call them 'piss horns'. The usual pattern is that you wake up with an erection and if you go to the toilet it goes down to its resting state. What happens to me now is that I wake up, sometimes from a dream which I usually can't remember, with a stiff penis, which I take off to the toilet to act as a drain for my bladder. It then subsides a little, as it is expected to do, but it remains firm, if not really hard. But when I get back to bed, I think of you, focus my thoughts on you, not always in a sexy way. I can be thinking about you in any of a hundred different ways. But always the hardness returns and I squirm about and turn on my front and rub against the bottom sheet. Quietly so I don't disturb Nola. It's totally involuntary, and I have this strange mélange of feelings. I am keenly aware of missing you terribly and knowing I won't be seeing you when I go to work. All in all Linda, a bit of a turmoil, and it is repeated day after day after day.

Thank God for emails. At least they kept us in touch, even if we had to tone down our messages. I nudged the boundaries of carefulness in a few of my messages and I thought, and hoped, you would read and delete quickly so they were not logged into some server file for a long time.

6 April
Michael: You have not yet commented on the intimate greetings I send sometimes. Is it OK? Safe? Dangerous? Embarrassing? Essential (to us both)? A quick comment please. I miss you to the point of pain and beyond. Can I make love with you again? Oh God!

For Nola
Love and Happy Anniversary

Reborn to love
To honour and to cherish
And in that love
The hurts, the sorrows perish.

Another year
Of life that's worth the living
Your hand again my dear
So loving and so giving.

MIW 6.vi.98

29 June email
Michael: I am depending on your powers of deduction, your memory and your intuition to fill in the gaps in what I write in this message. As I type, I have a turmoil going on in my head. Perhaps more accurately in my mind, because clearly they are not the same thing.

It wouldn't take a genius to work out that this time of the year is the anniversary of some significant events in the lives of several people, but especially in yours and mine. How momentous, how huge they were, can be known only by those personally involved. I have been through two of the most soul-searching and life-affirming weeks of my life, and I make no qualification of that extravagant description. May I say how vital it is for me to have love for and know that I have the love of a faraway person. Vital because I have shown some of the characteristics of depression in recent times, brought on by separation from the person, a sense of failing the person in some ways and of dread of the loss of that closeness with that person.

30 June

Michael: Also in my emails I have mentioned my concerns about depression . . . I began to wonder if I was suffering from a version of depression myself. There were signs, as there always are when you are actively looking. Mood swings, displacement activity, procrastination. I'm sure you know the experience. But complicating my life and underlying this self-analysis was the huge factor of missing you just terribly. Obsessively. Overwhelmingly. And what to do about it?

. . . I can't ignore my home life, even if my love for Nola is fundamentally different from the GL we share. I can't help becoming involved with my grand-children and children and Nola's family. I can't ignore the work I am expected to do at the university, and I certainly can't set aside the matters which affect you and your future. And in the same way, you are a wife, a parent, a researcher, and one with a social conscience. At mid-career you have so much you can achieve, and many decisions to make for the greatest personal and professional fulfilment.

And now I call upon your indulgence and permission to ramble on further about love and love-making. At this time of year I can't dismiss from my mind the beauty I shared with you in making love. Oh sure, every time was not sensational, but it was always very, very special. I still wish we had more time in the duration of the GL-in-Canberra period to express our love in that way. It would have become better and better and very deeply satisfying. Though we reached very high points of experience, we certainly would have gone higher and higher still. Our surrender, without inhibition or guilt, would have been full.

3 July email
Michael: The GL is safe, in both spiritual and written form. There may come a time when I decide to ship it to you, but not yet. Meanwhile I added a # to the folders on Tuesday. Can we resume a regular letter exchange? Please?? It is difficult to say what I need to say by email. I see Annette several times a week, and help her with transport and shopping. We both wish you were here to brighten up our spirits. We NEED you Linda!

He could not bear to let go of those letters. Until Linda received my email in 2010, I wonder if she ever gave a thought to what he'd done with them.

9 July email
Michael: Annette will complete the statutory declaration soon. She emphasises that she will be guaranteeing that she will house and support you on your visit to Canberra. She will make no mention of the airline ticket which Kaye has undertaken to provide. I have undertaken to provide money to Annette, and indirectly to you, to support your visit

expenses, but that will not be explicitly stated in the stat dec to keep it as simple as possible.

Purple Book: 'He's giving her money.' I won't deny that reading this seriously annoyed me.

15 July email
Michael: The graduate school told me today that you had been ADMITTED and that the notification was going out this week. Finally!

Linda replied sounding upbeat and relieved. She wanted to celebrate, saying how excited she was.

22 July
Michael: Good afternoon Dr Linda. Good to be in touch again. I do badly need to be in touch. The recent anniversaries hit me very hard. Sorry to be so weak, but I couldn't help it. I didn't get depressed; I didn't kick the dog; I didn't shout at my friends and loved ones. But I felt hollow and incomplete and had the severest miss-feelings. Only you Linda can reach so deeply inside me and your home deep in there is a permanent dwelling place.

I do hope you won't strike any difficulties in making your travel plans. I am worried by the 'black mark' you got for not renewing your visa on time last year. Even though it was an oversight and you had no thought to become an illegal immigrant, such mistakes are always capable of coming back to haunt you. Please find out as soon as possible if the Aust. Embassy tries to delay things so we can write quickly to verify any explanation you give. So long as you have official approval from the institute for a defined period of leave, and a return ticket, you should be OK.

Oh GL forgive me! Oh Linda, forgive me! But I DO!!! I DO want you and I want to hold you close. I want your breath, your taste, your aroma your touch, the look in your eyes. And of course I want to make love with you – love that is multidimensional. I am not a sexual athlete, and neither are you. But we're one in reaching to the stars . . . Love.

A month later Linda emailed Michael to ask if he'd received the form for a graduation dress, and asked how much it would cost to buy the dress. She said again she was excited and, probably to Michael's horror, added, 'Did Annette tell you Roy is coming for my graduation? He surprised me last week about this, isn't this great?'

25 August email

Michael: Could you please ask Annette specifically about Roy's coming, because that has implications for 'quality time' with you. I'm not including myself in any of this. I'll be grateful for any 'crumbs' that there may be time for.

Purple Book: 'Not happy about Roy coming.' Reading between the lines, it seemed that Linda and Roy were rebuilding their marriage. If Michael suspected this, he appeared to be refusing to accept it. There was a little irony here. Michael had given her money to help with the travel to Canberra for her graduation and, whoops, suddenly there was enough money for her hubby to come as well! That was not part of the plan.

Linda wrote back the same day to say that she didn't want Annette to worry about accommodation for her and Roy, or to be concerned about her during their stay. Roy would be with her, and she would ensure everything would be 'fine'.

26 August email

Michael: Please don't think there is anything unwelcome about the visit(s). Quite the contrary Annette is hugely looking forward to it all, and hoping like mad Kaye can be here. I guess she is most anxious that she can have MAXIMUM time to sit down, preferably with Kaye as well, and just 'girl talk' and 'talk talk' up to the point of exhaustion.

You must know that we have all been missing the indefinable, transcendental quality you bring to our every-day living experience and we have been waiting with huge anticipation for the ending of our 'Linda-drought'. Roy only comes into the equation insofar as his physical presence during any of the talkfest might lead to inhibition of frank expression of views on some topics.

I await further instructions on the hire or purchase of the graduation finery. As I said yesterday, my more personal anticipations about your visit will be better described in a more comprehensive way by letter, so be patient for that. I have 'booked' myself to be available for the duration of your visit.

Purple Book: 'Pathetic.'

On 1 September Linda emailed to ask Michael to order her a new bonnet and hood for the graduation, which Roy had apparently insisted she should have. She comforted him that they would still be able to talk about taboo subjects 'like ehemmmm he he he he'. She signed off rather breezily 'bye and cheers', followed by kisses and hugs.

Linda's increasingly emotional distance was obviously taking its toll on Michael's vanity. On 15 October he called his letter a 'cry of anguish'. He was missing her and only Annette kept him sane and he was grateful to her. I seemed to have become a peripheral character in his life.

It is clear to me that . . . for months now, you have been under very great pressure because of me and your love for me . . . without really knowing, I was making it even worse for you. In my naivety, I was cherishing the one means I had to 'touch' you, that of email messages. And occasional letters. To discover that the emails were not secure, that my affectionate greetings had a readership, was rather devastating. Not so much the being 'found out' because it was well past that stage, more that the words were sent by one person to one person, and so were, by definition personal . . . I prefer they are received and enjoyed privately. It's nothing to do with secrecy or conspiracy or deception.

I feel very deeply sympathetic towards Roy. I can truly understand that he wants this nightmare complication removed from his life and especially from his marriage. No amount of explanation of the specialness of the GL would make any sense to him. You simply have to choose as far as he is concerned – it is your duty to your family. You must give up this other love. . . . I did once believe we could continue this 'spiritual' union while at the same time giving all the love and attention reasonably expected by our respective partners and families. When it was clear that we had little choice but to conform to those expectations, I was in no doubt, no doubt at all, that in our core being, the GL was untouchable, unchangeable, inviolate and eternal. A position for us both that was not as good as a lifetime together in every sense, but a worthy second prize.

Is it not possible for us to embrace that position and still keep in touch somehow? . . . I was hoping that Roy could be persuaded that he has you in every real sense. If he does not understand, and regards the GL as a threat, or an unreal fancy, or worse still, a shameful exercise in exploitation willingly entered into by you, then we have little choice but to limit contact . . . I am crying out to you for help . . . Staying silent avoiding contact, hoping the situation will go away, are not real options. If you are trying to spare my feelings you are failing miserably. If you are hoping I will tire of the difficulties and voluntarily withdraw from a too-hard situation, you are sorely mistaken. If you are confused and sorry and concerned for how I feel, as I believe you are, then for God's sake *talk* to me!!

His suggestion that if Roy thought the affair was a 'shameful exploitation' into which she had 'willingly entered' then they would have little choice but to limit contact sounded like a threat to spur Linda into action. I found his comment about being devastated that his emails were not secure and had a 'readership' a bit naive; he had a lot to learn about the internet.

The graduation was over by the middle of October. For obvious reasons I was not invited. Michael wrote that he was surprised by the level of Roy's animosity towards him. What an absolutely crazy thing for him to say. He had been having an affair with this man's wife for six years, had been sending her a steady stream of letters filled with erotic fantasies for fifteen months and he was 'surprised by the level of his animosity towards him'. What planet was he on?

On 16 October Linda wrote her final letter to Michael before returning home with Roy. She was sitting under the she-oaks by Lake Burley Griffin, marvelling at the way the sun 'strikes the lake making it glitter and dance' – something Michael and I used to admire a long time ago now.

She had seen Michael at the graduation and during her stay but had made a promise to Roy that she would not see him alone. At the end of her two-page letter, her writing was barely legible and the ink was smudged. 'I came to celebrate the beauty of the GL, not to regret it but to acknowledge the GL is a gift of nature to make our lives better. She told him the GL would always 'reign' and urged Michael to get on with his life, adding that one day they would have the GL 'for just the two of them' (did she mean in death?). She finished, 'Go, and live my dearest GL. Be alive.'

1999

Purple Book: 'Michael wrote three letters; Linda did not write or email.'

Our life continued as normal. We had a growing number of grandchildren between us so family events were a little noisier. Michael had begun to write his family history and spent a lot of time in his office. We used to buy annual subscriptions to concerts but this stopped after he retired and instead we would cherry-pick the ones we wanted to go to – a bit of belt-tightening due to the fact that Michael was no longer earning an income. I was still working, and planned to retire in 2000. I realise now that he was probably giving her money around this time and that was another reason for him to watch his pennies.

Michael wrote his first letter to Linda of this year on 19 March. In it he mentioned depression again. I was not aware that he was depressed. The only time I do remember him being seriously depressed in our twenty-nine years together was in 2007, when he had more heart problems. There seemed no reason to worry about his mental health at the time these letters were written, so he must have either worked very hard at hiding his sadness from everyone, or he was exaggerating. Indeed, nothing he said in this letter came across in his 'real' life. But I know now that I was married to two different people.

Perhaps I should begin with my mental state; I am not a psychologist or a psychiatrist, but I think I am suffering from a form of depression. Not just sadness, which I believe is both healthy and appropriate, but something more. Having begun with a self-diagnosis, I may as well press on with further analysis. Basically I am having severe difficulty coming to terms with the *reality* of not having you as a loving, beautiful, enriching transcendent presence in my life . . .

I always thought the GL would heal my mind when you went away, and I guess I was led some of the way to acceptance. But, in the end, no matter how I look at it, no matter how I assess the reality of US, I come up against the impossible stumbling block of separation. Nola has said to me why don't you fly up to see Linda? But of course that would solve nothing. As I said earlier I never felt our separation, so keenly as when you were physically back here. The couple of brief moments of closeness only served to underline the hard reality.

While my conscious self is having such a hard time, my subconscious knows exactly where it is. I have the most vivid dreams of you, mostly just communing and enjoying in a sweet and spiritual way. But there are times when my dreams are very erotic. Usually these are waking-up dreams in which we make love endlessly and with infinite variety. I wake up with raging erections and massive pelvic congestion. My dream life is dominated by images of you. The unforgettable look in your lovely eyes. The fullness of your lips. The sensation of your nipples in my mouth. The aroma and delicious taste of your cunt (that's not a nasty word when applied literally, so don't be shocked). I literally feel the sensations in my own body as well as recollected images. It is thrilling at the moment of waking – but I nearly yell out loud soon after. Why? Why? Why? I *need* you Linda.

I think I am still healthy in mind and spirit despite my self-diagnosed depression. As to the latter I hope you have a word, a gesture, a piece of Linda-wisdom to be a therapeutic

help to me. I am confident on the one hand that you empathise with me because I do know you. But you are also a
very deep well of natural wisdom, and I long for you to share
some of that with me.

When he wrote this poem for me in April, I thought he was
merely having a moody reflection:

Depression and Dispersion

A sad or happy life may still bear hope of pleasure new or
    else of joy sustained.
This limbo though, wherein I find myself, prolongs uncertainty
and daily takes from me the joys so longingly desired.
My anguish and complaint in all unfair and disappointing
    times becomes
for me a blind, instinctive howl against the Fates that
rule our lives. And, like old Lear, I rail against ingratitude,
    as if to halt
the gathering clouds of dark frustration.
Oh God, this hell-bent mood must not persist to spread its
    amplifying
wave abroad so all around me flounder in the gloom.
Creation, bursting with autumnal pride and burnished
    colourings
can not provide sufficient warmth to bathe the stricken soul.
One only light can quench this Stygian dark and show me
    beauties without parallel.
My Nola can, with just one tender touch dispel the clouds
    and
light the darkening sky with shining radiance, while chains
    that bind
my heart just melts like ice before the sparkling sun-storm
    of her smile.

MIW 29.iv.99

6 September

Michael: Dearest Linda. You probably know how desperate I am to hear from you, but you have your reasons for not wanting to communicate with me. Usually I can tell why, or have a good guess at the reason, but I am at a loss this time. I would prefer to experience your anger or complaint than your silence. Silence can mean so many things – indifference, hurt, anger, punishment, illness, inability to cope, loss of love, loss of even interest etc. etc.

Dearest one. You continue to be constantly in my thoughts from the moment(s) of waking (there are several), to the last moments before going to sleep, and very often each day. It is especially strong at the university and near the lake as I drive past. I have gone into the Black Mountain Park by myself and walked around the shore, stopping at 'Holy Ground' spots, and into the trees where we exchanged vows. Both my heart and my eyes are full as I make these pilgrimages.

It would be wrong to give the impression that I have no opportunity to express love. Nola is and always will be very special and she is the reality of my physical future. She will be my home companion for the rest of my days, or I hers if she goes first.

But you must know the difference between fulfilling the daily expectations of home and family filling up the days and deriving many small pleasures and the deep abiding, passionate love that utterly engulfs the body soul and spirit and which I waited to experience until I was 56. O God Linda, your utter specialness which extends to eternity defies description and categorisation. Please tell me I am not just a deluded old man! Well even if you did see me that way, I would know my own reality . . .

The reason I avoid 'we' and 'us' is that I could not bear to put a weight on you that you could not bear, or that you are attempting to unburden yourself from. I dread the daily arrival of all the 'if only' thoughts which overcome me. If only we were free agents; if only we lived nearby; if only we lived together as a married couple . . . you know the kind of thing. Then comes the guilt concerning Roy, Nola and our children, not to mention the people who surround us and depend on us in some way. But honestly Linda, I am still the richest man alive in spite of all those difficulties and regrets.

I hope you understand what I now tell you, I can make love with Nola only rarely, and then only to reassure her that I love her and value the shared life we have. She knows my love for you and respects it, but she wants to be valued as a loving companion who shares my day-to-day concerns and practical plans for the rest of our life together. Fortunately (??) her own libido is diminishing and making love is a bit like a kind smile or a gentle touch that cements our continuing commitment to one another. But all the time I know, or I feel I know, that the sacrament that was our love making, was only a beginning for what could have become immeasurably better and more and more blissful. Yet I shall be ever grateful for that experience and I will not dwell on the 'what might have been', or I shall certainly go mad.

I can hardly write now because of the tears in my eyes. Sorry darling – I must finish now. Sorry sorry, sorry. I love you, I love you, I love you, I LOVE you. Have mercy on me, and love me always.

The crushing and unnecessary comments about our personal life had resurfaced. By now I was almost too exhausted to write of my rage in the Purple Book.

10 December

Michael: Dear Linda. I have destroyed many half-written letters over the last few months. I can't exactly tell you what was wrong with them, and it could be that I should have at least kept them, but too late now. Anyway, I am here now and I am going to post this, no matter how it turns out, I long to 'talk' to you – indeed I am desperate to do so. I just hope it can be a two-way conversation.

Dearest darling Linda, I must call you that because there is no other way to think of you. My mind is obsessed by my love for you, made so much more poignant by your ongoing unavailability.

In my more rational moments I say to myself that yes, the thoughts *do* get through, and you *do* want them to keep coming, but I confess to the need for some reassurance sometimes . . . just as Abelard was separated from Heloise, he was assured of the 'fact' of the love they shared. At least I haven't been castrated!!

Which brings me to my body. When we crossed over that boundary from a spiritual merging to a bodily one, we triggered something very, very special. It has been the cause of terrible strain in your marriage and a challenge to the focus of mine, but I can have no regrets, only celebration. I really don't know what state I would be in if we hadn't made love.I fantasise about pleasuring you with my tongue, fingers and penis, and recall the deliciousness of your mouth, your down-there lips, your juices, I do so knowing that it is not just some skilful erotic performer I am with, but the greatest love of my whole life.

I hope this letter has two effects (1) to bring you some pleasure and (2) to prompt you to write some of your own thoughts. I have so much more to say but there's always next time. Keep well, keep loving and keep in touch.

So he had found the affair a challenge to his marriage, after all. His admission of this negated everything he had claimed over the past seven years.

Purple Book: 'No more letters after 10 December 1999.'

2000

To my darling Nola on our 19th anniversary.
A day of celebration, just like every other day
We have been together. How we have been blessed
and continue to be.

A Retrospective Symphony

Celebrate the years with music of
Shared experience,
The counterpoint of memories,
With our heart's tempi pulsing
A scherzo here, a crescendo there,
Adagio and vivace
Ever changing, ever engaging, but
always integrating.

Marvel at the inspiration unfolded
in our love.
How could we have known where
life's music would impel us?
But now our symphony is
resolving and unfolding;

A whole is now emerging, though
yet incomplete.

Our final hymn to joy, and the
blessing of our fullness
Are revealed in our serenity
born of understanding.
Two lives intertwined are now
scarcely separable;
Our coda, foreshadowed no
more than final chords.

MIW 6.vi.00

2004–10

I have never been a good sleeper, and by the time I'd read all 741 letters (some more than once), I wished I could slip into a very long sleep and on awakening find the whole thing had been a horrible nightmare. But at least the letters were over. I packed them back neatly in date order. All the poems, cards and notes Michael had written to me, I filed separately, but as I reread the sonnet he had given me on our special anniversary in December 2004, I was overcome with sadness for the loss of my precious memories.

For Nola
December 7th, Then and Now
A Sonnet

Your presence, then so precious, came to be
A sacred contemplation for each day,
A prompt for deep thanksgiving as I pray
In humble gratitude for all you are to me.

Your love so nearly missed, so nearly lost,
Became my very life force, deepest well,
With power to lift me up whene'r I fell.
There is no way I can repay the cost.

But let me serve and love you with my all,
And stand with me against the world's cruel blows.
Your strength increases mine as Heaven knows.
With you beside me, can we really fall?
When tribulations come, we rise above
Abiding in the strength of long-learned love.

MIW 7.xii.04

When I had finally gathered my courage to tell the children about what I'd found in some of the boxes in the garage, and with the book I planned to write about the letters and Michael's affair in mind, I began printing out Michael and Linda's emails of 1998. Imagine the unpleasant surprise I got when I found that the correspondence was not over after all. It went on in a series of emails beyond those I'd discovered up to 1999. By accident I discovered a new email account Michael had set up after his computer had had a hard-disk crash in 2004. There may have been emails between 1999 and 2003, but there is no record of them. The intermittent emails over the subsequent six-year period were between Michael and Annette, with a few brief ones from Linda.

Annette's and Linda's emails were for the most part extremely short; Michael's were generally fairly brief as well, and his emails to Annette always asked her, sometimes almost begged her, for any news of Linda. I had packed away the Purple Book by then, but found much worthy of comment.

First, I was more than a little bemused to find that Michael had taken to writing to Annette, who had moved to Brisbane, in the similarly overblown way he wrote to Linda, without the sex. It was as if, in his compulsion to write in this same effusive way, he had replaced Linda with Annette as the recipient of his prose.

For example, in an email to Annette on 11 October 2004, he wrote:

> Dearly beloved. Not for the first time, I feel chastened by the receipt of your latest personal message. I have known for weeks, nay months, I should be feeding my loving thoughts directly into the communication networks, and not just casting them randomly into the ether, hoping for them to land randomly in your lap . . .
>
> And now to Linda. Thanks so much for the update on her recent past and more immediate past and present. No brief message could possibly have expressed the flood of feelings I have for her on a daily basis. She and I used to talk about the Great Love and how it was unassailable despite the complications of our lives and the impossibility of our geography. We always believed the Great Love would sustain us at either end of the arc that separated us, and those close to us would not be harmed or threatened by such a spiritual bond. (I hope you are not too put off by this soppy talk but I know no other way to share my thoughts with you.) To fall into a laid back, long time no see friendship role would be painfully unauthentic for me and probably uncomfortable for Linda as well . . .
>
> Much love. I miss you too.

And he sent this one on 20 December 2004:

> Let me now compose a short message to one of the really special people who have come into my life, whose physical presence I miss to a degree not far short of compulsive grieving. Oh God, Annette, I long to see you again. I can feel the hugs as we greet each other and the matching ones when we separate. But most of all I miss the buzz generated by just sharing each other's space.

My opening paragraph probably seems like oily schmoozing and the outpourings of a prize bullshitter. Please, if you can, suspend disbelief and take my sentiments at face value. To lose both you and Linda in so short a time frame were cruel blows. I'm glad you both managed to ride out the storms that followed your moves from Canberra, but I'm claiming my right to wallow just a little in self-pity.

On 20 September 2005 he wrote to her:

My main message is not self-flagellation but an announcement . . . Nola and I are selling and moving from our lovely house, which we designed and built and paid off, to a slightly more modest townhouse and much, much more modest garden.

The move isn't likely until October, at the earliest; so, my lovely one, hold that Christmas card until I say so . . .

Talk again soon.

In early 2006 we moved from our beautiful home, in which we had shared so many wonderful times, to the new two-bedroom townhouse, in a quiet and pleasant suburb in outer Canberra but still close enough for us to drive into the city to go to the theatre or to concerts and exhibitions. Michael commented to Annette that it had been 'an all-consuming, time-gobbling affair'. It was with a rather wry smile that I read his mention of the 'house shifting', as he called it, now that I was painfully aware he'd moved the box of letters along with us.

The emails to Annette in late 2005 also generally consisted of requests for any news about Linda, whose few, short messages to Michael pained him greatly.

Dearest, wonderful, ever-patient Annette. The answer is definitely 'NO' to the Linda question. She does not routinely email me, and seldom responds to messages of concern, though I'm willing to try another. I'd appreciate any inkling you may have of her state of mind or being, and whether her anxieties are largely due to do with job, money, family, matters too personal to mention or all of the above.

By now I had been retired for six years and life in retirement went on at its own pace – one I enjoyed and, I thought, Michael did too. I had taken up lawn bowling and Michael sometimes joined me; I was a very enthusiastic bowler but I'm not sure it was his cup of tea. We both did volunteer work at the local charity op shop. Michael had finally finished up as a Visiting Fellow at the university but replaced that work with a whole list of other things, including a lot of voluntary work, either helping people individually or assisting various charities, and he was still working on his family history. Between our seven children, we now had nine grandchildren (and another expected), so there were lots of family celebrations – birthdays and so on. We loved catching up with old friends and of course we were still very involved with the church and its activities. We travelled a bit within Australia but were not able to go overseas as Michael couldn't get travel insurance due to his heart.

We had both found the big garden at the house in which we'd once thought we'd see out our days together was beginning to eat into our other activity time and, once established, our new courtyard garden was pretty and easy to manage. On warm mornings we would sit in the courtyard as the sun streamed down while we drank coffee and read the papers together.

In April 2006, Linda sent Michael a brief email advising him her papers would soon be in print. Michael responded with an email on her birthday, 29 April:

Hi to the birthday girl. Today is a grey cloudy day in Canberra, much different from the beautiful autumn days we have been experiencing for the last few weeks. But I would be more than usually remiss if I didn't send you my very warmest greetings on this birthday. HAPPY BIRTHDAY LINDA!!!

I'm glad to hear your papers will be in print soon. Your great work in Canberra seems so long ago now – was it really nine years since you submitted your thesis? It was a truly momentous year, 1997, for many reasons – your thesis, my retirement (though I hung around for another five years longer) and much, much more . . .

It has been good to 'talk' to you again. Once more – Happy Birthday!

On 4 November 2006 Linda sent an extremely offhand letter with a completely different tone to that of the years of impassioned outpourings: 'Gdday!!!!' she wrote. She asked after the family and explained she'd sent Michael a shirt and me a batik shawl. She signed off with 'Cheers and thank you'.

I found it very odd that she should be sending me gifts. Naturally he never gave me this batik shawl and I have no idea what he did with it. Maybe he gave it to one of the charities. He responded on 10 November:

Dear Linda, thank-you so much for the surprise email. I don't know that I should be surprised except that we do leave it a long time between messages. It would be wonderful to catch up with you and all your news some time. Is email the best way, or a letter? I am not sure of your postal addresses anymore – lost in old computer files. Please take care and stay beautiful.

Linda replied breezily the same day, passing on another greeting to me and asking if we had liked the gifts she had sent.

5 December 2006

Michael: Dear Linda. Sorry to be so late in thanking you for the gifts you sent. Thank you so much for thinking of Nola and me in this way. But you taught me to treat each day as a gift. So I have been practising that as best I can. I have much to be thankful for in my life, past and present, and you Linda are right up there on the list. How I wish I could see you again, but failing that, I have my thoughts, my moments to remember. Go joyfully and gently.

PS. I nearly forgot. Both Nola and I have worn the gifts you sent and they are great! Thank you again.

Michael sent Linda another email on her birthday the following April, again asking her to stay in touch.

16 May 2007

Michael to Annette: My news is meagre but arguably important. I had a melanoma excised from my left forearm last week, along with what seemed like the target lymph node, should any bodgie cells have migrated from the site . . . the chunk hacked out of my arm should satisfy the 'better safe than sorry principle'. I expect to hear the results of the pathology report on 25 May. My expectation is that it will be clear and if not I expect to hear before 25 May. So there you go, or as Kurt Vonnegut used to write 'And so it goes . . .'

Nothing from Linda last year but I *did* remember her birthday.

Much, much love.

By the end of 2007, Michael was gravely ill with an unknown infection. He was eventually hospitalised in early 2008 and diagnosed with endocarditis. Shortly afterwards he underwent cardio-thoracic surgery to have the mitral valve replaced. It was a long and slow recovery, and he wrote about the illness in great detail in a long and rather sad email to Linda on 18 August. He did credit me with being 'a tower of strength' and said he would not have survived without me. That was a bit kinder than the way he'd totally excised me from his recovery after his heart failure in 1994. But if he was expecting this email to elicit sympathy from Linda, he was sadly mistaken. She wrote nothing.

I received some rather effuse gratitude in an email to Annette, too, in which he detailed the tribulations of the year. On 26 November 2008 he wrote to her:

Dearest One. The year 2008 has been one to forget for Nola and me. I include Nola as a right because she endured all that I did and more and my gratitude knows no bounds . . .

I have an almost pathological desire to be in your physical presence to be able to have our well-remembered and sorely-missed chats more easily, and to give each other the occasional sincerely-felt hug. Oooooooohh well. Take care and keep smiling.

And there was a New Year surprise to come from Linda. In a brief message on 6 February 2009 she told Michael that she could be coming to Brisbane for a meeting, and might also get down to Canberra. He responded immediately:

Hi Linda. What a lovely surprise to get your message. I was wondering if your busy life prevented you from keeping in touch with your Australian fan club. I received an email from Annette not so long ago in which she said, inter alia, that she hadn't heard from you for some time either. So wonderful to get your greetings and with them a promise to visit the great south land.

I will be hoping and praying that you will be able to make that trip to Australia, and an extension to Canberra would be especially welcome. You could of course stay with us, but you may prefer to stay with someone who lives closer to the city. The only cloud on the horizon for me is that Nola and I have plans already in place to travel to North Australia beginning about 17 August to early September. As you didn't mention dates, I am unable to say if it clashes with your plans . . .

After a horror year, I am hoping for a better one in 2009. It has already looked up with your email.

I could not believe it – he had actually invited her to stay with us! He then immediately sent an excited email to Annette:

Linda has finally broken her silence this week to tell me she is hoping to get to Oz, principally Brisbane, in August for a meeting and would like to add Canberra to the visit . . . I do hope it comes off, but I hope even more that if she does get to Canberra, I am not out of town.

Love, love, love – your Michael

But unfortunately for Michael, we were in Broome for the annual Opera under the Stars concert when Linda visited Canberra. On our return he contacted a former colleague at the university, enquiring if he had heard from her. He had not, but had heard she was coming to town. Michael emailed Linda on 15 September saying how deeply disappointed he was:

I was just back from the West on 2 September and was busy with appointments and arrangements we had made before we left but no way would I have missed a chance to see you. I suppose I must remain optimistic about the prospect of seeing you some time in the future, but my health has been so unpredictable I must be ready for any outcome.

Please stay in touch as often as you can. You remain an ongoing part of my life, not just an exciting early chapter. Thank you for your greetings to Nola. She is, of course very precious to me, and she was wonderful during my long periods of illness.

Please remember me to Roy and the family.

Then the final blow. On 26 February 2010 Michael sent Linda what was to be his last email to her:

Dear Linda. I see it was 3 February when I fired off the very brief reply to your last message. I was pretty pressed for time then, and seem to have been ever since. But I have no proper excuse, so will not bother to say one.

As I think I mentioned earlier, I have had enough of being unwell to last the rest of my lifetime, especially from the beginning of 2008 until about August 2009. Since then I have felt much better, but I am still weak and lacking in energy. I am coming to terms with being the age I am and accepting that how I feel is perhaps appropriate for someone of my age. Fortunately Nola is in very good shape and I am trying very hard not to be any further burden on her. She was a tower of strength during my illness but it must have cost her own health and wellbeing.

Dearest one, it seems such a long time since I saw you and I long to see you again. I am realistic enough to think that is unlikely, but hope springs eternal!

Fondest love from Michael, and Nola joins my best wishes.

I found this email heartbreaking. It would seem from the last sentences that Michael's yearning for his lover remained to the end of his life. How sad it must have been to live out those final years pining for his great love, knowing it was no longer reciprocated. But he could not let go, which is probably why he did not dispose of the letters – they were all he had left of her.

In the last years of his life, Michael had a lot of ill health and sometimes when I was sitting with him, he would take my hand, look me straight in the eye and with a gentle smile say, 'I love you.' Had I not read that last email he wrote to Linda, I may have been able to convince myself that, with these expressions of love towards me, which I never thought were anything other than heartfelt, he had, at the end, come back to me. But any thoughts that this might have been so were shattered by knowing of his expressed longing for Linda just a few months before he died.

Two days after Michael sent that email, Linda responded with an offhand, dreadfully patronising message, telling him to 'keep going, life is beautiful!' She asked if he could still write a letter, commenting, 'Maybe you can make that as your past-time; writing about how beautiful is the world.' She added that he could write anything, and said he could send the letters to her. She finished, 'Cheers, Linda.'

The great love of Michael's life had demonstrated cruelly that she was long gone in every sense. She had moved on; Michael was a distant memory – an old man in ill health, possibly not long for this earth. She was right: six months later Michael was dead. But 'best friend Nola' was there to look after him, bury him and slip into the role of grieving widow.

Turn out the Light

Turn out the light.
I need the darkness –
need to know now who I am –
need to forget the landscape of love
and the flowers in your eyes.

Turn out the light.
Let the silence
teach that being is alone
where love is song and dance and wonder
in the hollow of the stone.

Turn out the light.
I need to love now –
need to love what I don't know –
need to love my dream of wholeness
till I'm white, till I'm snow.

Turn out the light.
the world is darkness.
Your eye's no longer home.
The centre's out of focus.
I go blind. I go alone.

MIW (undated)

Epilogue

While this event in my life is not a tragedy, it has been a bewildering emotional experience and I realised after finding the letters that my life was never going to be the same. Naturally, I knew my life would never be the same after Michael died. I was a widow, but I was a grieving widow with dignity. But when I read those letters, my memories of my life with Michael became sullied and my dignity and self-esteem were crushed, and more so with every one I read.

When someone you love dies, it is the memories that you cling to; read any death notice, it is always the memories that the loved ones left behind are so grateful for. Having lost my wonderful memories, I found myself grieving for a second time.

There are many questions to this story, the main one being – why didn't Michael let me die with my wonderful memories intact, in blissful ignorance of his affair? This he could have done so easily by destroying the letters; instead he chose to leave them for me to find. It was a deliberate act on his part and I will never know or understand why he did it. He brought them with him from our former home and he knew I would one day find and read them; he would also have known the distress and heartache they would cause me.

He has not only burdened me with the knowledge of his affair, he has burdened me with a terrible feeling of guilt. What, I wonder, could I have done to keep it from happening? What was he searching for that I didn't provide? Did his dreams not match his life with me? Did he feel so unful-filled that he was reaching for a happiness not yet found? It's difficult not to analyse – even though I know there is no point.

And still today, when I find myself dwelling on why and how this could have happened, I cannot help thinking that much of the reason for Michael's affair was to do with me. I also wonder if other women who discover their husbands have had extramarital affairs feel the same way. In my comfortable happy-marriage delusion I knew these things happened – but only to other people. How could I have been so blind?

The other question is, of course, how can I ever get over what I found and live out the rest of my own life with any peace of mind? Both characters in this love story were highly intelligent people and both reveal themselves as deeply flawed, extraordinarily deluded and selfish. Both displayed a disregard for the family and friends who loved them; they did not deserve the love of the people who trusted them. Such disloyalty and betrayal is difficult to understand.

Betrayal is painful. Betrayal has tentacles that reach out and sting so many people. It can result in a crisis within a family and everything changes: people change, they take sides, some want to know, some do not want to know, the dynamics change and you wonder how it is all going to end. I have had time to reflect on Sally Parson's urging when I spoke to her soon after finding the letters that I must try to find it in my heart to forgive Michael. I read somewhere that forgiveness is a gift of temperament, but do I have the temperament to forgive? Michael himself considered forgive-ness one of his personal virtues. The process of forgiveness has become very important to me; it will affect the degree to which I can move forward. I feel I have to forgive Michael as I do not like the alternative. Without forgiveness, the knowl-edge of what he has done will fester inside me and all the negative feelings will sap my emotional energy for whatever years I have left.

Distressingly closer to the end of my life than to the beginning, Michael's morally bankrupt behaviour has left me feeling demeaned and undignified. The question of why he chose to embark on this reckless affair in which he risked so much will always be asked; it will always linger and will never be answered. Nor will the question of why he left the letters for me to find. But the reality is that he did, and in my own mind I have to work out how to deal with the consequences.

While it has been very unsettling to learn so many disturbing things about Michael so late in my life, I must now try to remember the redeeming qualities of the person who has hurt and disappointed me; there were many redeeming qualities and they are worth remembering. I will try to focus on what Michael brought into my life and to the lives of my children, and remember what we shared together.

In his book *Overcoming Life's Disappointments*, Rabbi Harold Kushner writes, 'What happens to you, no matter how hurtful or unfair, is ultimately less important than what you do about what happens to you.'

What I have chosen to do about what happened to me is to write about it. I acknowledge that many people who knew Michael – family, friends and colleagues – will not understand why I would want to reveal this terrible secret so very publicly; people will ask why I didn't just burn the letters and bury my feelings. But setting down some of my feelings and reactions in this book *has* been my catharsis. And a way of regaining some of my shredded dignity.

It has also been a way of writing Michael and Linda's story, the Great Love story that Linda so desperately wanted Michael to write. In 1997 Linda begged Michael to 'write our story soon. Make it tangible in its true sense . . . It would be so good to see copies of the book in front of my eyes.'

Well, her wish will now be fulfilled. They often speculated how they would be judged when their Great Love story was revealed. I wonder too how I will be judged for revealing it. Now we shall know.

No matter how painful the details are and how difficult they are to comprehend, our stories are part of who we are. I am sure the pain that Michael has caused will not last forever – one day it will be gone. Life may not be fair, but it is not without all sorts of possibilities and compensations. I will do my best to concentrate on what I have left and not just on what I have lost.